If you have a home computer with Internet access you may:
- request an item to be placed on hold.
- renew an item that is not overdue or on hold.
- view titles and due dates checked out on your card.
- view and/or pay your outstanding fines online ($1 & over).

To view your patron record from your home computer click on Patchogue-Medford Library's homepage: **www.pmlib.org**

EMOTIONS IN THE MORAL LIFE

ROBERT C. ROBERTS first presented his vivid account of emotions as "concern-based construals" in his book *Emotions: An Essay in Aid of Moral Psychology* (Cambridge University Press, 2003). In this new book he extends that account to the moral life. He explores the ways in which emotions can be a basis for moral judgments, how they account for the deeper moral identity of actions we perform, how they are constitutive of morally toned personal relationships like friendship, enmity, collegiality, and parenthood, and how pleasant and unpleasant emotions interact with our personal wellbeing (eudaimonia). He then sketches how, by means of their moral dimensions, emotions participate in our virtues and vices, and, for better or worse, express our moral character. His rich study will interest a wide range of readers working on virtue ethics, moral psychology, and emotion theory.

ROBERT C. ROBERTS is Distinguished Professor of Ethics, Baylor University. He is author of *Emotions: An Essay in Aid of Moral Psychology* (Cambridge University Press, 2003), *Intellectual Virtues: An Essay in Regulative Epistemology* (2007), and *Spiritual Emotions: A Psychology of Christian Virtues* (2007).

EMOTIONS IN THE
MORAL LIFE

ROBERT C. ROBERTS

CAMBRIDGE
UNIVERSITY PRESS

CAMBRIDGE
UNIVERSITY PRESS

University Printing House, Cambridge CB2 8BS, United Kingdom

Published in the United States of America by Cambridge University Press, New York

Cambridge University Press is part of the University of Cambridge.

It furthers the University's mission by disseminating knowledge in the pursuit of
education, learning and research at the highest international levels of excellence.

www.cambridge.org
Information on this title: www.cambridge.org/9781107016828

© Robert C. Roberts 2013

First published 2013

Printed and bound by CPI Group (UK) Ltd, Croydon CR0 4YY

A catalogue record for this publication is available from the British Library

Library of Congress Cataloguing in Publication data

Roberts, Robert Campbell, 1942–
Emotions in the moral life / Robert C. Roberts.
pages cm
Includes bibliographical references.
ISBN 978-1-107-01682-8
1. Virtues. 2. Emotions (Philosophy). I. Title.
BJ1521.R58 2013
171′.3–dc23
2012048499

ISBN 978-1-107-01682-8 Hardback

Additional resources for this publication at www.cambridge.org/9781107016828

Table of contents

Figure

Acknowledgments

This book has been long in the making and many debts have accumulated in the process. Versions of some parts date back to 1999–2000, when I enjoyed a fellowship from the Center for Philosophy of Religion from Notre Dame, then directed by Alvin Plantinga; the manuscript was completed under the benefit of another such fellowship in 2011–12, from the same Center, now directed by Michael Rea. I am grateful also for sabbaticals from Wheaton College (1999–2000) and Baylor University (2011–12), and for a fellowship from the National Endowment for the Humanities (1999–2000).

Parts of the book were presented at Åbo Akademie University, Turku, Finland; a Summer Seminar of the Baptist Association of Philosophy Teachers; Baylor University; the Bled Epistemology Conference; the Brackenridge Philosophy Conference, the University of Texas at San Antonio; the Catholic University of Leuven; Colorado College; George Fox College; the Institute for Advanced Study, Notre Dame; the Ohio State University; the Technical University of Delft; the University of the Andes, Santiago, Chile; and Wheaton College.

For comments, questions, and conversations that made a difference, I am grateful to Mark Alfano, Michael Almeida, Robert Audi, Mike Beaty, David Cockburn, John Deigh, Lindsay Cleveland, Scott Cleveland, Richard Cross, Brandon Dahm, Justin D'Arms, Steve Evans, Peter Goldie, Brad Hadaway, John Hare, David Lyle Jeffrey, Bob Kruschwitz, Blake McAllister, Adam Morton, Martha Nussbaum, Adam Pelser, Michael Rea, Jonathan Sands-Wise, Tasia Scrutton, Greg Smith, David Solomon, Robert Solomon, Carlos Steel, Jim Sterba, Bill Tolhurst, Ryan West, Jay Wood, and Linda Zagzebski. For especially extensive or intensive commentary, I am particularly indebted to Audi, S. Cleveland, and Dahm, McAllister, Pelser, and West.

Part of Chapter 7 appeared in *Emotion Review* 1.3 (2009): 279–86 in a special issue edited by Sabine Döring and Rainer Reisenzein.

Studying virtues

This book is a prolegomenon to a study of human virtues in their connections with emotions and related affective / motivational states. Accordingly, it is a contribution to the broad and diverse field of "ethics," in particular to the subfield sometimes known as "moral psychology." Initiated (or rather, revived) fifty years ago by Elizabeth Anscombe's "Modern Moral Philosophy" (1958) and given increased momentum by several works of Alasdair MacIntyre (1981, 1988, 1990, 1999), the study of virtues is now a major part of moral philosophers' business. In this introductory chapter I will explore the question of how to study the virtues and defend this book's approach.

To ask *how* the virtues should be studied immediately raises the more basic question of *why* study the virtues. Our way of studying them will surely be affected by what we take to be the point of doing so. What is the point of studying the virtues? What do we want to accomplish in studying them? This question, in turn, leads to a broader one: why study moral concepts? Why study the concept of the good, or of obligation, or of supererogation? Maybe we ought to study the virtues for the same reason we ought to study these other concepts. And this question really comes to why we should do moral philosophy – assuming that moral philosophy is in large part the study of moral concepts.

Virtues and theories

Many philosophers these days would say that the point of studying moral concepts, including the concept of a virtue or the concepts of the virtues, is to produce a moral theory. This answer raises a couple of other questions, namely, what are moral theories? and what good are they?

If we look at recent writings on the virtues – say, Michael Slote's *Morals from Motives* (2001) and Rosalind Hursthouse's *On Virtue Ethics* (1999) and many papers on virtue that have appeared in professional journals in recent years, we note frequent recurrence of words like "derive," "derivative," "depend on," "subordinate," "define in terms of," "construct out of," "based," "grounded," "grounding," "independent," "conceptually prior," "supreme," "fundamental," "foundation," and the like in connection with moral concepts. That is, we find authors preoccupied with *ordering* moral concepts in such a way that some of them are subordinated to or derived from other concepts or some single other concept so that some one or small number of moral concepts become the source, the ground, the foundation, the base, the site of derivation, of the others. This ordering will also be an order of justification. The foundational concept presumably does not need justifying, or is self-justifying, and it justifies the other, derivative concepts. Ethical theories will then differ according to which concept or concepts provide the foundation, and which ones are derivative. They will also differ as to how the derivations work and which concepts are closer to the foundation and which more distant from it.

This is one standard model for ethical theory. The pattern is widespread in the modern period. David Hume tends to derive ethical concepts from the human passions, Immanuel Kant from a certain conception of practical reason or obligation, utilitarians from the concept of quantified pleasure, and social contract theorists from the concept of harmonious social functioning. Mark Murphy (2002: 6) comments that "The principle that God is to be obeyed is, on normative versions of divine command theory, supreme due to its status as an independent moral principle that is the source of the correctness of all other moral principles." Some thinkers have tried to avoid the implausibilities entailed by such a broad divine command theory by deriving only the concept of obligation or duty – not, say, the concept of the good or the concepts of all the virtues – from the idea of a divine command. See Adams 1999: chap. 10 and Evans 2004: chap. 5. On this hierarchizing model of moral theory, in "virtue ethics" the concept of virtue somehow becomes the source or foundation of the other concepts of ethics.

A particularly clear example is Slote's 2001 book, whose project is to defend an "agent-based approach to virtue ethics," which "treats the moral or ethical status of acts as entirely derivative from independent and fundamental aretaic (as opposed to deontic) ethical characterizations of motives, character-traits, or individuals" (5). Slote's proposed moral theory accounts for the moral status of acts (good or bad, right or wrong) by deriving it "entirely" from aretaic construals of motives, etc. Thus if we wish to know whether a particular action is a good one, we will try to ascertain the agent's motive in performing it. If his motive was virtuous, then the action was good, and if it was vicious, the action was bad. So, if I give $10 to a beggar out of a morally indifferent motive such as a desire to lighten my billfold a bit, my action is morally indifferent; and if I do so out of a virtuous motive, such as compassion for the beggar, my action is good; and if I perform the action out of a vicious desire to humiliate my walking companions, my action is bad. And this is the *whole* story about the moral goodness or badness of the action, on the sort of theory that Slote is promoting. These moral qualities of the acts do not derive at all from the social consequences of the acts – say, the benefit or harm I do to the beggar or the damage to my relationship with my walking companions – nor do the acts have an "independent" moral value. Furthermore, the moral status of the motives of compassion or cruelty is not derived from any ethical concepts at all. It is "independent [of other moral concepts] and fundamental." This arrangement of the concepts may seem rather artificial and even paradoxical, but it has the merit of bringing a simplifying order to the conceptual array, an order, furthermore, that is *secured* at a certain point. The whole idea of a base or foundation is that of something that needs no securing or deriving, something that will stand fast by itself and give orientation and steadiness to the whole, keeping everything else from slipping. And Slote's theory is an example of *virtue-*ethics because of the place the virtue-concepts occupy in the conceptual system: they (or rather, their motivational aspect) form the base or foundation.

Slote's thought is a particularly clear example of this understanding of moral theory, but we find many examples of it in the literature. Gary Watson (1990) says that an ethics of virtue is "a set of abstract theses about how certain concepts are best fitted together for the purposes of understanding morality ... [in which] the concept of virtue is in some way theoretically dominant" (451). "An ethics of virtue is ... the ... general claim that action appraisal is derivative from the appraisal of character" (452). Watson attributes to John Rawls the view that moral theories differ according to the direction of conceptual derivation. Linda Zagzebski (1996) says that her favored type of moral theory "makes the concept of a right act derivative from the concept of a virtue or some inner state of a person that is a component of virtue" (79), and that "pure virtue theorists deny that virtue is an excellence because it is a means to some external good" (99). Robert Louden's (1997) critique of virtue ethics assumes that it is a theory analogous to deontology and utilitarianism, thus characterized by "conceptual reductionism." For a heroic defense of the foundation proposed by "pure" virtue theory, see Kawall 2009.

We see this pattern in Rosalind Hursthouse's (1999) comment that "according to virtue ethics – and this book – what is wrong with lying, when it is wrong, is not that it is unjust (because it violates someone's 'right to the truth' or their 'right to be treated with respect') but that it is *dishonest*, and dishonesty is a vice" (6). (Note the exclusions. But isn't injustice as much a vice as dishonesty?) Later in the book she affirms vegetarianism "on the grounds that (i) temperance (with respect to the pleasures of food) is a virtue, and (ii) for most of 'us', eating meat is intemperate (greedy, self-indulgent)" (227). But her theory is not a virtue ethics in the strong sense of Watson and Slote, since it makes human nature even more fundamental than the virtues (see her chaps. 9–11).

However, Hursthouse appears to me to be inconsistent in her advocacy of any moral theory at all. For she advocates peaceful coexistence among utilitarianism, deontology, and virtue ethics (5) after, however, earlier noting that virtue ethics has now "acquired full status, recognized as a rival to deontological and utilitarian approaches" (2), and she does do the characteristic theoretical thing of deriving other ethical concepts from her privileged one – virtue – *to the exclusion* of others, even if she does not make that concept foundational. On the purer, Watsonian or Slotean conception, virtue ethics could not peaceably coexist with the other theories because each theory's defining structure – its exclusive derivation of all other concepts from its foundational concept – is incompatible with each other theory's defining structure.

Sometimes, of course, the conceptual regimenting move typical of modern theory is directed *at* the concept of virtue. Thus the concept of virtue is derived from some other single item in the array of ethical concepts. Kant's reduction of virtue to strength in the sense of duty is one historical example. Another is Hume's somewhat indecisive reduction of it to traits that we respond to with positive emotions. A contemporary example is Julia Driver's consequentialist theory (Driver 2001). On Driver's theory, a trait is a virtue exactly to the extent that it generates good consequences, given a "normal" world for its operation. It may accomplish this by a variety of mechanisms that have been thought by many people to contribute non-instrumentally to a trait's status as a virtue – say, by way of benevolent desires, or intentions to perform virtuous actions, or sound moral opinions, or skillful practical reasoning, or morally good emotions. In principle, *any* dispositional mechanism that regularly produced good states of affairs would be a virtue. It could be a disposition to get pleasure, to reason fallaciously, to wish other people ill, to believe falsehoods, or to intend harm to others (see Driver's example of the Mutors in 2001: chap. 3).

Julia Annas (2011: 110–11) points to some "intuitions" about virtues that we must give up if virtues' only value is their good consequences. No doubt *one* consideration that favors counting a trait as a virtue (Slote notwithstanding) is its tendency to generate good consequences, but we praise people not just for the good results of their traits, but for their motives (as Slote would note); and if the results are very good but the motives stink, we don't call the agent virtuous. We praise people for their virtuous motives even while lamenting the outcome of their actions. Another consideration that favors judging a trait to be a virtue is that it constitutes an aspect of its bearer's being an excellent specimen of the human kind. Furthermore, as Driver herself notes, we insist more strongly on appropriate motivation in attributing some virtues (for example, generosity) than others (say, justice). These aspects of our moral practice would have to be revised if we took Driver's theory seriously. In my view, we are less likely to distort the moral concepts and their associated practices if we follow Annas's policy of aiming

> to build upwards from our conceptions of virtue, rather than start on the level of abstract discussion of already developed theory. From this point of view losing such central aspects of virtue [as are lost through theorizing in the modern style] makes it at least unclear what the point is of having a theory of virtue at all. (Annas 2011: 111)

I try to exemplify Annas's approach in Chapter 9, looking at the virtues individually to see how they actually work and interrelate, rather than trying to develop a monolithic theory that runs the risk of unhappy exclusions and procrustean adjustments.

Why theory?

In general, ethical theories differ from one another according to which concept is taken to be the foundational source for the other, derivative, concepts, but they tend to have this common basis-and-derivation structure. Why think ethics ought to have this structure? What is to be gained by trying to order the concepts in this way? One possible answer is "the truth about the concepts." Maybe the ethical concepts just *are* ordered in one of the ways that the various ethical theories say they are, and the point of ethical theory is to ascertain and clearly present these properties of the moral concepts, much as a point of any science is to ascertain and clearly present the properties of the things in its domain. It seems to me that moral concepts do, clearly, bear relations of logical or quasi-logical dependency on one another and that the moral philosopher is the chief investigator of these conceptual relations. An interest in the truth about such relations seems respectable enough. But the effort to find a single, exclusionary ordering of the hierarchical kind that I have been illustrating appears always to generate implausible claims and paradoxes which are then leapt on by theorists with rival agendas. Thus we get the interminable disagreements characteristic of discussions between deontologists, conse-quentialists, social contract theorists, and most recently virtue theorists. Perhaps the truth about the moral concepts is that they are not orderable in the way aspired to by moral theory. Besides the implausibility of moral theories as truth-claims about concept-order, most ethical theorists, if pushed, would be unwilling to think of philosophical ethics as merely a "pure science" of concepts; they want more than just to know, for intellectual satisfaction's sake, what the logical ordering of the moral concepts is; instead, they tend to think that moral philosophy – and therefore presumably moral theory – has some *moral* point.

One possible moral point for ethical theory is "foundationalist": if we can find a foundation that is genuinely secure, and then derive from it, by equally secure methods, everything else that is crucial in ethics, we may have a defense against the moral skepticism and relativism that otherwise seem implied by the deep disagreements that arise in a morally pluralistic society. And as a solvent of moral disagreements, the theory might also be thought a powerful antidote to the social conflicts that can arise from them. This explanation of moral theory's allure is initially plausible if applied to the older theories, in their original contexts. If it were true, as Kant thought, that practical reason is a singular auth-oritative structure that is universally accessible to human minds and that lays down a categorical imperative of duty from which all particular obligations can be derived, then from this foundation of reason it might be possible to resolve all moral disagreements and thus dispel the skepti-cism or conflict that fundamental disagreement seems to entail. Something similar might be admitted if it were true, as the early utilitarians thought, that there is a single, universally plausible concept of human happiness from which, by an incontestable application of universal logic, all particu-lar attributions of the good and the right can be derived. But at the present day, I take it that not even the most confirmed Kantian or utilitarian thinks that the proposed foundation of his or her theoretical structure has the incontestability and universally accessible obviousness that it needs to perform the foundationalist function. In fact, the debates about Kantian and utilitarian ethics concern, to a great extent, the viability of the proposed foundations in light of what appear to be unacceptable moral judgments that derive from them by the rules of derivation that they employ.

Hursthouse points out that if our ethical evaluations of human beings are to follow the naturalistic model, we have to have some conception of human nature. And she admits, ever so briefly, that this can be controversial:

> There is, of course, room for disagreement over what we are. It might be said, for example, that what human beings *are* are possessors of an immortal soul through which they can come to know and love God for eternity. But "ethical naturalism" is usually thought of as not only basing ethics in some way on considerations of human nature, but also as taking human beings to be part of the natural, biological order of living things. Its standard first premise is that what human beings *are* is a species of rational, social animals and thereby a species of living things – which, unlike "persons" or "rational beings", have a particular biological make-up and a natural life-cycle.
>
> If all the above is basically right, then . . . we would expect the structure of our ethical evaluations of ourselves to resemble that of a sophisticated social animal with some differences necessitated by our being not only social but also rational. (Hursthouse 1999: 206)

Hursthouse eschews the foundationalist project, but here she is trying to reduce the number of possible interpretations of "human nature." The argument is weak. People may agree that human beings are "part of the natural, biological order" and yet think that the most important part of our nature is something else. It's perfectly possible to think that we are natural biological beings *with* an immortal soul. And the doctrine of the immortal soul is not necessary for religious conceptions of human nature. With much of pre-Christian Judaism, one might believe that human beings are created in the image of God, without having any opinion about whether the soul is immortal. And part of that concept of human nature would be that human beings are not *just* biological entities, distinguished from the other animals by being a bit smarter in some ways, but are created with a disposition to worship God and a need to do so and to obey him if they are to function well *qua* human beings. To religious people, the idea of leaving out this dimension of human nature is laughable. Believing in a God like the Judeo-Christian God will significantly affect one's list of virtues, for in that case we need not just virtues that fit us for our human-human social life, but also virtues for our divine-human social life: faith, hope, love (of God), and this reference will alter all the other virtues in various ways.

And the numerous religious conceptions of human nature are not the only variants that can affect our ethics and our list of virtues. Aristotle's sexism and belief in natural slaves is not just a result of cultural myopia. His teacher Plato had already called Aristotle's brand of sexism into question, and in the nineteenth century the very sophisticated Nietzsche revived something like Aristotle's belief in natural slavery. Some people still take Stoicism seriously as an account of human nature, and it doesn't fit very well Hursthouse's biological reduction. And Buddhism seems to have yet another way of construing human nature – or perhaps denying altogether that there is such a thing.

Hursthouse adds to certain biological features of human beings that we share with the other animals the attribute of rationality, but what rationality consists in and what its norms are is highly contested. Inspired by economic theories (Becker 1978), sociologists and political scientists have been proposing "rational choice" explanations of human behavior for several decades, but the concepts of practical rationality in the literature are rife and every one of them is contested by one theorist or another. Studies in empirical social psychology have challenged most of the axioms of rationality proposed by rational choice theorists (see Tversky and Kahneman 1986). In the light of all these things, Hursthouse's attachment to "naturalism" as a kind of biological philosophy can begin to look a little parochial or simplistic.

As I said, Hursthouse does not in the strictest sense advocate a virtue-based ethical theory. But the real virtue ethicists, the advocates of a "pure virtue theory," would have an even harder time making plausible the idea that their theory can fulfill foundationalist aspirations. Proposed lists of virtues are as controversial as other kinds of moral claims. Just as there are multiple rival concepts of human nature, practical rationality, and human happiness, so there are multiple and rival concepts of the virtues. Even where two moral traditions agree that, say, courage or justice is a human virtue, it is not so clear that they are agreeing on a virtue. Philosophical analysis will readily show differences in virtue-concepts belonging to different moral traditions, even when the names of the virtues are the same across traditions.

The vices of moral theory

The derivations that are motivated by the theoretical mind-set are notoriously problematic. Earlier I quoted Hursthouse to the effect that "what is wrong with lying, when it is wrong, is not that it is unjust (because it violates someone's 'right to the truth' or their 'right to be treated with respect') but that it is *dishonest*, and dishonesty is a vice" (1999: 6). It seems clear that *one* thing wrong with lying is that it expresses a vice (when it does express a vice). But it seems equally obvious that other things are or can be wrong with lying: its wrongness can derive from its being a violation of somebody's right, either to have the truth or be respected or both. It can also be a violation of God's will. And surely its wrongness derives also from the nasty consequences that so often follow, including human suffering, waste of resources, and the disruptions of social life and degradation of human relationships.

The theorist's exclusivist mind-set closes off promising avenues of reflection and insight. Hursthouse tells us that vegetarianism is right because temperance is a virtue and meat eating is intemperate (1999: 227), but it seems more plausible to ground the value of vegetarianism in the supposition that animals have a right not to be killed for food, or that meat eating causes animal suffering, or that meat eating cuts down on the overall food supply in the world by feeding one kind of food to another kind of food. If we don't appeal to any of these consequences or rights, it is not clear how meat eating, in itself, is intemperate. On the dependency of temperance on other kinds of moral considerations, see Roberts 2013.

Slote notes an objection to his agent-based virtue ethics that follows the pattern of my criticisms of Hursthouse's theoretical exclusivism. The objection is that if to do the right thing *is* to act with virtuous motivation, as agent-based virtue ethics holds, then it's not possible to do the right thing for the wrong reason. But this happens all the time, and the philosopher's ethical reflections ought to allow a place for this, and even illuminate how it's possible. An example from Sidgwick is a prosecutor who does his duty in prosecuting a defendant, but does it from malice. Slote's answer to this objection seems to be that if the prosecutor prosecutes, he does it from *some* sense of duty; because if, horrified by his malice, he decided not to prosecute at all, his inaction would be motivated by "insufficient concern for the public . . . good" (2001: 14). If he does his duty at all, then, he must be motivated by a sense of duty – so this is not a case of doing the right thing for the wrong reason. This defense depends on the fallacy of inferring that if somebody *has* a duty and acts in conformity with it, the act must be motivated by a *sense* of duty. It's bad philosophical practice to construct the moral concepts in a way that rules out distinguishing the value of an action from the value of its motive. In Chapter 6 I'll show how emotions can give various moral identities to an action, but nothing that I say rules out evaluating an action independently of its motivation. Many actions are complex enough to be evaluated in a variety of ways – in terms of what they express, how well-thought-out they are, and their human relational character, in addition to the two ways we've been discussing.

Much of moral theorists' energy is expended in trying to make plausible the implausibilities created by their conceptual reductions. Slote is aware how implausible it is to regiment the moral concepts in a way that rules out evaluating actions in terms of their consequences. To avoid this conclusion, he points out that people who are virtuously motivated just *do* consider carefully the likely consequences of their actions (2001: 17, 34). He thinks this observation protects the priority of motivation while fully acknowledging the importance of consequences, but he seems not to notice how arbitrary this construction is. Rather than say that consequences of a certain kind are good because they are the kind virtuous people aim at, why not say that virtuous people's aims are virtuous because they take good consequences as their objects? If certain kinds of consequences, such as disease and disability and despair and loneliness, were not bad independently of the motivations of people who bring them about, it is hard to see how the desire to avoid such consequences and promote their contraries would be virtuous. Virtues seem to be, in part, patterns of appropriate response to the way the world is, dispositions to avoid bad states of affairs, to correct defects in the world and to make the world approximate better the way it ought to be. Again, it's desirable to be able to acknowledge this kind of plausible explanatory conceptual connection (between motivation and consequences), and Slote's derivational theoretical mind-set rules it out. Our understanding of moral concepts would be better served by having no theory at all, if every theory must prevent our acknowledging some of the ways the moral concepts work.

An argument for moral theory

Slote offers one argument in favor of moral theory in general: the concepts of commonsense morality are disordered, and moral theory can clean up the mess. He gives two examples. Of two equally negligent acts, non-theoretical morality has us blame much more severely the agent whose act results in a disaster than we blame an agent when, by good luck, no disaster occurs. Slote regards this as an incoherency in commonsense morality. The other example is the asymmetry between our judgments of obligation, as regards others and ourselves. We think we sometimes have an obligation to do good for others and always an obligation not to harm them; but non-theoretical morality does not hold that we sometimes have an obligation to do good to ourselves and always have an obligation not to harm ourselves. To Slote it seems unreasonable that we should have obligations to others without having symmetrical obligations to ourselves. He concludes, "we do need some sort of theory in ethics and *have to abandon some intuitions* if we are to gain the sort of paradox-free understanding in that domain that has been and is being sought in set theory, confirmation theory, and a host of other areas in philosophy" (2001: 13; italics added).

What shall we say to this argument? It is less than crystal clear to me that the workings of the concepts that Slote here points to are actually incoherent. In the case of blame for negligence, a premise in Slote's argument is the supposed moral principle that only "voluntary" action or omission, and not accidental circumstance, can contribute to blameworthiness. So we might ask why people are as complacent as they are about their lucky negligences. I think that morally sensitive people do blame themselves fairly strenuously for harmless but potentially harmful negligences, though, of course, when disaster occurs, they feel even worse. So, maybe we create the appearance of inconsistency by consulting the response-patterns of less than ideal exemplars of non-theoretical morality. And maybe part of what makes people of more exemplary character feel more blameworthy than others do for their lucky negligences is the good working of their moral imaginations: they "realize" more vividly and with greater concern and self-transparency than others what they might have done. But the impact of "what they might have done" on their emotions shows the seriousness about consequences of action that is characteristic of non-theoretical morality at its best, and thus why even the morally exemplary obsess less about unconsequential negligences than about disastrous ones. Non-theoretical morality, unlike Slote's reduction, does accord an independent value to consequences, so the conclusion that what happens in the world is irrelevant to blameworthiness denies an essential aspect of such morality. We do appeal in some circumstances to the principle that people are not to be blamed for what is accidental, but the notion of the accidental does not apply in the case Slote describes, since the negligent person is in fact responsible for whatever nasty consequences result from his negligence. I conclude that the first kind of case does not show non-theoretical morality to be incoherent in the way Slote supposes. Morally serious people are less complacent about their lucky negligences than he supposes, and consequences of action bear more on responsibility and blameworthiness than his theory allows.

What about the asymmetry of our obligations to others and to ourselves? The non-theoretical morality that Slote has in mind says we have greater obligation to others than we have to ourselves, and that we have more obligation to close others (friends, family) than we have to other others. Slote thinks that this combination of implications of our concept of obligation is incoherent. If we have no obligations to ourselves (presumably because we usually love ourselves so much that we need no obligation to induce us to treat ourselves right), then we ought to have less obligation to our friends (whom we're at least a little bit inclined to treat well) than to strangers. What shall we say to this argument?

Non-theoretical morality does allow for some obligations to ourselves. We are under some obligation not to destroy ourselves by drinking ourselves into oblivion nightly or smoking cigarettes, and these obligations come into play when we are inclined to abuse ourselves in these ways. Still, obligation probably does apply less to ourselves than to others. But the reason we are under more obligation to others than to ourselves is not the same as the reason we are under more obligation to close others than to distant others. Let us say that obligation applies less to ourselves than to others because we are more inclined, apart from the pull of obligation, to do what obligation requires in our own case than we are in the case of others; but we have stronger obligations to our friends than to strangers because they are "closer" to us: they are more in our sphere, more closely connected to us and dependent on us and so we are more responsible for them. Thus two different kinds of reason bear on strength of obligation, and have implications with different directions. Is this incoherent? It has a certain complexity, but it does not seem to be incoherent.

So, I don't think Slote has shown that we need moral theory to comb out the conceptual tangles in non-theoretical morality. But let's think for a moment about the implications of accepting this as a task of moral theory. Given the two defects that Slote perceives in our non-theoretical moral concepts, the proposed reformation would seem to involve, first, ceasing to blame people more for consequential negligence than for nonconsequential, and, second, taking obligations to ourselves as seriously as we currently take our obligations to others. We might think of the task in one of two ways. The proposed reformation of our ethical thought might be merely academic – just a matter of theory, aimed at giving comfort to conceptually fastidious philosophy professors without touching the moral grassroots. Or it might be a full-fledged campaign of moral reformation aimed at re-educating the masses in the new symmetrical morality.

It seems a little fatuous to think of the task as merely theoretical; after all, the point of the ethical concepts is the pursuit of ethical practices and the formation of ethical character. So, let us say that Slote's reformation will have to get down to the moral grass roots. What are moral grass roots? A natural answer to this question, especially for a virtue ethicist, is "the moral character of individuals." Slote's agent-based virtue ethics, with its reductions, eliminations, and revisions of non-theoretical morality, will have to take root in *people's moral dispositions*. The task of getting people really to think and feel and act in accordance with ordinary, given, traditional, and proven-viable moral frameworks is daunting enough; getting them to grow into a framework theoretically concocted by a philosopher is an exponentially greater task, a nightmare of social complications. We do not know in advance what the psychological and behavioral consequences of revising the moral concepts would be. A revisionary theory like Slote's would be only a beginning; its completion would involve an almost unimaginably complex, socially dangerous, and arduous program of character-reeducation.

No moral philosophers these days, virtue theorists or others, are very serious about the prospect of using moral theory to dispel deep moral disagreements. Very few think of themselves as chemists of the moral concepts in search of the objective and universally accessible truth about their hierarchical ordering. They see too clearly the essential contestability of any foundations that may be proposed. We might wonder, then, why they do moral theory. The answer, it seems, is often something like an appeal to tradition: This is what moral philosophers do. It's what with much sweating lucubration we learned to do in graduate school. If I didn't do this, what *would* I do? I'm too weak to dig, and ashamed to beg. I have a Ph.D. and need to eat; and, besides, the puzzles are challenging enough to be interesting for a long career.

Exploring moral concepts: moral frameworks

Maybe we can find another way to approach ethical concepts, one that avoids the pitfalls of moral theory and yet is recognizably philosophical enough to keep us respectably, maybe even usefully, employed. Let me propose the idea of a *moral framework* or *outlook* or *tradition* as contrasted with that of a moral theory in the modern sense.

Examples of moral frameworks are the outlook represented in the *Iliad* and *Odyssey*, the outlook that Aristotle tries to distill in his ethical writings, the Judaism of the Hebrew prophets, Roman Stoicism, New Testament

Christianity, the outlook expressed in the Qur'an and the Hadith, Puritan Christianity of the seventeenth century, perhaps Nietzsche's attempted revival of the heroic outlook, contemporary democratic liberalism, various contemporary "therapeutic" outlooks, and so forth. All of the outlooks just mentioned have variants, and some of the variants may result from debates that arise between outlooks or within a shared outlook. A moral framework has a vocabulary and is composed of a number of interdependent (mutually defining) ideas that give shape and understanding to the living of its adherents. This notion of living includes such things as acting, thinking, and feeling, and the dispositions to act, think, and feel in ways prescribed by one's framework are personal traits (virtues).

Like moral theories, moral frameworks are ordered sets of concepts that bear on ethics or morality. However, they differ (usually) in origin and in the character of the conceptual order from moral theories. Typically, they have *evolved* over long periods of time in particular moral communities (communities of moral *practices*), though there are sometimes sages or prophets who, more or less suddenly (from a historical standpoint), inject innovations and striking formulations. But even such sages and prophets inherit much from previous moral tradition. Examples of such sages and prophets are Confucius, Socrates, Lao Tzu, Moses, Jesus, Paul the Apostle, Mohammed, and Benjamin Franklin. I think Friedrich Nietzsche regarded himself as a kind of sage or prophet who drew on, developed, and formulated moral concepts from Greek and Germanic heroic traditions. Moral frameworks are "traditional" in this sense, not the sort of thing that a philosopher concocts in his or her study and lectures. They evolve in the course of moral *use*, and thus avoid the existential artificiality that we have noted in moral theories.

The existential artificiality of moral theories – their unlivability – is, of course, a function of the deformation that moral concepts suffer at the hands of philosophers attempting to adjust them for placement in a moral theory. I have argued, using some examples from recent "virtue ethics," that the reductive derivational hierarchical structure of modern moral theories is to blame for the interminable disputes in modern moral philosophy, and for their morally unworkable character. By contrast, moral frameworks, as conceptual systems that have guided and partially constituted moral lives, sometimes over quite long stretches of history, don't have the factitious neatness of moral theories. The concepts are no doubt related in systematic ways: by studying them, one can discern a "logic" or "grammar" in the ways the concepts interlock and support one another. But the order of conceptual interaction in a moral framework cannot be depended on to have any preconceived structure such as modern moral theories preconceive moral concepts to have, and I hypothesize that no moral framework will be found to have the structure of a modern theory.

In Table 1 (p. 16) I have arranged some of the concepts (or rather, concept-types) that typically feature in moral frameworks. I have arranged them under some general headings, with more specific categories underneath. The table does not try very hard for completeness, nor is it fastidious about categorization. It is just a rough display of typical moral concepts.

Such concepts as these from ethical frameworks typically figure in ethical theories, and we have seen that on one major conception ethical theories are competing regimentations of such concepts characterized by attempts to privilege one concept or small cluster of concepts and to derive the remaining ones from the privileged one(s). These regimentations are artificial relative to the "original" concepts in their original order in the moral outlooks. The kind of ethics that I am commending and hope to exemplify in this book does not aim at such a basis-and-derivation regimentation, but instead at a description of the concepts in their interconnections, always with reference, at least implicit, to some moral framework or other. Moral frameworks will differ from one another in giving different places to analogous concepts, and may even lack some of the concepts displayed in the table. For example, Stoic frameworks will treat emotions differently from many other frameworks, and some frameworks will have no place for God, or will conceive God in different ways. Humility and gratitude figure, if they figure at all, quite differently in Aristotle's framework than in Christianity. Socratic humility is presumably a different trait from Christian humility. It should go without saying that moral frameworks not only differ from one another, but also have a great many similarities, among which is a sharing of many of the concept-types arrayed in the Table. No doubt these similarities have encouraged another thought typical of moral theory, namely, that there is some one such set of norms and practices as Morality or Ethics.

I hope is it clear that a moral theory is not the same as a moral framework. A framework is a set of concepts and practices belonging to a community such as Aristotle's city state, the Christian church or some other religious community, the fellowship of Stoics, or the rather loose community constituted by modern Liberalism. A moral theory of the kind criticized here is a hierarchical and derivational regimentation of concepts, most of which will have originated in one moral framework or another. While a framework is an order of concepts, it is not conceptually regimented in the way a theory is, and so is not subject to the conceptual

Table 1 *Table of moral concept-types*

Actions and Omissions
intentional, unintentional; deliberate, impulsive; responsible, negligent;
just, unjust; kind, unkind; helpful, hindering[1]; truth-telling, lying;
property-respecting, stealing, violating

Consequences of Actions and Omissions
good, bad; pleasurable, distressing; harmonious, conflictual; beneficial, harmful

Situations
just, unjust; harmonious, conflictual

Practices
making agreements, contracts, promises; activities like violin playing,
landscape painting, basketball; holding responsible, forgiving, praying,
counseling, seeking counsel

Institutions
just, unjust; as supporting practices

God
as creator, as redeemer, as law-giver, as model

Human Nature
one conception or another thereof
fulfillment, happiness, proper functioning

Exemplars
role model, mentor, sage, saint

Traits of Character (Virtues, Vices)
justice, injustice; kindness, cruelty; humility, arrogance; love, hatred; courage,
cowardice; truthfulness, mendacity; sense of duty, sense of entitlement,
sense of humor

Motives, Reasons, Concerns, Desires
love, hatred; friendship, envy; to help, to hinder; sense of duty; love of justice

Interests (that is, Objects of Interest as an Attitude)
self-interest, family interest, public interest, and the interest of humanity

Emotions, Attitudes
anger, fear, hope, gratitude, horror, pride, surprise, admiration, respect, contempt

Personal Relationships
friendship, enmity, collegiality, spouse–spouse, parent–child, child–parent

Generic Social Roles
parent, child, colleague, boss, employee, citizen, leader, husband, wife

Obligations, Duties, Rights
to do or refrain from doing this or that (actions); to be this or that (virtues);
to feel this or that (love, cheer, obligation)

Rewards, Punishments
honor, dishonor; pleasure, pain; goods, deprivations

Rules, Principles, Maxims, Codes
practical reason, natural law, God's commands

Judgments, Beliefs, Insights, Perceptions, Intuitions

---

[1] I intend this and the following "ing" words to be read as adjectives.

troubles that dog moral theories. Once the concepts reappear in the theory, they will not be quite the same concepts they were before; for some of their connections with other moral concepts will have been cut off and some new connections will have been established. A similarity between moral frameworks and moral theories is that frameworks are always normative and theories are sometimes intended to be normative. For provocative comments on the moral ills that attend efforts to make moral theories function normatively, and likewise the neglect of such application, see Stocker 1976.

Though the descriptive project that I envision does not aim at the one-directional derivations that moral theories exemplify, it will identify analogous relations of support and implication – often, *mutual* support and implication – among the moral concepts. If such relations did not exist "naturally" among the moral concepts, it is hard to imagine how moral theory would have prospered at all; it inherits whatever plausibility it has from such natural connections. For this reason also, reading moral theory can help the descriptive virtue ethicist. Even if moral theory tends to create conceptual tangles, it does at least involve careful consideration of concepts, and theoretical ingenuity in ethics can sometimes yield interesting insights – or at least incite the descriptive ethicist to interesting observations of her own.

Just about any of the concepts named in the foregoing Table are apt topics of philosophical reflection (and have been such), and a deft and colorful treatment of them might deepen our understanding of the moral life in some framework. Such a treatment will inevitably *focus* on the concept in question, but equally it will draw connections of that concept to other parts of the conceptual array. That is what conceptual description – and philosophical ethics in the mode that I am commending – would be. To focus on a concept, be it *responsibility*, or *God*, or *obligation*, or *virtue* (or one of the virtues) is quite different from trying to make that concept a foundation from which all the other concepts in the array can be derived. A book like the present one, that focuses on virtues, can thus be a "virtue ethics" in a sense quite different from that intended by Hursthouse, and even more different from that intended by Slote. But to call my kind of endeavor "theory" is not necessarily wrong, especially if one hearkens to the etymological suggestions of the word, since qewriva in ancient Greek meant something like "viewing" or "contemplating" (see Louden 1992: 85–86). For the aim of the kind of analysis I am attempting is a presentation of a concept that promotes a clear "seeing" of it, a presentation that Wittgenstein (1953: § 121) calls a "perspicuous representation" (*übersichtliche Darstellung*). But it seems to me more precise, in that case, to drop the article from "theory": if I do moral "theory," I do it without having a moral theory. (Not having a moral theory differs from not having a moral point of view, and not having a theory of virtue is not the same as having nothing insightful to say about it.)

Emotions, virtues, and moral understanding

This book and its intended sequel focus on the intersection of two families of moral concepts – that of the emotions and that of the virtues – and on the various relations of various members of these two families. The current volume extends the account of emotions that I started in *Emotions: An Essay in Aid of Moral Psychology* (2003), and explores the connections of emotions to such things as moral judgments, actions, personal relationships, and happiness. On the assumption that such relevancies of emotion to the moral life all bear in important ways on the virtues, its explorations should prepare the way for the discussions of virtues in Chapter 9, and the much fuller discussion of them in a successor volume.

In my view, the heart of any serious study of virtues will explore the virtue-concepts one by one; the present project aims at understanding the virtues with special interest in their involvement with various kinds of emotion. To me, it looks quite ironic how little of the writing on virtue ethics in recent decades contains sustained reflection on particular virtues. Instead, references to particular virtues tend to function as illustrations, since the philosopher's primary interest is not in the virtues, but in "virtue ethics" as a theory that rivals the main modern ethical theories. In the third edition of Christina Hoff Sommers's *Vice and Virtue in Everyday Life* (1993), she added a number of essays on particular virtues and vices. In the fourth edition these papers were removed. Professor Sommers has told me that the change was due to a publisher's survey of college teachers showing that the papers on particular traits were assigned significantly less frequently than the others. Such was the grip on philosophy teachers' minds that to "do ethics" is to "do moral theory." For signs that this attitude may be changing, see Timpe and Boyd 2013 and Austin and Geivett 2012.

At the beginning of this chapter I asked what is the point of philosophical ethics, and in particular what is the point of philosophizing about the virtues. I have argued that an ethical theory is not a very promising goal, and have proposed descriptive virtue ethics as an alternative. So far, however, I have argued for its superiority mainly on the grounds that it is a more "natural" approach to the conceptual array, less likely than moral theory to distort the concepts. But this is a rather "scientific"-sounding reason for preferring description, and I have also suggested that serious moral philosophy is not just a scientific enterprise, but ought to be contributing something to people's moral lives. I think that a plausible and worthy goal for moral philosophy is the enhancement of moral understanding and thus of wisdom (see also Roberts 1994; Roberts and Wood 2007).

Moral wisdom is a special clarity of mind about the moral life, not an abstractly intellectual clarity but one that has a strong affective and motivational dimension. It is an unusually good knowledge of one's way around in one's moral framework. I share with ancient philosophers (Socrates, Plato, Aristotle, the Stoics, the Epicureans) the hope and belief that philosophical reflection on ethics can contribute something to our wisdom. I think, also with most of the ancients, that the virtue-concepts are an especially fruitful focus for reflection that aims at moral understanding. Philosophical ethics as conceptual description (as contrasted with construction) can contribute to this condition of individual human minds because morality is deeply conceptual and conceptual description clarifies concepts. If it is well done, it can affect the thinking, feeling, and action of the person who engages it.

Among the many morally relevant concepts (see Table 1), the virtues, and the emotions that are relevant to their analysis, are two especially interesting and wisdom-generating foci. Since these foci gather together many important aspects of a moral outlook in a way that is personally involving, considering them can be an especially potent way for philosophy to contribute to moral understanding. As a combination, they are also a theme that has run through the history of philosophical ethics. In his *Republic*, Plato makes *dikaiosunê* (justice, righteousness) a matter of the proper integration of *to thumoeidês* (the "high-spirited part") with *to logisticon* (the "reasoning part") in allied governance of *to epithumêticon* (the "desiring part"). In *Nicomachean Ethics*, Aristotle makes virtue a mean with respect to action (*praxis*) and emotion (*pathos*). Thomas Aquinas devotes QQ 22–48 of *Summa Theologiae* 1a2æ to the *passiones*, in preparation for his discussions of the virtues. David Hume devotes Book 11 of his *Treatise of Human Nature* to the passions, in preparation for his discussion of the virtues in Book 111. *The Theory of Moral Sentiments* is Adam Smith's book on "virtue ethics." And when John Rawls (1971: chap. 8) comes to discuss justice as a personal virtue, the moral sentiments figure importantly in his discussion.

The question of style

To make moral wisdom an important goal of philosophical ethics is to heighten the question of philosophical style. Moral philosophy has been written (and spoken) in a huge variety of styles, including Plato's dialogues, the letters and essays of the Stoics, the novels and plays of the French existentialists, the highlighted propositions and fussy algebraic formulae of twentieth-century analytic philosophy, the history-of-thought approach of writers like Alasdair MacIntyre and Charles Taylor, the esoteric jargon of some of our contemporary "continental" philosophers, the edifying discourses of Søren Kierkegaard, the scholastic question-and-debate format of Thomas Aquinas's *Summa Theologiae*, and the theoretical essay that is currently so common in present-day books and professional journals. Much of this contains conceptual points that could be moral wisdom were they so digestible as to be rightly assimilated by the mind and heart; but these styles vary considerably in their aptitude to aid moral digestion.

It is possible to write as weakly and abstractly about moral character and the moral emotions as about other topics in ethics, but more difficult. Both of these concepts resist abstraction (especially when one is talking about particular traits and particular emotion types) and invite narrative investigation. Narratives have a natural immediacy and memorability that fit them especially well to promote wisdom. The philosopher will write little narrative snapshots to illustrate points, but I think he or she will also do well to exploit major storytellers. The great novelists of the nineteenth century – the likes of Jane Austen, George Eliot, Dickens, Dostoevsky, Tolstoy, and Henry James – are also great moral psychologists. Their stories embody an impressive understanding of emotions and virtues, and their narrative artistry presents these with vivacity and grip. In their graphic way, the novelists clarify moral concepts to a degree that few if any moral philosophers can achieve by purely philosophical means. The novelists' advantage is that they present characters, across significant stretches of time collapsed into a manageable few hundred pages, in the varying contexts of a lived life, and often with special reader access to the mental states of the characters. The philosopher can capitalize on such books, especially ones that are widely read, for his or her own perspicuous representations of the concepts under investigation. He can direct his conceptual remarks to features of the narrative presentation.

The following are some of the devices by which the philosopher constructs perspicuous representations of moral concepts. He formulates remarks on the conditions for the application of a concept, for example, the kinds of considerations that can be appealed to in making justice-claims. He locates the concept in question in relation to other concepts, for example, comparing the sense of duty as a passional virtue with justice or generosity as other, but different, passional virtues. The philosopher may formulate formal sentences representing the form of thought characteristic of an emotion of a given type (see my *Emotions* (Roberts 2003): chap. 3, for many examples, and many examples in the present volume). He may compare analogous virtue-concepts across moral frameworks, for example, Christian compassion with the compassion endorsed by the Greek tragedians. Or run counterfactual variations on narrative depictions of virtues and / or emotions to bring out special features of the concepts. For the kind of moral philosopher I am trying to conceive, all of these devices, and no doubt more, will be in the service of a clarifying presentation of the moral concepts that is compelling enough to deepen ethical understanding.

Apologetics and inter-framework debate

I have argued that the main reason for studying the moral concepts, including the virtue-concepts, is to deepen our moral understanding. But I want to end this chapter by noting another moral use for the kind of descriptive ethics that I endorse. Nothing that I have said about the diversity of moral frameworks should be taken to suggest that they are all equally coherent or deep. Serious people who are reflective about their own moral frameworks, and therefore realize that some others in the world disagree with them, not just in particular judgments, but in outlook, take their own moral outlook to be *correct*, and take outlooks that are in one way or another contrary to their own to be *incorrect* in some way or other (though any moral framework can be judged correct in some ways from the viewpoint of some other framework). And they may be right in these judgments. Out of concern for others they may want to commend their own outlook to them – or they may be interested in debating partisans of another framework because they suspect that the others' framework is closer to the truth, in some regard, than their own. The kind of understanding and articulateness that comes from philosophically exploring the moral concepts prepares one to formulate arguments for such purposes. Consider a couple of examples of a Christian moral apologetic. Notice that features of the Christian moral outlook are argumentatively exploited with the particular features of the opposing framework in view.

My first case involves not virtue-concepts, but the concept of obligation. In her famous article "Modern Moral Philosophy," Elizabeth Anscombe argues that a certain concept of moral obligation, to which some modern atheists and agnostics feel allegiance, makes no sense apart from the notion of a divine Obliger. The notion in question is that of an *unqualified* obligation, which might be formulated as "you must (or must not) do such-and-such *no matter what you want.*" We might say that my formulation indicates part of the grammar of the kind of obligation that Anscombe has in mind. Another part of that grammar could be formulated as "unqualified obligation is established by the will of God." This last formulation is a grammatical remark about the concept of obligation in a moral framework that is either Christian or a descendant of Christianity or some other relevantly similar form of theism. It seems clear that these two features of a theistic concept of obligation go hand-in-glove. If we ask, within the Christian framework, what is the ground of the unqualified character of moral obligation?, the ready answer is, it derives from God's will. So, Anscombe claims, in effect, that these two features – being unqualified by human purposes, and being commanded by God – are inseparable not just within the Christian moral framework, but in general. Any moral framework that includes the notion of unqualified obligation, and yet leaves out God as the Lawgiver, is inconsistent.

Anscombe proposes that, to avoid this inconsistency, modern atheists should give up the idea of unqualified obligation and resort to a kind of hypothetical obligation that has the logic, "if you wish to flourish as a human being, then you must . . ." But to modern people who find they cannot give up the notion of unqualified obligation, she might instead have insisted that they need to rethink their atheism. Perhaps Anscombe is right about the inseparability of unqualified obligation and theism, or perhaps other concepts of obligation are possible that approximate the unqualified character of the Christian concept, yet without bringing in a divine Maker of obligation. I won't decide that issue here, but we can see that the exploration of moral concepts within a framework could yield a kind of apologetic argument. Someone whose moral outlook included a strong sense of unqualified obligation, but without including God, might be brought, by a Christian *phronimos* (wise person), to see that he needs to allow a place for God in his moral life. Note, however, that such an argument would have appeal only for someone who already had a fairly strong sense of unqualified obligation and was not too strongly averse to the idea of God. The character of the argument, its relevance, and its potential to convince depend on particular features of the two frameworks in debate, and on particular conceptual-affective commitments of the parties to the debate.

A second example, which comes from Alasdair MacIntyre's book *Dependent Rational Animals* (1999), does bear on virtue-concepts. The Christian moral framework takes more note of human weakness and dependency than do some others. Consequently it has a special place for virtues of compassion and generosity (virtues of giving to others in need), and virtues of humility and gratitude (virtues acknowledging one's own need and others' contribution to one's wellbeing). MacIntyre calls such traits "virtues of acknowledged dependence." In moral frameworks such as those explored by Aristotle and Nietzsche, the stress is much more strongly on self-sufficiency and power over others, and traits like humility and compassion will not appear in the virtue-lists, and may even be among the vices. Aristotle may admit gratitude as something like a virtue in somewhat inferior people, but not at all in the best people, and both Aristotle and Nietzsche have very different conceptions of generosity (*eleutheriotês, die schenkende Tugend*) from the Christian one, in which generosity is essentially motivated by a concern for the wellbeing of the recipient. MacIntyre's exploration of these virtue-concepts is a sort of apologetic argument for the framework, directed at adherents of moral frameworks that tend to ignore or depreciate human dependency and devalue dependent persons.

It seems pretty obvious that we all start out weak and dependent, owing our very existence to our guardians' provisions, and owing the wellbeing of our minds and personalities to their nurture and generous care. As our lives progress, we meet again with periods of weakness and dependency if we are sick or injured, eventualities to which we are always liable; and we depend on others in countless ways, even when we are strong and healthy, for virtually all the aspects of our wellbeing. Finally, if we live long enough, we will inevitably again be weak and dependent on the ministrations of others in our old age. So, a pretty strong argument can be made against moral frameworks that major in self-sufficiency to the point of ignoring the virtues of acknowledged dependence or rejecting them as vices. The argument starts with the grammar of gratitude, humility, compassion, and generosity, and then points out their excellent fit with these broad diagnostic facts about human life.

But this argument, too, does not compel by its logic and evidence alone. It is very unlikely that Aristotle and Nietzsche are unaware of the cited facts of human dependency and weakness, and many moral outlooks, including Christianity, include *some* kind or degree of self-sufficiency in their character-ideal. (Another part of the character-ideal that looms large in *Dependent Rational Animals* is that of being an "independent practical reasoner.") So, the issue between Christianity and these other outlooks is not an exclusive choice between acknowledging dependency and vulnerability, and accommodating the human need for self-sufficiency. Both kinds of outlook have *some* way of accomplishing both tasks. The issue is one of evaluative emphasis and interpretation. Aristotle and Nietzsche *revere* strength and self-sufficiency and think of weakness and dependency as rather accidental to human nature and as at best a necessary evil (shameful), something to be got through. So, an argument like MacIntyre's needs to catch the Aristotelian or the Nietzschean in the right mood, or manage somehow to create one, or encourage by rhetorical means a "seeing" of the issue in his own way. There is argument here, and from time to time it may effect a conversion or a partial one. But it will do so, if it does, as much by mood and rhetoric as by facts and logic.

Apologetics and inter-framework debate is a legitimate moral reason for studying virtues, but to me it seems an auxiliary reason. The chief reason is to understand the virtues better and thus to deepen and confirm our moral understanding and that of our readers. In the chapters that follow, I will be exploring two kinds of morally relevant concepts – that of emotions and that of virtues – and I will treat these concepts as important and integral members of the larger array of concepts that make up moralities. My own framework is Christianity, though often my remarks will apply also to a theologically attenuated moral framework inherited from Christianity. I will also, from time to time, comment about the grammar of counterpart concepts from other moral frameworks, on the assumption that such juxtaposition and comparison can function as a "perspicuous representation" of some aspect of the frameworks. My approach will be nontheoretical, grammatical, and exploratory, and I will try to anchor my discussions in bits of realistic narrative that aid understanding by keeping the discussions on solid human ground.

2

The roles of emotions: an overview

Introduction

The Stoics hold a minority view on the place of emotions (passions) in the moral life. They are notable for their blanket moral rejection of emotions from the morally perfected human being. In this brief chapter I will present an argument of the apologetic kind that I mentioned in the last pages of Chapter 1. It consists of several smaller arguments, all using the standard philosophical strategy of counterexample that appeals to the reader's intuitions. Taking the point of view of frameworks that share the feature of allowing that emotions of most types may have *either* positive *or* negative moral value, I'll argue against the Stoics' evaluation of emotions.

The Stoic sensibility is recurrent in the history of thought. It is present in the feeling that emotions are in some kind of basic opposition to "reason," and that to be morally perfected is to be tranquil, disinterested, objective, detached. The Stoics' own word for this ideal state of character is *apatheia*: passionlessness. The most famous moral philosophical heir of the Stoics is Immanuel Kant. In defense of the moral idea of apathy, in a section titled "Virtue Necessarily Presupposes *Apathy* (Regarded as Strength)," Kant says,

> An affect always belongs to sensibility, no matter by what kind of object it is aroused. The true strength of virtue is a *tranquil mind* with a considered and firm resolution to put the law of virtue into practice. That is the state of *health* in the moral life, whereas an affect, even one aroused by the thought of what is good, is a momentary, sparkling phenomenon that leaves one exhausted. (Kant 1996a: 536 [*Doctrine of Virtue* XVII, 6: 409]; italics original)

Sensibility is for Kant the non-rational area of the human mind, which he associates with sensation, sensory desire, inclination, heteronomy, self-interest, and passivity; and he dissociates sensibility strongly from reason, agency, duty, limitation of self-love, and autonomy. But Kant is a mild sort of Stoic in his moral attitude towards emotions. Unlike the original Stoics, he doesn't think emotions to be positively morally pernicious as a class, and even allows one emotion type – respect for the moral law – an essential role in morality and a special connection to rational agency. Emotions of all other types, however, he classes as "inclinations" and thus as essentially non-moral, merely "pathological" motives, and thus prone to displace the properly moral motive of duty, though Kant does ascribe such motives, when aroused by the thought of what is good, an instrumental value in getting duty done (Kant 1996a: 49–50 [*Groundwork* 4: 393]). He also says that if we always only acted from duty, never feeling any benevolence for each other, "a great moral ornament ... would then be missing from the world" (Kant 1996a: 576 [*Doctrine of Virtue* § 35, 6: 458]). But, despite these non-Stoic elements, Kant is like the Stoics in ruling out the epistemic, motivational, and aretaic roles of emotions in morality that I argue for in this chapter and, more extensively, in this book.

The Stoics' blanket rejection of emotions from the morally perfected human being is the official position; their distinctions of real emotions [passions] from "first movements" (Seneca 1995: 42–45 [*On Anger* II.1–4]) and "*eupatheiai*" (Sorabji 2000: 47–51), and of goods and evils from preferred and dispreferred indifferents (Sorabji 2000: 169–75) are more or less slippery conceptual devices for softening the position without abandoning it. A little more cynically, we can see them as pedals designed for backing away from implausibilities.

My argument will serve as an introduction to the theme and main chapters of this book. The overall argument of the book is that emotions play a variety of roles in the moral life, for *better* and for *worse*. They can serve both to enhance and to block or degrade our moral knowledge. They can play a crucial role in the motivation of our actions, giving us reasons both morally good and morally bad for action. They can play a constitutive role in our interpersonal relationships, both in good ones like friendship and in bad ones like enmity. They can make for human happiness and fulfillment, or for misery and dysfunction. And, finally, gathering together emotions' epistemic, motivational, relational, and eudaimonic functions in a rich variety of ways, the variously structured virtues get their structures in large part from the involvement of emotions in them.

Let's begin by considering the Stoic's backpedals.

First movements. We might think that the Stoic project is doomed from the start by the fact that human beings are fundamentally emotional in our nature, so that no kind of discipline is up to making us passionless. Seneca heads off this objection at the beginning of Book 11 of *On Anger* by admitting that "involuntary movements can neither be overcome nor avoided" (11.2.1) and reels off a list of what appear to be emotional states: we hear bad news and our hair stands on end; we hear indecent language and blush; we peer into a precipice and feel vertigo; we feel a "mental jolt" (11.2.2) when we think ourselves wronged or when we read of terrible injustices; we're moved by a martial sound of trumpets or by the grim sight of a just punishment; we laugh when others laugh, sink into depression at the sight of a crowd of mourners, and "boil over at conflicts which have nothing to do with us" (11.2.5). Here the "we" includes the sage, the fully mature Stoic, for even he (if such a person exists) has no control over such "movements." But, says Seneca, none of the above is really an emotion; so far we have mentioned only "first movements," the reflexive non-rational preludes to emotion. An emotion can follow such movements, but only if the subject assents to the impression that evokes the movement. For a true passion to occur, the subject must credit the first movement with rationality and truth, and consent to it with his will. He must voluntarily engage the first movement. Only then has the subject come into a passion and thus enslaved himself.

Eupatheiai. Even the Stoic, whose moral ideal is detached tranquility vis-à-vis the vicissitudes of the world, can't quite get over the intuition that some things are worth being glad about, at least in a relatively quiet, calm-spirited sort of way. Since the Stoic wants to indict passions wholesale, it will be handy to have a term other than "passion" (*passio, pathê*) for those passion-like states that need to escape the indictment. The word "*eupatheia*" means something like "good emotion." Sorabji (2000: 47) tells us that they come in three kinds: joy, will, and caution. They are not, however, what we call joy, will, and caution. These are states that only the Stoic sage can have, and most of us are very far from being Stoic sages. For example, the objects of eupathic joy are such things as the rational order of the universe and the deeds of temperate persons, and eupathic joy is supposed to be a very stable state, not changing into its opposite. One might think that a disposition to feel joy at the deeds of temperate persons would be also a disposition to feel distress at the deeds of the intemperate, but the Stoics don't allow such distress to be a *eupatheia* because it would disturb the Stoic's tranquility. For two reasons, worldly joys such as joy in the health and wellbeing of one's children are not good: because the object is not truly good, and because such passions are prone to turn into disturbing passions like sadness and despair, in case one's children become ill or die. The person who is subject to such joys and sorrows is spiritually a slave of the vicissitudes of life.

   Preferred and dispreferred indifferents. According to the Stoics, nothing is good except the rational order of the universe and the conformity of the mind to that order (that is, wisdom, virtue); and, conversely, nothing is bad except the unconformity of the mind to that order (vice). "Thus it comes about that all of the following are for the Stoics indifferent: life, health, pleasure, beauty, strength, well-functioning sense organs, wealth, reputation and their opposites, death, disease, pain, ugliness, frailty, disablement, poverty, low repute, and ignoble birth" (Sorabji 2000: 169–70). Epictetus expresses this view when he says,

> When you see anyone weeping in grief because his son has gone abroad, or is dead, or because he has suffered in his affairs, be careful that the appearance may not misdirect you. . . . As far as words go . . . don't reduce yourself to his level, and certainly do not moan with him. Do not moan inwardly either. (Epictetus, *Enchiridion* 16)

Epictetus suggests that someone who weeps because his son has died shows thereby a deficiency in wisdom, and that it would be similarly unwise for an associate to sympathize with him in his grief. This judgment can seem harsh, even to the Stoic. Since the list of indifferents is a list of precisely the kinds of things that most people value, positively or negatively, including people widely thought to be good and wise, the Stoic needs a conceptual device for softening the shock to common sense.

   The device consists in saying that while life and health, for example, are not strictly *good*, they are to be "preferred," and while death and illness are not strictly *bad*, it is appropriate to "disprefer" them. The distinction between "preferred" and "good" raises the question of how they are related. In this connection, Sorabji discusses the Stoics' approval of suicide and notes that they were divided in their opinions about how to justify it. Cicero took what we might call the soft or more commonsense line and said that suicide was justified for someone faced with a preponderance of what is dispreferred over preferred. This opinion tends to transform the dispreferred into the bad, and so to abandon the distinction, along with Stoicism. Seneca, by contrast, took a more orthodox line and said that suicide in the face of illness, senility, or pain was justified only if these dispreferred things prevented one's exemplifying virtue, which is not just preferred, but good. This rationale also seems questionable on Stoic grounds in allowing that virtue can be held hostage to things that are, strictly speaking, indifferent.

In this chapter I choose to focus on an emotion (type) that comes in for especially vehement rejection by the Stoics, one that non-Stoics too are likely to find problematic, namely, anger. In the Preface of Book 1 of his treatise *On Anger*, Seneca offers a number of reasons for extirpating this emotion from our lives:

> Raving with a desire that is utterly inhuman for instruments of pain and reparations in blood, careless of itself so long as it harms the other, [anger] rushes onto the very spear-points, greedy for vengeance that draws down the avenger with it. . . . oblivious of decency, heedless of personal bonds, obstinate and intent on anything once started, closed to reasoning or advice, agitated on pretexts without foundation, incapable of discerning fairness or truth . . . Now look at its consequences and the losses which it occasions. . . . You will see slaughter, poisoning, charge and sordid counter-charge in law-courts, devastation of cities, the ruin of whole nations . . . Anger changes all things from the best and justest condition into the opposite. Whoever falls into its power, forgets all obligation. Allow it, and a father turns into an enemy, a son into a parricide, a mother into a stepmother, a citizen into an enemy, a king into a tyrant. (Seneca 1995: 17–18 [*On Anger*, Book 1, Preface])

We can read Seneca in this passage as claiming that anger has negative moral value of seven or so kinds: it impedes epistemic processes, provides bad motivation for actions, has bad consequences, fouls up personal relationships, and creates human misery. We can generalize these five failings in terms of two others: anger makes us dysfunctional and unhappy and puts us out of tune with the universe we inhabit. Let's look at each of these accusations in turn.

Epistemic value

Seneca notes that anger can make a person "closed to reasoning or advice, ... incapable of discerning fairness or truth," "oblivious of all decency," and forgetful of all obligation. We've all seen instances of such epistemic incapacitation at the hands of emotion, and especially anger. But consider the following kind of case. Two white persons are watching a documentary on the history of the civil rights movement in the latter half of the twentieth century in the USA. The video shows the horrors experienced by blacks in Mississippi and Alabama in the 1950s and 1960s, but also documents the real progress that some parts of the black community have made over the last six decades.

One of the watchers tracks the narrative with the following emotions: he responds to the clips of church bombings, mourning of the victims, and fire-hosing of the crowds by feeling such uncomfortable emotions as guilt, pity, and indignation (a variant of anger); and he tracks with pleasant emotions of hope, joy, and gratitude the later clips of prosperous middle-class black households enjoying family fun. In contrast, the other watcher is amused by the sight of the protesters being scattered pell-mell by the powerful streams of water turned on them but feels nothing much in response to the later scenes of family happiness. Which of these two persons *understands* better the values that inhere in the situations presented in the video? Which of them has higher quality *knowledge* of what went on in black communities in the fifties and sixties in the USA? I will argue, in Chapters 3, 4, and 5 that emotions are a kind of perceptual state through which we can be acquainted with the values (positive and negative) that situations have. They thus play a crucial role in our epistemic wellbeing – our fitness to know and understand certain truths, and to deliberate rationally.

Thomas Aquinas, in a critical discussion of the Stoics on anger, concedes that anger always "prevent[s] judgments of reason" in cases where the anger *precedes* the judgment, "since the soul can best judge truth in a certain tranquility of mind" (Aquinas 2003 [*On Evil*, Question 12, Article 1, reply]), but he criticizes the Stoics for neglecting the cases in which the judgment comes first, and the anger follows. Since in these cases the judgment of reason comes first, it is not disturbed by anger, and instead shapes and guides anger. But Aquinas concedes too much to the Stoics. If a person's emotional sensitivity with respect to justice is well formed, the emotion may trigger the judgment, rather than vice versa. It might well happen that our emotionally sensitive video watcher feels indignation well up in him, and only thereafter, as in response to a moral perception, forms the judgment that the actions of the authorities were highly unjust. If his anger springs from a genuine sensitivity to injustices (namely, the virtue of justice), then it may be analogous to the perceptions of an expert bird-watcher which give rise to the birdwatcher's judgments about the species to which birds belong – an excellent basis for the judgment. See Gladwell 2005 for several compelling examples of emotional perception that precedes explicit judgment and far from degrading its rationality contributes rational justification.

Brandon Dahm has pointed out to me that Aquinas's claim that the judgment of reason must precede the emotion for the emotion not to "disturb" the judgment may allow of a broader interpretation than I have given it. Dahm proposes that *Summa Theologiae* 2a2ae 157–58 may be read as suggesting that in the gentle person (the person whose anger-disposition tends to produce anger at the right objects, for the right reasons, with the right intensity and duration, etc.), reason "precedes" the anger-disposition insofar as that *disposition* is formed in accordance with reason. This could be so even if, in the particular instance, the anger precedes the judgment. If this reading of Aquinas on the judgment's precedence of anger in giving rise to a moral judgment is correct, then his view would resemble the one I offered in the preceding paragraph.

The Stoics are right to point out that anger and other emotions can blind us to what is just, close our minds to reasoning and advice, and cause us to "forget" the values that we know. Perhaps emotions' "perceptual" character is itself what equips them to do this epistemic harm. If emotions always present situations to us in a certain "light," then if that light is a false, distorting light, a light that colors things in evaluative colors not their own, emotions can be an epistemic liability as well as boon. The proper remedy, then, is not to extirpate emotions altogether – not even "nasty" ones like anger – but to become the kind of person who, as Aristotle says, "is angry at the right things and with the right people, and, further, as he ought, when he ought, and as long as he ought" (Aristotle 1980: 96 [*Nicomachean Ethics* 1125b 32–34 (Ross)]). See aretaic value, below. Part of the excellence of being such a person, I will argue, is the access that it gives to epistemic goods. Of course, the Stoic will think that there *aren't* any right things, people, etc. to be angry about, because the very fact that the so-called "(dis)value" is grasped with anger is enough to show that it is not really a (dis)value, but an indifferent. Aristotle, like the New Testament (see Eph. 4:25–27), is cautiously aware of the liabilities of anger, but, believing that some of the occasions of anger are not about indifferents, but about real values, allows for occasions on which it is appropriate. Anger is a partially epistemic response to wrongs, and wrongs are sometimes real.

Intrinsic practical value

Seneca says the angry person is moved to action by the prospect of pain and harm to the supposed offender, a pain and harm with the character of revenge or "getting even," and he paints this desire in the bloody terms of spear-points and the like. He is all too obviously right that anger sometimes accounts for murders and tortures. I think he is right to suppose that it involves desiring the offender to have unpleasant experiences. But it is less obvious that all anger wishes actual harm to the offender. Plenty of unpleasant experiences are not harmful – indeed, can be beneficial – and besides, unpleasant experiences admit of an enormous range, all the way from lethal torture on the end of the spectrum that Seneca stresses down to the mild embarrassment that a dirty look may be calculated to cause. From time to time, perfectly loving parents get angry with their children, and thereby wish the children, not harm, but various kinds of discomfort and inconvenience. Analogous points can be made about the civilized anger that occurs between friends or colleagues, and determines the moral character of the actions that emerge from it. It seems plausible to suppose that such anger is sometimes justified by the situation and the action or inaction or negligence that it responds to. The justification (or lack thereof) possessed by the emotion can transfer to the action that it motivates, as I will show in Chapter 6, giving actions an enormously rich spectrum of possible values, some of which are contraries, though simultaneously possessed by a "single" action.

The colorful imagery with which Seneca prefaces *On Anger* is calculated to turn the reader absolutely and totally against the emotion, and is part of the larger project of making plausible the Stoic program of eradicating emotions across the board. But this effect depends on feeding the reader a rather narrow diet of examples. If we take a more balanced diet, as I try to do in this book, I think we'll be inclined to favor moral outlooks that allow emotions of almost all types (possibly excluding such types as *Schadenfreude* and unfriendly envy) to have positive moral status – while also allowing some instances of almost all types (including, for example, joy and gratitude) to have negative moral status.

Consequential value

Emotions have good and bad consequences, and can thus have extrinsic value, for better or worse. Anger can result in destruction of life and treasures, as Seneca notes. He doesn't note that anger can also procure the righting of wrongs and prevent exploitation and future disasters. Think again of the civil rights movement in the USA and the anger that was instrumental in its accomplishments. Fear, which is a natural response to anger, can forestall the doing of good, but also the doing of harm. Even envy, which may arguably never convey intrinsic good to the action it motivates, may bring on good consequences by motivating the envier to self-improvement. When detailing the consequential evils of anger, Seneca rightly stresses evils brought on by *actions* motivated by the emotion. But actions are not the only way that emotions mediate consequences. A person who "controls" his anger to the extent of not acting on it may nevertheless express it in gesture, voice, and face, thus depressing the spirits of his associates and discouraging worthwhile actions on their part. By the same token, though, a better functioning person's expressions of anger may throw proper caution into the company, depressing poisonous mirth and foolishness and discouraging ill-advised actions.

I'll briefly discuss the extrinsic value of emotions in Chapter 6, but that chapter will give most attention to the way emotions invest the actions they motivate with intrinsic practical value.

Relational value

Seneca comments on the relational (dis)value of emotions when he comments, "Allow [anger], and a father turns into an enemy, a son into a parricide, a mother into a stepmother, a citizen into an enemy." He uses the relational terms "father," "son," "mother," and "citizen" in a moral sense. To be a father or a son in this sense is to stand, not merely in a well-known biological relation to another human being, but in a moral or spiritual or personal relation to the other, a relation that is severely strained (to put it mildly) by hatred. By contrast, there's no conceptual strain at all in the idea of hating someone who physically begat you or whom you begat.

People very often figure in our emotions. When we fear, envy, get angry, rejoice, or hope, it's often *people* we fear or for whom we fear, *people* we envy, *people* we're angry at or on whose behalf we're angry, *people* we rejoice over, *people* we hope for or on whose behalf or in whom we hope. Furthermore, we're enormously sensitive to *other* people's emotions in which *we* figure: to the fact that people fear us, or fear for us, that people envy us, that people are angry with us or with others on our behalf, that people hope on our behalf or place their hope in us. And our sensitivity to others' emotions with respect to us is an emotional sensitivity: we are glad or sorry that people fear us or fear for us, regret that people are angry with us, or hope or fear that they are angry on our behalf; we are glad or angry or sad that they envy us; we rejoice that our friends rejoice with us in our successes or sad or resentful that they don't; we are glad that they hope with us for what is dear to our heart. In the passage I quoted earlier from Epictetus, the grieving person whose Stoic associate refuses to grieve with him is likely to feel that his associate is no friend of his. In short, we care about how others feel about us and about what we feel strongly about.

In Chapter 7 I'll explore how such facts about persons and their emotions constitute, in significant part, the "moral" relations that we bear to one another: friendship / enmity, moral parenthood, moral filiality, moral siblinghood, moral collegiality, and the like. I'll explore how certain co-ordinations of emotion on the part of two or more persons constitute good relations among them, while other co-ordinations constitute bad relations. Moral outlooks that value good relations of these kinds among their practitioners will not want to extirpate the emotions wholesale.

Eudaimonistic value

If we understand "happiness," as I will in Chapter 8, in the sense of what Aristotle calls "eudaimonia" or the kind of wellbeing that a person has when functioning properly *as* a human being in an environment that is approximately conducive to such proper functioning, then the eudaimonistic value of emotions will encompass all the main moral values of emotions: the epistemic, the intrinsic practical, and the relational – assuming that to be human involves very centrally being an agent who knowingly, intelligently, and practically relates to fellow human beings in a variety of norm-governed personal ways. Emotions do not as such make us miserable and dysfunctional, as Seneca and the Stoics would have it. Rather, it is the poor having of emotions or the having of poor emotions that makes for misery, while the virtuous having of emotions or the having of virtuous emotions is a necessary condition for human happiness, as Aristotle and representatives of many other moral outlooks would have it. It is also true, as Aristotle says, that pleasure is an important element in eudaimonia; so the so-called "positive" emotions will have a special place in the life of the happy person. Proper functioning as a person implies the capacity to feel "negative" and "unhappy" emotions when situations call for them; but if they are overwhelming, they are not compatible with happiness.

Aretaic value

The primary Stoic virtue – *apatheia* or emotionlessness – is the corollary of the Stoic conception of value. If none of the objects of emotions has the values that emotions attribute to them, then a right attunement of the individual personality to the world will be one in which, as the Stoic believes, the emotions play no part. But if we believe that some situations – a flourishing family, healthy children, friendships, relationships that are just and generous, thriving crops and animals, and wilderness – are good, while other situations – sickness, war, conflict, malnutrition, unjust arrangements and greedy actions, natural devastation, and extinctions of animal and plant species – are bad, then we must think it important that our emotions track the values of the world. Our attunement to reality must be to a large extent a matter of the emotional formation of our hearts. Such attunement, and differential adjustment among the objects of our emotions, is a challenging task and not a condition in which we automatically find our hearts. It is a task of discipline, of education, and of proper institutional formation. And understanding it is a task of ethics as an intellectual discipline, a task of philosophy and psychology.

In Chapter 9 at the end of this book I will sketch a conception of the virtues that reflects the moral roles and values that I identify in Chapters 3–8. That chapter will be only a sketch, an anticipation of much fuller individual portraits of the virtues in their individuality and their familial relations to one another. The individual portraits will be the business of another work. The excellences of a human being as such will bear in different ways on the four main dimensions of human functioning that I focus on in Chapters 3–8: the epistemic, the practical, the relational, and the eudaimonic. If emotions have the functions that I've outlined in this chapter, they are as important to the constitution of the virtues as classic writers like Plato, Aristotle, Thomas Aquinas, David Hume, and Adam Smith have taken them to be. The virtuous person will be perceptive and rational as only an emotionally well-formed person can be. She will be an agent whose actions are more than excellent behavior because well motivated. By her emotional dispositions she will be capable of excellent relationships with her fellow human beings in a variety of social contexts – as friend, as lover, as parent and child, as colleague, as citizen. As a result of these modes of proper human functioning, she will tend to experience the joy, hope, satisfaction, admiration, wonderment, love, gratitude, and pride that are the most obvious emotional manifestations of a well-lived life. Some virtues, like justice and compassion, will be positive dispositions to emotions. Others, like courage and forgivingness, will be abilities to transcend and adjust and correct emotions like fear and anger. Practical wisdom will both depend on the perceptual capacitations of right emotion and direct itself reflectively to the evaluation of one's emotions in context. Humility will consist primarily in *lack* of disposition to experience a certain class of emotions – the emotions of vanity, snobbery, domination, arrogance, and conceit – and to implement this lack by virtue of some ruling passion.

Intrinsic value

I earlier quoted a saying of Aristotle that presupposes that there can be such a thing, in a situation, as the right reason for being angry, the right person to be angry with, and the right offense to be angry about. When the anger satisfies such conditions, it matches the world, so to speak, and this matching makes the anger good in one way. Correspondingly, anger is bad to the extent that it fails to match the situation to which it is directed. The Stoics justified their rejection of anger and other emotions by a metaphysics according to which the world is excellent in every respect – a beautiful whole rational system beyond human control – including all the things at which human beings take umbrage. Here is Marcus Aurelius:

> That which happens to (or, suits) every man is fixed in a manner for him suitably to his destiny. For this is what we mean when we say that things are suitable to us, as the workmen say of squared stones in walls or the pyramids, that they are suitable, when they fit them to one another in some kind of connexion. For there is altogether one fitness, harmony. And as the universe is made up out of all bodies to be such a body as it is, so out of all existing causes necessity (destiny) is made up to be such a cause as it is ... And so accept everything which happens, even if it seem disagreeable, because it leads to this, to the health of the universe and to the prosperity and felicity of Zeus (the universe). (Marcus Aurelius 1997, *Meditations* 5.8)

Thus anger, by attributing badness to what is not bad, always fails to match reality.

If emotions can match or fail to match reality, this will be a very basic kind of value or disvalue. It seems to be especially close to the epistemic value, which, as I will argue in the next two chapters, is based in the perceptual character of emotions. I don't think we have any entirely emotion-independent access to the reality that emotions, at their best, represent. But we may well be adherents of some moral tradition that, like Stoicism, makes claims about the nature of reality; and if we are confident of our moral outlook, then I see no reason not to be confident also that the emotions of the morally best among us often represent moral reality as it is in some aspect or other. When, through the emotion, the morally properly functioning subject accurately perceives the situation with its value, he knows and understands the situation. But the matching of emotion and reality will also usually characterize the other basic kinds of emotional value: the emotions constitutive of excellent relationships will represent the persons involved in some of their actual aspects, and this emotional "truth" will be essential to the personal bond. Similarly, the emotion that motivates, and thus defines, an action will, to the extent that the action is virtuous, usually match reasons for action that actually inhere in the situation to which the action responds.

In the above paragraph I insert the qualifiers "often" and "usually" in describing the correspondence between the intrinsic value of emotions and their relational, motivational, and eudaimonistic values. I want to resist the temptation to reduce the other kinds of value to the intrinsic. At least in the flawed world that we currently inhabit, it can happen that for the good of our personal relationships, for the good of our actions, and for our happiness, we must compromise the intrinsic value of emotions and settle for emotions that give us something less than perfect evaluative truth. Thus the different kinds of value that emotions can possess are genuinely, irreducibly distinct one from another.

3

Emotions, perception, and moral judgment

Introduction

In the last chapter I sketched Stoic intuitions that in several ways emotions are primarily if not always enemies of the moral life. I acknowledged the truism that emotions sometimes impede the good life, but rejected the "primarily," suggesting that each moral liability that the Stoic detects actually marks an area of impingement of emotions on morality, salutary *or* pernicious. I might now have turned to a "sentimentalist" account of the relation of emotions to the moral life, which is a sort of symmetrical opposite of the Stoic moral rejection of emotions, namely, the view that emotions are somehow the normative *basis* of the moral life. I've done that in Roberts 2010 and will consider the matter again in Chapter 5. My chief aim in this book is not moral theory, but an understanding of the basic emotional psychology of the virtues. So, I will instead begin to discuss the moral dimensions of emotions that emerged from Chapter 2's sketches.

The first of those dimensions is the epistemic. I will explore how emotions may function as a basis for moral judgments in much the way visual and auditory perceptions function as a basis for judgments about things that can be seen and heard. My primary account is particularist in that the judgments it explains are about particular moral situations, but I will try at the end to see how it might apply to moral generalities, at least "default generalities" (Dancy 2004: 111–17). It also treats evaluative judgments, as contrasted with deontic ones, as primary, and I'll say a little at the end of the chapter about deontological judgments. The explanation of the emotion–judgment relation that I'll offer is based on my notion of emotions as concern-based construals (Roberts 2003: chap. 2).

After getting oriented with some examples, I'll discuss first the kind of perception that I call construal. Then I'll turn to emotions, proposing that we understand them as concern-based construals, which are thus perceptual experiences of values possessed by situations. Next I'll examine the possibility that emotions might be a perceptual basis for particular moral judgments of an evaluative kind. Then I'll consider a complication for this proposal, and, finally, I'll try to see how the view I've sketched might apply to moral generalities and to deontological judgments.

Some examples of moral judgments

It is plausible to imagine each of the following judgments as having an emotional background:

> *What the Underground Man did to Liza the prostitute* [Dostoevsky 2008, *Notes from Underground*, Part II] *was outrageously unjust.*

Upon hearing of, or remembering, what the Underground Man did, I felt **indignant** towards him about it.

> *Mother Teresa's compassion for the poor and suffering is saintly.*

When I consider Mother Teresa's compassionate life's work, I feel **admiration** (or **reverence**) for her and **gratitude** to God for her devotion to Jesus Christ.

> *Mrs. Bennet's pride in her culinary arrangements is so disproportionate to their value as to suggest that she is a rather silly person.*

When I hear her going on volubly and proudly about them, I feel a mild **contempt** for Mrs. Bennet (or **embarrassment** on her behalf, or **amusement** at her pride).

Perception as construal: conceptual perception

Sensory perception can support judgments in several ways. First, I can be told that the double-crested cormorant has a longer gular area than the neotropic cormorant, and, once I have learned what the gular area is, I have the wherewithal of a judgment. But I will certainly *understand* this judgment better if given the opportunity to see examples of the two species side-by-side. Second, if a reliable cormorant-spotter tells me that the birds on the river behind my house are double-crested cormorants, I still may gain some *justification* for my belief by stepping out back and looking. Third, even if my reliable informant is so much better than I at spotting these birds that I gain no justification for my belief by seeing them for myself, I still seem to enjoy a certain epistemic upgrade by seeing them for myself. We might call

Figure 1 Duck–Rabbit. Joseph Jastrow (1863–1944). Private Collection.
From Joseph Jastrow, "The Mind's Eye," *Popular Science Monthly* 54 (1899): 312.
Fine Art Images / Superstock

this upgrade *personal acquaintance*. There's nothing quite like perceiving for yourself, whether what's perceived is the flavor of a fine whiskey, the nastiness of a case of racial injustice, the gular area of a cormorant, the necessity of a necessary proposition, or the grace of God. The upgrade here seems to be a matter of epistemic proximity or intimacy with the object. Thinking of Linda Zagzebski's phrase, "cognitive contact with reality" (Zagzebski 1996: 167), the upgrade is that the contact is *closer* or more *intimate*.

Emotions, I propose, are a kind of perceptual state that is, in its essence, non-sensory, though it often involves, or is associated with, sensory experience in some way or other. Let me try to make clear the kind of perception I have in mind. Consider the famous duck–rabbit (Figure 1). Most people can see this figure either as a duck, or as a rabbit, at will. I will make three points about this seeing.

First, the difference between the experience of seeing the duck and that of seeing the rabbit is a difference in the way the figure *presents itself* to you. It *looks* different in the two construals; the two construals are different perceptual *impressions*. The difference is not well characterized, for example, by saying that when you see the figure one way you think of a duck, while when you see it the other way you think of a rabbit. In the one construal it has that rabbit look, while in the other it has the duck look. Presentation or impression is a characteristic of perception, and I suggest that construal more generally is a kind of perception. In this sense, perception is not necessarily factive; false perceptions are still perceptions (they are misperceptions). The point is that as perceptions they have impression content. Mere judgments don't have impression content.

My second point is that the duck–rabbit shows that perception is *not entirely sensory*. The different "looks" of the duck and rabbit don't result from a sensory difference, because the two different perceptions have exactly the same sensory content while having different impression (perceptual) contents. So, there must be a kind of perceptual "input" that is non-sensory. Thomas Reid requires this input to include belief. Perception, he says, requires,

> First, Some conception or notion of the object perceived. Secondly, A strong and irresistible conviction and belief of its [that is, the object's] present existence. And, thirdly, That this conviction and belief are immediate, and not the effect of reasoning. (Reid 1997: II.V.III–12)

I agree with Reid that no one who lacks a concept of a duck will see the duck in the duck–rabbit. But it seems wrong to think that my beliefs or convictions change as I switch back and forth between the duck- and rabbit-perceptions of the figure. What is the relevant belief? – That the figure [these particular blotches on this white background] is before me? – That the figure can be seen as a duck (or rabbit)? – That there is a duck or rabbit before me? I submit that none of these beliefs or disbeliefs needs to change as I switch perceptions of the figure. My belief *might* change if, having seen only a duck in the figure, I suddenly see the rabbit for the first time. In that case, I might be said now to have acquired a new belief: that the figure is or can be seen as a rabbit, as well as a duck. But then if I switch back to seeing the duck, it doesn't seem that the perceptual change results from now *believing* that there is a duck there to be seen; I already, while seeing the rabbit, believe (occurrently, let us say) that the figure is or can be seen as a duck. See Pelser 2010, especially 369–71, for an argument that Reid would have done better to make construal the non-sensory input.

Some people say that they can't switch the construal without moving their eyes slightly from one part of the figure to another. (I owe this objection to Richard Cross.) I admit that moving one's eyes helps, but I think I can switch construals without moving my eyes. But even if the eyes had to move for the construal to change, this difference wouldn't be sufficient to explain the perceptual difference between the two construals, because the construal difference is that between having a rabbit-impression and having a duck-impression, and it is implausible to think that *that* difference is merely mechanical. Whence, then, comes this difference in presentational content?

My third point is that the perceptual difference between the two construals is made by the way in which the features of the figure are *organized* in perception, and that the organization in turn depends on how the features are *conceptualized*, or to put the matter a little differently, what *roles* the features of the figure are assigned in perception.

For example, the protrusions on the left side of the figure are assigned the role of beak if you're seeing it as a duck, and they are ears if you're seeing it as a rabbit. The darker spot in the upper middle of the rounded area is the eye in either case, but it appears to be looking in somewhat different directions depending on which animal you're seeing, and this is plausibly explained by the "use" you're making, in the different cases, of the elements of the drawing – the different roles you're perceptually assigning to them. When you perceptually "assign" any crucial feature of the drawing a different organic role, the *whole* "look" of the drawing changes; and vice versa, when you make a different whole of it, the significance of each part changes. Role-assignments to features are interdependent with the character of the whole.

We might say that construal is *conceptual* perception, as distinguished from *sensory* perception, inasmuch as it depends, in the duck–rabbit case, on conceptualizing those protrusions on the left either as ears or as a beak; or, alternatively, on conceptualizing the whole figure as a picture-duck or a picture-rabbit.

Still, sensory information is involved in the construals of the duck–rabbit, so the experience is a kind of visual (sensory) experience, despite its conceptual nature. Furthermore, the duck–rabbit works by way of resemblance; it looks a little bit like both a duck and a rabbit, and if it didn't, it would be very difficult, if not impossible, to construe it as such. For example, if we try to construe it as a bowl of gerberas, we run up against the limits of visual conceptual perception, because the drawing doesn't provide the visual resources for such construal; it doesn't look enough like a bowl of gerberas for us (most of us, at any rate) to construe it visually in these terms. The sensory information in the drawing (minimal though it is) provides the needed resemblance to a duck and rabbit, but not to a bowl of gerberas.

The main contrast between construals and other perceptual states is that construals have their impression content by way of structure, the organization of the parts of something complex into a whole, whereas sensory perceptual states have their impression content by way of sensory impressions. This being so, while not all construals are sensory, most sense perceptions are construals. The only ones that aren't construals are the "pure" sensory impressions. Imagine that upon opening your eyes an undifferentiated red field presents itself. This might be an example of a sensory impression that was not a construal. I say "might" because if you're a normal human being above the age of two years, you probably *recognize* the color of the field *as* red. In doing so you introduce into your impression the complexity of *placing* this color field into *relation* with *other* color fields. And that too is a kind of construal. Even though the visual field doesn't have parts, the perception does in a sense, the other parts being the relata in terms of which this undifferentiated field is construed.

More purely conceptual perception

Consider now a case that doesn't depend on resemblance. Some people, upon hearing or seeing the following sentence, do not hear or see it as a syntactically correct, meaningful English sentence:

Fish fish fish fish fish.

It doesn't make sense to them. It strikes them as just a string of words that doesn't say anything. But it can make sense to you, if you hear or read it in the right way. To make sense of it, you must *organize it perceptually*, and you do this by perceptually assigning parts of speech and differential word meanings to each of the five word tokens. One possible assignment is as follows:

Fish	*fish*	*fish*	*fish*	*fish.*
Main subject noun	*subordinate clause subject noun*	*subordinate clause verb*	*main verb*	*main clause object noun*

Filling in connectors brings out the syntax of this reading:

Fish [that] fish fish fish [for other] fish.

Or, translating the verb "to fish" with the verb "to catch," we get,

Fish [that] fish catch catch fish.

We see here the same conceptual perception phenomenon noted in the case of the duck–rabbit. Just as the construal of the figure as a duck requires the assignment of roles to the aspects of the figure, so the construal of the whole string of words as a meaningful English sentence requires that each of the word-tokens be assigned an appropriate grammatical and semantic role. It happens that, like the duck–rabbit, the fish sentence can be construed (read, perceived) in more than one way. It can also be read using the following assignments:

Fish	*fish*	*fish*	*fish*	*fish.*
Main subject noun	*main verb*	*main clause object noun*	*subordinate clause subject noun*	*subordinate clause verb*

Paraphrasing again, this time we get,

Fish catch fish [that] fish catch.

(Think of a fish's "catching" a little fish by catching a bigger fish that caught the little one.) Grammatical and semantic roles are concepts, so such assignment is a conceptual activity. But it is performed perceptually. In hearing (or reading) the word string as an English sentence, one assigns each word token its grammatical role by *perceiving* it properly, and in perceiving each token properly one relates it properly (that is, hears or sees it in some sense-making relation) to its companions and thus perceives (hears or sees) the whole as a well-formed English sentence.

The relatively unsophisticated construals of the duck–rabbit exploit the same conceptual–perceptual capacities as the much more sophisticated construals of the fish sentence. It is the ability perceptually to organize into a meaningful whole the parts of something that admits such organization. A pervasive example of normal people's ability to do this is facial recognition. Neurologically normal people are extremely competent at recognizing human faces, and this is a non-analytic capacity that nevertheless obviously exploits differences among noses, eyes, forehead size and shape, distance-proportions among face-parts, etc. In virtue of such differences, many of which we don't even notice explicitly, when we see someone we know, his or her face has that Gary-look or Linda-look. The difference between the linguistic case and the more simply visual cases is that in the fish sentence the conceptual assignments are not made on the basis of resemblance ("fish" in no way resembles a fish or the activity of fishing) and, indeed, the words in the sentence are not differentiated from one another by any strictly visual or auditory marks. They all sound and look the same. Unlike the visual cases, even their spatial–temporal placement in the sentence doesn't determine the meaning of the sentence; each word token, taken on its own, is indistinguishable from all the others. The perception of the word string as a sentence results from your assigning grammatical and semantic roles to the word tokens. And yet, note that even here there are right and wrong ways to construe the string of words; not just any set of role-assignments makes sense.

If we try, for example, to construe the sentence according to the following conceptual schema, we reach the limits of construal:

Fish	*fish*	*fish*	*fish*	*fish.*
main verb	*subordinate clause verb*	*subordinate clause subject noun*	*main clause object noun*	*main subject noun*

Paraphrasing as before, we get

Catch catch fish fish fish.

That is beyond my powers of construal, at least. The crucial indication of failure here is that the ordering doesn't *feel* sense making. It doesn't *satisfy* the way the two successful construals of the word-string do. This is apparently a conceptual scheme in conformity to which the fish sentence can't be understood.

Perhaps we can see better the point about perception by imagining a contrasting case. Imagine somebody who can't hear the fish sentence as a sentence, but by some method of calculation and inference can figure out the grammatical assignments of the words. Beginning students of Greek, when "construing" a sentence for a teacher, sometimes figure out the grammar and vocabulary of a Greek sentence in this sort of way (looking up the words in a dictionary and the noun- and verb-endings in an inflection table). That would not be construing in the sense that I'm trying to construct, which essentially involves "hearing" the sentence as a grammatical whole, and, further, as grasping the sense that *Fish [that] fish catch catch fish* or *Fish catch fish [that] fish catch.*

Construal in this sense is a kind of perception, an impression that results from a power of the mind to synthesize the diverse parts of something that "works" as a whole into an impression of the whole that it works as. Here, perceptual organization differs from purely intellectual or calculating organization.

So, the ability to hear the fish sentence as a sentence is strongly analogous to the ability to see the duck–rabbit as a rabbit (or a duck). An inability of either kind is both a failure of understanding and a failure of perception in the broad sense that I am proposing. In each case, the person who construes the object in a sense-making way undergoes a phenomenal presentation, a holistic impression, as a result of perceptually organizing a body of "data."

The two features of construal – its organic, structural, or gestalt character, and its non-sensory presentational or phenomenal character – are not separable, and they conspire to endow construals with the power to yield three potential epistemic goods: *understanding*, *acquaintance*, and *justification*.

Emotions as concern-based construals

Let's now turn to emotions. On the view of emotions that I endorse, they are *concern-based* construals. That is, they are perceptions, in the construal sense of the word, in which one or more of the elements going into the construal is a concern. Christine Tappolet (2010: 329) doesn't reckon with this perceptual integration of the concern when she comments that "The problem [with the view that emotions are construals] is that construing or seeing something as fearsome would not explain why, when we experience fear, we are nonetheless tempted to avoid what we fear. If I construe or see a cloud as a horse, I am not likely to be tempted to try to ride it." I take it that the construals we've looked at so far are not concern-based, and so are not emotions. (If you're a duck or rabbit lover, or have a duck or rabbit phobia, you perhaps got a mild affective buzz out of seeing the duck–rabbit. Otherwise, I doubt that your seeing it as a duck or rabbit was an emotional experience, any more than Tappolet's construing a cloud as a horse.)

The idea that emotions are *concern*-based construals is that, for example, you will never feel fear if you don't care about the thing that you see as threatened, nor anger if you're not concerned about the thing you construe as offended against, nor shame if you don't care about being worthy of respect. You come into a situation that has emotional potential for you with a dispositional (or possibly occurrent) concern or desire, or an attachment; you then construe the situation in the terms characteristic of some emotion type, and the situation emotionally appears to you as it does because the terms in which you see the situation impinge on, connect with, that concern. Consider a parent watching his toddler totter towards the edge of a wall with a three-foot drop to the ground on the other side:

Basic concern	Construal	Motivation
I care dispositionally about this child's **wellbeing** →	I construe X as **threat**ening the child's wellbeing →	I am moved to **protect** the child against the threat

Each emotion type has a package of concepts. *Threat* is the lead concept for fear. *Wellbeing* and *protect* [*avoid*] are correlative concepts inasmuch as threat is *threat to wellbeing* and protection or avoidance is *protection of wellbeing against threat* or *avoidance of loss of wellbeing in the face of threat.* Here is what I call the "defining proposition" for fear:

> **Fear of X for Y**: *X presents a threat to Y of a significant degree of probability; may X or its threatened consequences for Y be avoided.* (Roberts 2003: 195; modified)

The defining proposition for an emotion type outlines the way the elements of the situation are sense-makingly ordered in an emotion of that type. The defining proposition for fear outlines the way a person sense-makingly orders a situation in which he is afraid of something (X) on something's (Y's) behalf. (The reader who thinks the talk of defining propositions and conceptual packages too "intellectualist" to be plausible of the whole range of emotions, I refer to the section titled *The beasts and babies objection* in Chapter 4.)

On the construal view of emotions, when a person fears something, he perceives (feels, understands) the situation as having the form expressed in the above defining proposition, and typically wants the situation changed in a way suggested by the propositional form as integrated with the basic concern, that is, concern for the wellbeing of Y. The concern is unexpressed in the defining proposition, though suggested by the word "threat." Just as seeing the duck–rabbit as a duck consists in perceptually assigning roles to the elements of the drawing, and hearing the fish sentence as saying something coherent about fishes' fishing activities consists in perceptually assigning grammatical and semantic roles to its word tokens, so fearing that one's child will fall off the wall consists in perceptually assigning roles to aspects of the situation, and thus arranging them in the conceptual order of the defining proposition for fear: the child is Y, the threat to his wellbeing is his treading near the edge of the wall, and the avoidance of the threat to the child or the protection of the child's wellbeing against the threat is some action that will prevent his falling off the wall. The parent who experiences this fear cares about the wellbeing of his child and perceives the whole situation, with its aspects thus perceptually assigned, through the lens of this care.

We can easily imagine an adolescent watching the child treading dangerously close to the edge of the wall, seeing that the child is in danger of falling off and thus in need of protection, without experiencing any anxiety or fear. Perhaps the adolescent is just watching idly, with the most minimal interest, or perhaps he is curious to see whether the child will fall. In the latter case, he will have some emotion, but it will not be fear (it might even be hope). The difference between the adolescent's construal and the parent's is less in the purely propositional structure of his perception of the situation than in the adolescent's lack of appropriate concern.

The drawing, the sentence, and the situation of the child are all configurations of elements that invite and enable further sense-making configuring by a perceiving subject.

Affect

As a *concern*-based construal, an emotion is a perception that is "colored" in value. If the basic concern were not picked up in (integrated into) the construal – if, for example, the concern for the child were not an element in the perception of the situation – then the construal would be merely a construal, like the perception of the duck–rabbit or the fish sentence. It would be a non-affective construal of the child's wellbeing being threatened, like the adolescent's idle watching of the unfolding scene. The coloration that the construal derives from the integration of the concern is *affect*. Affect is not something in addition to emotion, but is the way the concern-based construal feels to the person experiencing the emotion. Just as in the visual experience of a house one is appeared to in the way characteristic of house-sightings, so in fear one is appeared to (in feeling) in the way characteristic of threat-confrontations (the threat being directed at something one cares about).

Notice how different this account of affect is from that of Jamesian theories such as those of William James (1884: 190), Antonio Damasio (1994: 145), Jesse Prinz (2004: 206–07), and Jenefer Robinson (2005: 29), accounts that in various ways make affect a matter of the sensations of the bodily concomitants of emotions. I don't think the bodily sensations are pleasant or unpleasant enough to explain the intense positive affect of emotions like joy over the healthy birth of one's baby or the intense negative affect of grief over a child's death. On the present account, emotional pleasures and pains are a matter of the *meaning* ("positive" or "negative") that a situation has for the emotional subject, not the sensations of his body (though those sensations do contribute something to the overall feel of the emotion). And that meaning is a function of the synthesizing, constructing, qualifying, of factual perception in terms of concern.

In the case of most emotions, affect is pleasant or unpleasant. Fear is usually unpleasant, hope pleasant. When the propositional content of the emotion thwarts the basic concern, the affect is unpleasant; when the propositional content indulges the concern, the affect is pleasant. Affect makes the construal feel like an *emotion* and like the particular *type* of emotion that it is (e.g., fear) and the *particular* emotion that it is (e.g., fear for this dear child as he treads too close to the wall's edge). Affect is the phenomenal or qualitative experiential difference between an emotion and a non-emotional construal.

Affect is crucial to the epistemic value and role of emotions, because it is the way that the distinctively evaluative aspect of the perception is registered so as to become perceptually available to the subject. Felt emotions are the subject's perceptual access to the goodness and badness of situations, and the pleasantness or unpleasantness of the situation's meaning for the subject is the registration of that goodness or badness. But if so, what shall we make of the fact that emotions that are not felt lack affect, and yet they too seem to be, in some sense, evaluative perceptions, inasmuch as they are concern-based construals? I think the subject's epistemic relation to an emotion that he doesn't feel is like a third party's perception. If you see a deer grazing in the back yard, then I can profit epistemically from your telling me what you see. If you don't inform me of your perception, then I can't profit from it, and if you do inform me of it, the kind of profit it can afford me is not the same as it would afford me were it my perception. The same is true of my own unfelt emotion. My epistemic relation to the information it contains is this: If I don't know about my emotion, then its information is unavailable to me; if I do know about it (say, my therapist informs me of it), then I can profit from it epistemically, but not in the perceptual way I could if I felt it. Thus I bear to my unfelt emotions a relation to the evaluative information they contain similar to the one I bear to the perceptions of a third party. I'm grateful to Adam Pelser for helping me see this point.

Affect is not the same as motivation. As I have commented, the concern that is basic to fear generates not only fear's affect, but also the motivation characteristic of fear. But at the moment I refer only passingly to emotional motivation, because this chapter is about emotional perception and affect is what makes possible emotional perception of value qualities like *threat, culpable offense, good prospects, the beloved,* and *enhancement of self.* In Chapter 6 I will discuss the difference between affect and emotional motivation in the section titled *Reflections on affective motivation.*

Emotions and moral judgments

Let us now try to see how an emotion may be the perceptual basis of a moral judgment. Consider the following judgment:

What the Underground Man did to Liza the prostitute was outrageously unjust.

The emotion type that seems most appropriate to this judgment is probably indignation, or at least some form of anger. Here is the defining proposition for indignation:

> **Indignation**: *S has very culpably offended in the important matter of X (action or omission), and is bad; I am very confident of being in a moral position to condemn; S deserves (ought) to be hurt for X; may S be hurt for X.* (Roberts 2003: 215)

The situation type depicted in the above propositional form needs to be filled out in a narrative that instantiates the offense and the offender and suggests reasons for attributing culpability for the offense to the offender. Such a situation is narrated in Dostoevsky's (2008) *Notes from Underground* (Part II, sections v–x). To enhance its emotional impressiveness, I'll summarize the story as though you know the man and Liza, though I think most sensitive readers of Dostoevsky's novella will have felt something like the indignation I'll talk about.

Imagine that someone tells you the following story. A man you know personally has been insulted and rejected by his associates at a dinner party, and afterwards follows them to a brothel to start a fight, only to find that they have already dispersed into the rooms of the brothel. While there, he falls in with a prostitute, Liza, whom you also know well enough to be concerned about her wellbeing. The man wants to assuage his wounded vanity, and has been in the habit of doing so by exercising power over others. After he has slept with Liza he preaches a little sermon to her on the glories of family life and the degradations of prostitution. He pours it on really thick, and by his rhetoric reduces her to a condition of bitter remorse, and of gratitude and admiration towards himself. Overplaying his assumed role of judge and savior he gives her his address on departing, indicating that she may come to him. When she does come to his room several days later in hopes of pursuing the relationship with her sage redeemer, he is humiliated by her seeing his poverty and turns on her with vindictive anger, telling her that she never cared for her at all, doesn't mind if she degrades herself in prostitution, and was only using her to salve the social wounds he had received at the drinking party. In her disillusionment she is devastated and leaves.

Let us say that your response to the story is indignation against the man for falsely raising Liza's expectations, shamelessly jeopardizing her to relieve his own emotional pain, and punishing her for doing just what he had invited her to do. In your indignation you are vividly impressed with the situation's nastiness, Underground Man's blameworthiness, and Liza's victimization. (This evaluative coloring of the facts of the situation is what I call the emotion's affect.) Your indignation is based on a concern for Liza's wellbeing and a more general concern for justice. These prior concerns are dispositional in you, and prior to your hearing the story are neither a feeling of any kind nor a desire to do anything in particular. But now, upon hearing the story, you not only feel strongly about the situation, but want to do something in particular. You would like to get hold of the man and make him regret deeply and intensely what he has done to her. Towards Liza you feel an aching compassion, which has been aroused by the narrative, and it too involves a desire to do something in particular – in this case, to console her, to assuage her suffering, to let her know that you support her.

John Riker has pointed out to me that a rather different emotional reading of the story is possible: John says his reaction is not indignation, but compassion for Underground Man as well as for Liza. This is a possible reading of the story. Underground Man is a truly pathetic character; even if he is in some sense responsible for the corruption of his character and personality, his overall miserableness and dysfunction may be what most strike the reader. Dostoevsky seems to explain his state, in part, by reference to corrupt cultural trends in contemporary Saint Petersburg. A non-indignant construal of Underground Man will yield different moral judgments while still involving the attribution of injustice. But my purpose here is philosophical, not interpretive, and in the following discussion I will assume what I take to be the more natural reading, in terms of indignation.

Notice that the terms of this construal are just as far from being sensory as the grammatical and word-meaning terms of the construal of the fish-sentence. We perceive the meaning of the fish-sentence without the sentence in any way resembling the situation it depicts – namely, the fact that fish that are caught by other fish catch (have caught) still other fish. In the experience of being angry at the Underground Man for his treatment of Liza, he appears to you as culpable, bad, and deserving of hurt for what he has done in a way that is strongly analogous to the way the duck appears to you when you see the duck–rabbit as a duck, and one of the meanings of the fish sentence appears to you when you construe it as a grammatically correct sentence. In your concern-based construal, the situation appears to you as a structured whole with a certain complex value. A notable difference between the construal of the duck–rabbit and the construal of the Underground Man is that the relevant parts of the drawing appear to you simultaneously, while relevant aspects of the Underground Man's action are collected serially in the course of the narrative. You perceive the situation thus:

> *Underground Man has very culpably and shockingly rejected Liza after manipulating her and causing her to trust and care for him, and is a complete jerk; I am very confident of being in a moral position to condemn him; and he deserves to be made to regret vividly and painfully what he has done, as repayment for his vile behavior. May he be made so to suffer regret.*

This summary is what I call the emotion's material proposition; it is the actual propositional structure of the emotion token. In your indignation, the parts of the situation depicted in the narrative have come together for you into a whole that impresses you powerfully with its (dis)value.

As you read the final sections of *Notes from Underground*, the narrative unfolds, yielding the features which, brought together, become the material for the indignation construal. Nowhere in the text does the word "injustice" occur, and it may not occur to you, the reader, either. But if you are normally compassionate and have a sense of justice, you will feel the indignation that is expressed in the material proposition above. This felt indignation is then the perceptual basis for your judgment that the Underground Man has treated Liza very unjustly. What do I mean by "basis"?

Let's admit that it's possible to make this judgment, and to derive it from the story, without feeling indignation towards Underground Man or compassion for Liza. Perhaps we can imagine a highly intelligent person with severe frontal lobe damage who reads the story without emotion and is able to come to the conclusion that Underground Man has treated Liza unjustly. (Perhaps he was reared among normal people who taught him to recognize injustice by its empirical marks, or perhaps earlier in life he was emotionally normal.) He can point to all the right evidence, give all the appropriate reasons, if asked to justify his judgment. So, let's admit that someone could be epistemically justified in making this moral judgment without his own emotion being the basis for the judgment.

Still, one who feels the injustice for himself, by way of his indignation, has an epistemically *higher-quality* judgment than the emotionless person. The perceptual experience of the injustice gives him deeper understanding and more intimate cognitive contact with this moral reality. He is like the person who has seen the double-crested cormorants for himself, as compared with the person whose true beliefs about the birds are based on less direct contact.

I think that in normal cases, "base" might mean two more things. It is true that, by telling the reader the "facts" of the case, the narrative supplies the information necessary to make the judgment. But emotions, as construals, are integrating, synthetic mental states in which these data are organized into a meaningful whole. They are the form in which the understanding of the situation occurs to the reader. In the normal case, this is the priority. It is much less normal for the reader first to come to a non-emotional judgment that Underground Man has mistreated Liza, and then, on the basis of that judgment, begin to feel indignation towards him. So, one sense in which the emotion is the basis of the judgment is that in the normal case it *precedes the judgment*, just as in many cases sensory perceptions precede empirical judgments.

But if the person who makes the judgment is morally normal (virtuous), then his perceiving the injustice by way of the emotion actually *adds justification* to whatever justification he may derive for the judgment by other means (say, legal evidence, testimony, and whatever calculations may support these). The added justification is like that which a well-trained scientist gains when, after amassing enough less direct evidence to justify a judgment that p, he looks in his microscope or other perception-enhancing device and *sees*, by way of his scientifically trained visual powers, that p. Emotions in general are the way we get perceptual (presentational, noninferential) moral information. This thesis is perfectly compatible with the thesis that only the emotions of the virtuous are highly reliable in this role. The vicious, because their emotions are morally distorted or under-developed, have less access to moral information than the virtuous; they understand less and are less "in touch" with moral reality.

A complication

So far, my point has been that emotions function as a kind of perception in which situations are presented to the subject in their evaluative aspect. On my account, the evaluative aspect depends on *the subject's concern*, as well as his ability to perceive the situation in the *required conceptual way*. Daniel Jacobson (2005) has proposed that we think of virtues as skill-like capacities and of moral perception as an output of such capacities. In this chapter we have seen that construals are a kind of conceptual perception and so depend on conceptual capacities. Some such capacities (or skills, if you will) are fairly simple, while others are demanding. The capacity to see injustices, on the account I have presented here, thus has a skill-like aspect. The perceiver needs to have mastery of the concepts essential to the relevant emotions, and this mastery is subject to considerable development and sophistication. But on the present account, this is only an aspect of moral perceptual capacities. The other crucial aspect is the moral concern, and it would seem to me odd to think of *that* as skill-like. Virtues have a skill dimension, but most virtues are not *just* skills. The example we've considered accommodates these two suppositions nicely. Indignation matches injustice because the concern basic to indignation is a concern for justice, and the main concepts that indignation trades on are *offend* (against justice) and *culpable* or *blameworthy* (of injustice).

But two of the examples with which I began this chapter mention more than one emotion type that might be the perception that corresponds to the moral judgment, and these emotion types may be quite diverse, both with regard to their conceptual structure and with regard to the basic concern. For example, for the judgment that

> *Mrs. Bennet's pride in her culinary arrangements is so disproportionate to their value as to suggest that she is a rather silly person,*

I suggested that we imagine someone commenting, by way of explanation, that "When I hear her going on volubly and proudly about them, I feel a mild **contempt** for Mrs. Bennet." But, alternatively, someone might respond to the situation by feeling **embarrassed** on her behalf, or **amused** at her silly pride, and make the same judgment that *she is a rather silly person*. So, contempt, empathic embarrassment, and amusement are all possible ways of emotionally perceiving Mrs. Bennet's silliness. But contempt, empathic embarrassment, and amusement are very different emotion types. Here is the defining proposition for contempt:

> **Contempt**: *S is markedly inferior and unworthy in X important way, yet he (she, it) obtrudes, pretending to equal status and worth; may he (she, it) be put in his place.* (Roberts 2003: 256)

The defining proposition for embarrassment is

> **Embarrassment**: *Being concerned to be approved by others or not too apparent to them, I am appearing to others in an uncomplimentary or too revealing light; may I cease to do so.* (Roberts 2003: 233)

And that for amusement is

> **Amusement**: *X, which is at most minimally tragic, disgusting, immoral, or otherwise painful, appears in a delightfully incongruous aspect.* (Roberts 2003: 308)

Note: Amusement is similar enough to paradigm emotions that most thinkers, including me, class it as an emotion, but it is not based on a concern as the paradigm emotions are, and so doesn't have a consequent concern. It is based, instead, on a sense of the normal that, being contravened by the incongruity, yields a pleasant affect. This deviation from the paradigm is one of many reasons that I don't call my account of emotions a "theory": the basic formula doesn't perfectly cover all the cases. For discussion, see Roberts 2003: 300–08. However, because amusement is pleasant, it can be *blocked* by a concern, as indicated by the formula above, and this fact is relevant to the possible virtue status of a sense of humor.

As we can see from the defining propositions, contempt is an alienating perception of another, while embarrassment takes the perspective of its own object (namely, oneself if one is embarrassed on one's own behalf, or another, as in the case of feeling embarrassed for Mrs. Bennet). Contempt is a species of antipathy, while embarrassment is a species of (self- or other-) sympathy. Thus *empathic* embarrassment is an uncomfortable sense of solidarity with the other person. Contempt arises out of a concern for some kind of superiority or excellence, a concern that the object of contempt contravenes; unlike empathic embarrassment, it does *not* arise out of an attachment to, love for, or pro-attitude towards the object of contempt, and is rather predisposed by a lack of positive concern for the other or even a concern to diminish the other. Empathic embarrassment presupposes a concern that the other appear in a good light, and is therefore an uncomfortable construal of the other as appearing in a bad light.

But emotions of both types can be the perceptual basis of the judgment,

> *Mrs. Bennet's pride in her culinary arrangements is so disproportionate to their value as to suggest that she is a rather silly person.*

The following material propositions indicate how contempt, embarrassment, and amusement might be instantiated in this case:

Instantiation of contempt: *The pride that Mrs. Bennet shows in insisting on the excellence of her culinary arrangements is so disproportionate to their value as to suggest that she has a silly mind; in this she is alien to what is excellent and should be apportioned the trivial status among us that she deserves.*

Instantiation of empathic embarrassment: *The pride that Mrs. Bennet shows in insisting on the excellence of her culinary arrangements is so disproportionate to their value as to suggest that she has a silly mind, but she is my friend [family member, associate, fellow human being]; if only she did not appear so silly to our fellows!* (Notice especially the sympathetic "our.")

Instantiation of amusement: *The pride that Mrs. Bennet shows in insisting on the excellence of her culinary arrangements is so disproportionate to their value as to suggest that she has a silly mind; the incongruity between the excellence she pretends to and the mediocrity she exhibits is delightfully comical.*

Emotions are situational construals with the phenomenal or qualitative character of affect. The affect colors the situation with value: Mrs. Bennet's silliness in making such a fuss about her culinary arrangements comes across *as* silliness. In a way analogous to the way that seeing the cormorant for oneself may yield a higher quality judgment that it *is* a cormorant than merely judging it to be so, say on the basis of testimony, "seeing" the silliness by way of the contempt, empathic embarrassment, or amusement yields a higher quality moral judgment than merely judging her, without affect, to be silly. In the emotion we *feel* (perceive) her silliness in its bearing or import. Thus we go beyond merely registering or noting that she is silly.

But what about the fact that emotions of more than one type can supply the affect with which the evaluative quality of Mrs. Bennet's silliness is perceived? After all, silliness seen through the eye of empathic embarrassment has a pretty different appearance from silliness seen through the eye of contempt. Can all three perceptions really be perceptions of *silliness*?

We may be tempted to deny this – to suppose that if emotions can be the perceptual basis of moral judgments, then the emotion types and the moral judgment types should correspond in a regular way. Linda Zagzebski (2003) seems to make this assumption. She divides the judgment types along the lines of division of the thick evaluative concepts and then, to make the connection to emotions, calls these "thick affective concepts." Examples of thick affective concepts are *pitiful, dogmatic, contemptible, rude, petty, tacky, brutal, lie [mendacious?], kind*, etc. (108–09, 114). Then she says that to each thick affective concept corresponds an emotion type (115). For Zagzebski, emotion types are "defined" by the thick affective concepts that shape the intentional objects of their instances. For example, there is an emotion corresponding to *kind*, an emotional way of responding to someone who, or some action that, is kind; and another for seeing people and actions that are dogmatic, another for those that are petty, and so forth. Many of her emotion types are nameless; and they differ from the ones that are lexically identified in natural languages.

For example, she says we perceive an action as rude only when we feel offended by it. But it seems to me that rude remarks and actions can be evaluatively perceived in many affective ways. One sometimes responds with offense, but also one might feel contempt for the speaker, or amusement, gratitude, joy, or fear. Furthermore, in context, any of these affective responses might be the *right* response (or *a* right response), one that nails the (an) evaluative truth. I would think that rudeness has different kinds of value, depending on context.

Returning to Mrs. Bennet's silliness, here is what I think we should say: at a great enough height of abstraction, the persons who perceive her silliness with empathic embarrassment, contempt, and amusement all perceive the same evaluative quality, namely, her silliness. And so at that height of abstraction they will all make the same judgment: *she is silly* (or perhaps: *her pride is silly*.) But closer to the ground it is evident that they are not seeing exactly the same quality. Thus in a way Zagzebski is right. One person might be seeing contemptible silliness, another lamentable silliness, and another laughable silliness. If all three form a judgment on the basis of their perceptions, then they form three different judgments (that is, types of judgments). The differences are obscured by the abstract formulation "she is silly." They can all sincerely assert that, and they all "see" that, but the fuller truth about their perceptions and corresponding judgments will require further explanation to formulate.

But if we say this, haven't we created a problem for ourselves, a problem that will send us back in the direction of Zagzebski's claim that perception of such properties as silliness requires that a single emotion type be dedicated to each distinct evaluative property? (I thank Adam Pelser for raising this question, and for discussion of it.) The argument might go like this: silliness is perceived in each of the three cases: by way of contempt, by way of empathic embarrassment, and by way of amusement. But silliness is itself an evaluative property, and we have claimed that the most essential way to perceive evaluative properties is by way of emotions. But if silliness is perceived *via* each of the three quite *different* emotion types, and is in some sense the *same* property in each case, then it can't be right to think that these three types of emotion are the most basic way that silliness is perceived. There must be yet *another* emotion type that accounts for the perception of silliness *itself* – whatever is common to the contemptible silliness, the amusing silliness, and the lamentable silliness that are perceived by *these* three emotions.

The problem with this argument, as I see it, is that its conclusion is false. If we look for an emotion type that targets silliness *in itself,* apart from any context that lends one value or another to it, we come up empty-handed. Silliness seems to be always embedded in some context in which it emerges as having one value or another other than just plain silliness. If this is so, then the faulty premise is the one that claims that silliness is itself an evaluative property.

But if silliness is not an evaluative property, how does it come to be so at home in evaluative or even moral judgments like the one in our example? It is certainly a different kind of property from being five feet tall or having red hair, and the difference is in the direction of being evaluative. True, we can imagine somebody feeling contempt or empathic embarrassment for another because he is five feet tall or has red hair, but it would take a *very* special context to make sense of the idea that such a perception might be a veridical moral perception that could issue in the true judgment that the person is contemptibly or lamentably redheaded or five feet tall.

It is popular these days to distinguish "thick" evaluative concepts like *kind* and *tacky* and *silly* and *contemptible* from "thin" ones like *good* and *bad*. But perhaps we need more distinctions among the "thick" ones than we are usually given. It seems to me that *contemptible* and *lamentable* are rather densely thick, while *rude* and *brutal* and *petty* are less so, and *tacky* and *silly* and *dogmatic* are still less evaluatively dense. I say so because it seems to me that *contemptible* and *lamentable* are quite determinately evaluative in particular, pretty constant ways, while on the other end of the spectrum *silly* and *rude* admit of a wide range of evaluative variations. "Tacky," "silly," and "dogmatic" are perhaps more naturally or frequently qualified by "lamentably" than by "delightfully," but it is not hard to imagine something being delightfully tacky, silly, or dogmatic. It is harder or less likely for something to be delightfully brutal or petty, but perhaps not impossible. But delightfully contemptible or lamentable seems downright incoherent.

Yet all these concepts seem to be broadly evaluative, as compared with *redheaded* and *five feet tall*. They belong in contexts of evaluation; they invite, or lend themselves to, evaluation in a way that the merely factual concepts don't. Though silliness does not have, in itself and across all contexts, any determinate value, it lends itself to various values, and naturally takes on values, in a way that red and five feet tall don't. So, the premise in the objection is not exactly wrong in calling silliness an evaluative property, but it would be wrong to assimilate it without qualification to properties such as the contemptible and the lamentable. We might call silliness and rudeness *parasitically* or partly parasitically evaluative properties since as evaluative properties they live off of, depend on, more robustly thick evaluative properties. I think that evaluative properties can be more or less parasitic or dependent. Brutality seems to me to be a far more evaluatively independent property than silliness.

The idea of parasitically evaluative properties seems to lead to a distinction between two kinds of thickness of evaluative properties, descriptive thickness and evaluative thickness. Thickness in an evaluative concept is usually thought to be its descriptive specificity. *Bad* has little descriptive specificity, while *cruel* has a lot; to say "X is bad" is to convey little information about what kind of thing X is factually, while to say "X is cruel" conveys a lot. Silliness has quite a bit of descriptive specificity, but it's short on what we might call evaluative specificity, since its evaluative import can be specified in a variety of ways, as we have seen. Thus silliness is descriptively pretty thick, but evaluatively pretty thin. To belabor the point, *good*'s thinness consists in its being parasitic on descriptive concepts: thus we specify good *tea*, good *man*, good *axe*, etc. Similarly, *silly*'s thinness consists in its being parasitic on evaluative concepts: *lamentable* silliness, *amusing* silliness, *contemptible* silliness. That "X is silly" tells us little about X's value – though, I am saying, it does suggest that X has some kind of value, whereas "X is five feet tall" does not.

Deontological judgments and evaluative generalities

So far, this chapter has been entirely about the perception of evaluative qualities and the judgments that may be based on them. I have argued that, because of their perceptual nature, emotions can contribute to moral judgments such epistemic goods as justification, understanding, and intimacy of cognitive contact with reality. How might our ruminations apply to deontological judgments – judgments to the effect that someone ought to do something, or ought to have done something? How might emotions contribute here?

It seems to me that the range of relevant emotion types is much narrower for deontological judgments than for evaluative ones, and that the emotions apply in a different way.

Ethicists who have thought deontologically and also incorporated emotions into their account of moral judgments have often fixed on two emotion types in particular: anger (or resentment) and guilt (Rawls 1971, Gibbard 1990). So, we might start here. Our reaction to Underground Man's treatment of Liza is a graphic case. Evaluatively, our emotion tells us that he treated Liza unjustly; deontologically, we can conclude from this that he ought not to have done what he did.

Ought and *ought not* seem to me too thin, too abstract, to be objects of perception; that is why I say we would "conclude" the deontological judgment from our perception. Furthermore, if the question is about whether an as yet unperformed action is obligatory, permissible, or impermissible, then we might imagine (with sufficient narrative context) performing the action and not performing it, and our emotional reaction to it. If we see that we would feel guilty if we performed it, we could conclude that it is impermissible; if we would feel guilty if we didn't perform it, we could conclude it was obligatory; and if we wouldn't feel guilty in either case, we could conclude it is permissible either to do it or not to do it. This method presupposes that our responses to cases are reliable, and, of course, not everybody's are reliable, and perhaps everybody's are under certain circumstances unreliable. I would say that people with virtues like compassion, justice, and objectivity about themselves and their emotions would be the most reliable sources of correct deontological judgments here.

So, if our guilt-disposition is well formed, then the emotion will lend some justification to our judgment. But the understanding and the intimacy of contact with reality would seem to me to attach less to the oughtness than to the value from which we concluded the oughtness – again, because *ought* is such a thin moral property. Obligation by itself doesn't offer much to be understood or to have epistemic contact with.

Since the account of emotions and moral judgments that I've given is particularist, it says nothing so far about moral *principles*. But if I were pressed to say something about how evaluative principles might be generated on this chapter's account of emotions and judgments, I might say this: given a principle to test, the virtuous person might try instantiating it with as large an assortment of imagined cases as his or her time and imagination would allow (with special attention to counter-cases), testing each case with his or her virtual emotion response. Then he might tentatively generalize: it seems that proposed principle #1 is pretty general, whereas proposed principle #2 is less so, and so forth.

Emotions and moral reasoning

The purpose of this chapter is to explore how emotions are related to moral judgment. My most general thesis, in response to extreme Stoicism, is that emotions may *either* support moral judgment *or* impede it, though I have stressed the supporting relation. In stressing this, I have also focused almost exclusively on emotions' perceptual function in moral cognition – that is, on moral judgments as arising rather spontaneously in response to the situations of life. Of course, those spontaneous responses are highly prepared by what goes before – by background knowledge of the situation, possibly by hearing a narrative without which one would not understand the emotion-evoking situation well enough to respond with the emotion, and, of course, by an innumerable array of past experiences, developed sensitivities, powers of conceptual discrimination, and dispositional concerns, as well as more immediate factors such as one's present mood and powers of attention. Sense perception too can have such a complex preparatory background, at least the more powerfully cognitive kind of perception that I have taken as paradigmatic in this chapter, the perception of situated whole things in one or another set of terms. We don't think of this background, in either case, as a set of premises from which the perceptions in question or their associated judgments are arrived at by inference, nor as a comparing process in which alternative ways of reading a situation are weighed by considering reasons for and against each. Yet reasoning is an important process by which beliefs are formed, in moral matters as well as others. In the present section I explore briefly the role of emotions in moral reasoning.

I begin by considering how emotions can degrade moral reasoning. They can do so by *disruption of proper process* and by *misinformation*. Disruption can occur by stopping deliberation or de-motivating it or misdirecting it or motivating inferential mistakes. The misinformation by which emotions may degrade moral reasoning is primarily about values, though, as we have seen, facts and values are here not very clearly divided one from the other. Here the fault lies not in the *direction* of the reasoning, but in the *premises* from which it draws its inferences.

First, an emotion irrelevant to the issue to be reasoned about can distract the reasoner. Moral reasoning is no more susceptible of this kind of disruption than other kinds of reasoning. A person who is trying to solve a problem in economics or symbolic logic may find that anxiety about his sick child keeps him from thinking clearly. It distracts his attention from the problem, making it difficult to search diligently for relevant data, to pay adequate attention to what a text or a colleague says about the argument, to use his imagination in considering data and possible inferences from them, and to hold relevant considerations sufficiently in mind. All of this can apply as well to someone trying to decide how to advise a friend considering a divorce or whether to join a group opposed to US economic sanctions against a Middle Eastern rogue state. Since the disrupting emotion is internally irrelevant to the reasoning, its power to disrupt seems to come primarily from its *power to distract attention from the arguments.*

In a second kind of case, an emotion that is relevant to the moral reasoning (by having propositional content that belongs to the argument) can "prejudice" the reasoner. The prejudicing emotion may be rational or irrational. Let us start with an irrational case. A black man has been convicted (justly, let us say) of murdering a white woman, and a jury must decide his sentence. One jury member has an irrational dislike, almost amounting to hatred, of blacks. Blacks tend to look bad to him, even in the best of circumstances, and always look worse than they really are, but especially when they act in opposition to whites. The juryman's reasoning towards a sentence decision is of poor quality because his racist repugnance for the defendant distorts his view of the badness of the crime and the badness of the man. Any reasoning he does about whether one sentence or another is more appropriate is based on the false "premise" about the defendant's degree of badness (he appears worse than would any white man who had done the same crime). One effect of the false "premise" is that considerations that would favor a lighter sentence will tend not to have their proper weight with the juryman. In deliberating about sentencing, he will come to a correspondingly false conclusion. He will not see the moral point and (what we have argued is internally connected with this blindness) will not be moved to leniency of any sort. Despite the irrationality of the emotion, I say that in this kind of case its propositional content belongs to the argument because the proposition *the defendant has committed a crime and is a bad person* is both a proper premise of the reasoning toward a sentence decision and part of the emotion's material proposition.

For an example of a rational emotion that degrades moral reasoning by prejudicing the reasoner, let us say it is rational to fear that the rogue state will develop the capacity to destroy masses of its political neighbors. The emotion is rational because it has been shown to have stockpiled such weapons in the past, has shown that it is willing to use them, and because its neighbors are vulnerable. Let us say that this fear is primary in a person's approach to the question of whether economic sanctions against the rogue state ought to continue. On the other side is the destructiveness of the sanctions to the people of the state (let us say that the deaths of many children in the recent past are plausibly attributable to the sanctions). The rational fear of the rogue state's military exploits might keep a moral reasoner from seeing clearly (with full evaluative and motivational force) the reasons for lifting the sanctions. Here again the mechanism of disruption is not distraction, but something we might call essential premise-deafness. It is an inability to "hear" clearly the counter-argument, because the considerations in its favor are dimmed relative to the intensity with which relevant considerations against it are felt ("heard," "seen").

Someone might object that in this last case the emotion is still irrational, since it leads a person to reason poorly. But a distinction should dispel this impression. The ideal reasoner about this situation would not only fear the rogue state's being able to destroy its neighbors, but also be horrified at what the sanctions are doing to the people. So, it is true that the reasoner's *overall state of mind* is subrational. It is this one-sidedness of his moral sensitivity that makes his reasoning "prejudiced." But the emotion itself, unlike our juryman's repugnance for the defendant, is grounded in good reasons and well fitted to its object. Good moral reasoning depends on having not just some morally perceptive emotions, but on having wide-ranging and potentially conflicting emotions that ground the premises on various sides of a moral debate.

If disruption and prejudice are the chief ways that emotions degrade moral reasoning, and if, as I am arguing throughout this book, emotions' potential to hinder suggests a corresponding potential to help, these considerations suggest that emotions promote good moral reasoning chiefly by enhancing the process of moral inquiry and by supplying true premises.

Moral reasoning, like any other kind, is not likely to be excellent unless it is sustained over a period of time and pursued with concentration and energy. An acquaintance of mine has had a "passion" for the sufferings of the Palestinians under Jewish rule in Israel. This passion comes out in various moral emotions, such as his indignation against the Palestinian's oppressors, hope for improvement of their plight, compassion for them in their suffering, and satisfaction when a step towards their liberation seems to have been taken. Over the years, he has done some careful and high-quality moral reflection about the Palestinian problem. The quality of his reasoning is no doubt due in part to the excellence of his raw intellect, but it seems indisputable that it would not have been done as well, and probably not done at all, apart from moral passion, which focuses and energizes his reflection, making answers a matter of urgency. We should note that it is the dispositional concern for the problem, the concern that is the basis of the four emotions I have mentioned, that sustains the reflection over the years. But this observation does not gainsay the role of those emotions, since the emotions are episodic manifestations or versions of that concern, focusing the Palestinian situation in one particular way or another; as such they function as bursts of episodic impetus to reflection. Emotion is a pre-eminent way in which the mind is "occupied" with an object; this is why anxiety about a sick child can distract a person from moral reasoning, but it is also why an emotion with moral content can concentrate the mind in reasoning about its object.

Trading on something like the "occupation" theme, Antonio Damasio (1994) has proposed his "somatic marker hypothesis" about how emotions contribute to the process of practical reasoning. His idea is that emotions make feasible what would otherwise be an enormously cumbersome if not impossible task of considering options. The problem that emotions solve is that of how to reduce to a manageable number the options among which practical reasoning aims to decide. Consider Jean-Paul Sartre's famous case of the young man who must decide whether to join the resistance or stay home and be a comfort to his aging mother. What makes the case so simple? How come the boy has only these two serious options? Why doesn't he have to consider also whether to commit suicide, leave for America, stay with his mother and torment her, devote himself full time to the classical guitar, join the resistance and betray his comrades to the Germans, and any number of other possible courses of action? Damasio's answer (1994: chap. 8) is that his emotions have pre-selected these two options as the only serious contenders. Most of the other options I mentioned probably don't even occur to him, because they have no attraction for him; they do not speak to his concerns; and, if any did occur to him, it would be quickly dismissed as either uninteresting or positively repugnant. Damasio's hypothesis is that the thought of these various options is "marked" with a pleasant or unpleasant bodily sensation that sorts them into categories: those worthy of consideration and those that aren't. I have criticized that part of the hypothesis at Roberts 2003: 155–57. But if we subtract the somatic marker part from the idea, the rest has merit. Because of the young man's concern for French autonomy, and perhaps because of many other concerns of his, joining the resistance is an attractive option. And, because of his love for his mother, and perhaps his sense of duty, staying home for her comfort also has its attractions. By contrast, the classical guitar prospect leaves him cold, and the idea of betraying his comrades to the Germans positively disgusts him.

Moral reasoning often occurs in a social context of discussion – one person gives advice or offers a proposal, and another raises objections or suggests an alternative; and the first person responds with further suggestions, rebuttal, or revision. Envy, distrust, anger, embarrassment, contempt, and shame stemming from the interaction can impede the process and degrade the reasoning, while self-confidence, friendly feeling, admiration, trust, and respect for one's interlocutor can foster depth, creativity, and thoroughness of deliberation. Thus the first general way that emotions foster good moral reasoning is by facilitating process – motivating it, keeping it relevant, and producing a social atmosphere in which hard, honest exchange can occur.

The second general way that emotions support moral reasoning is their involvement in the production and enforcement of premises. Emotions can play a role analogous to the one sense perceptions play in some non-evaluative arguments. I see a person come into the room with a dripping umbrella and conclude that it must be raining. The visual perception provides a premise – *The arrivés are wet* – which I put together with an assumption or two, from all of which I infer that it must be raining. Similarly, I feel anger at someone for speaking condescendingly to me and, putting it together with an assumption or two, conclude that I should not again put myself in a position to be spoken to like that. It is true that I might have formed the premise – *the condescension with which he spoke to me is offensive* – without feeling anger or any other emotion, but the emotion is a very basic way to form it, and one that gives the premise prima facie immediacy and conviction, as also in the case of sense perception.

We sometimes reason morally by weighing options in imagination. It is a little like a person deliberating about where to hang a picture, who tries it in one position and then in another, then looks at it from another angle, and so forth, consulting her reactions in each case and comparing them. In the moral case, the reactions consulted are typically emotions or virtual emotions. Shall I shoot the deer that devastates my garden? I am vexed by the devastation, but the deer would not vex me if I gave up gardening; but would I be vexed about giving up gardening? If I harvest her for the freezer, I will not be vexed about the garden, but how will I feel about the deer, and myself? And which is the heavier emotion, the vexation I will feel about not gardening, or the regret I will feel about shooting the deer? All of this is weighing options – testing them imaginatively – by reference to emotion. It is highly personal: I am using my "heart" as a testing instrument. I may, of course, understand this reasoning in a non-moral, merely "therapeutic" way: My ultimate aim in deciding what to do may be to feel comfortable. But this is not the only way to think of the procedure. If I trust my emotions, I may use them in the hope of drawing correct moral conclusions. And some people's emotions *are* trustworthy, or at least approximately so.

Just as empirical anomalies create premises from which a revision of existing theory may emerge by reasoning, so emotions that conflict with our moral opinions may prevent our drawing moral conclusions with confidence, and keep us investigating. For example, a person may be convinced by historical and theological considerations that Muslims ought to be treated with suspicion; yet in personal interaction with a Muslim, one may find oneself feeling respect and trust. If we take the emotion to be an impression whose propositional content includes something like *this Muslim has dignity and character and is worthy to be trusted*, it creates a new premise that calls out to be made consistent with one's other beliefs. Sidney Callahan has noted that seemingly flawless arguments to the conclusion that torture is justifiable or that dead babies may be harvested for their parts or that AIDS patients may be refused treatment can come up against emotions in response to imagining or seeing actual torture, actual harvesting of dead babies, and actual AIDS patients refused treatment, that strongly discourage us from assenting to the conclusions (Callahan 1988: 12). Justin D'Arms has suggested to me that a difference between emotions and sense perceptions is that sense perception may seem to provide an *independent* check on empirical theory that emotions cannot provide on our evaluative outlook. One would need to qualify carefully the ways in which sense perception is a truly independent check on empirical theory, but no doubt it does sometimes so function (see Alston 1991: chaps 3–4). Callahan's remarks suggest that our emotions sometimes function as an analogous check on our moral beliefs.

So far, we have been reviewing ways emotions generate moral premises in their capacity as analogous to perceptual states. The theme of Roberts 2003: 323–28 was that feelings of emotions can be used in the production of self-knowledge (much of which is a kind of moral knowledge in our broad sense of "moral"). But here the emotion provides evidence not in virtue of its similarity to a perceptual state, but rather as something perceived, that is, as the object of perception. It is now the *feeling* of the emotion that is analogous to the sense perceptual state. In that passage I pointed out that emotions are evidence of character traits, and so feelings of them can be a source of self-knowledge. Often, though not always, the relation between the felt emotion and the self-knowledge is one of inference: one concludes from one's emotion what one's own character is like.

Last, I would mention an indirect way that emotional experience makes premises for use in moral reasoning. In our interactions with others, information about their emotional states is crucial to our deliberations about how to judge them and how to act with respect to them. From a look on my wife's face or a tone in her voice and a little further reflection I conclude, "This is not the time to broach the subject I had in mind." People vary in their sensitivity to the often subtle and fleeting cues to emotion supplied by tone of voice, body posture, eye movements, and facial expression. But the considerable "intuitive" ability most of us have to detect others' emotions seems to depend on our own history of emotional experiences. This thesis is suggested by the case of autistic persons, who typically do not experience the range of emotions that occur in normal people in the context of social interaction, and consequently (so it seems) lack the ability to perceive those emotional states in others.

Conclusion

The most basic thesis of this chapter is that emotions are perceptual states that can in principle be true or false perceptions of the values that inhere in situations. The possibility of truth and falsity in emotions implies an even more fundamental value that emotions can have, the value that I identified briefly at the end of Chapter 2 in connection with a quotation from Marcus Aurelius. It is that an emotion may fit or fail to fit the situation it is about. It can be properly or improperly attuned to reality. This relation of fit or lack of fit, when thought of in epistemic terms, is truth and falsity. In what follows, I am going to call this kind of value an emotion's *intrinsic value*, so as to have a label by which to distinguish it from several other kinds of value that emotions can have. I call it intrinsic because this kind of value is an internal relation between the emotion and what it is about. As we move into the other kinds of value that emotions can have, in Chapters 6–9, by virtue of their relations to actions, personal relationships, happiness, and character, we will see that the intrinsic value of emotions is often in the background of these other kinds of value. But first I will address, in the next chapter, some objections to the perception thesis that is fundamental to this chapter. And then I will consider, in Chapter 5, how we can know that some emotions are veridical and others not, and what it takes for an emotion to be veridical.

4

Objections to the perception thesis

Introduction

In the previous chapter I sketched an account of one of the moral
functions of emotions, namely, their possible role as a kind of perceptual
basis for moral judgments and knowledge. I tried to give a compelling
account of the nature of the kind of perception that I have in mind.
Emotions, I argued, are concern-based construals. In the last couple of
decades philosophers have raised a number of objections to accounts of
emotions that make them perceptions or perception-like. First, it is said
that emotions, but not perceptions, are mediated by belief and imagination. Second, perceptions are about what is present to the subject, but
emotions are often about things absent – in the future and in the past.
Third, perhaps moral perception is most plausibly understood by analogy
with perception of secondary properties; but it's implausible to think of
moral "perception" as literally a kind of perception because moral properties are in many ways starkly different from secondary properties. Fourth,
when you depict your perceptual experience you depict something "out
there" in the world, but when you depict the content of your emotions you
describe only the state of your own mind. Fifth, perceptible predicates
present phenomenal content; but moral predicates, being dispositional, do
not. Sixth, beliefs can be justified by reference to sense perceptions, but
not by reference to emotions. Seventh, literal perception has a causal
condition that emotions can't meet. Finally, the special conceptual kind
of perception attributed to emotions in Chapter 3 can't be what emotions
are, because beasts and babies have emotions, but not concepts. I think
that the answers to all of these objections lie implicitly in the previous
chapter. The present chapter aims to make these answers more explicit,
and so to make the account of the previous chapter clearer and more
compelling.

Emotions are mediated by belief, memory, and imagination

If, for example, I regret having missed the opportunity to ask somebody's forgiveness before she died, the emotion depends crucially on my belief that I transgressed against her in some significant way, which in turn depends on ostensible memory of the offense and my ability to imagine what things would have been like had I asked her forgiveness. By contrast, when I see the rotten stump in front of me, the perception seems to be quite independent of my beliefs, my memory, or my imagination (Greenspan 1995: 194–96).

This objection ignores the phenomenon of conceptual perception that I expounded in Chapter 3 and in general the elements in perception that are not strictly sensory. Our ability to recognize things we've seen before, and to categorize things we haven't seen before depends on memory, and even very straightforward cases of sense perception are mediated by belief or imagination. Consider the visual perception of a motionless rabbit sitting in surroundings that are visually similar in color and texture to itself. One might stare at the scene for minutes, with 20 / 20 vision and in good lighting, and not see the rabbit. Then, upon being induced to believe a rabbit is there, or upon being told to imagine a rabbit in the setting, one comes to see the rabbit within the very same sensory display. The experience resembles that of "seeing" something new (to oneself) in a gestalt drawing. The rabbit "appears" or "takes shape." As to the perception of a rotten stump, a person with no previous experience (memory) of rotten stumps can certainly have the sensory visual impression in question without accessing his memory, but he cannot see (construe) the thing *as* a rotten stump without having the requisite concepts, and this will depend on memory.

Perceptions are of what is present, but emotions are often about what is absent

Patricia Greenspan argues that emotions cannot be perceptual because what they are about is often not present to the subject and may be abstract and conceptual:

> what emotional attention hooks onto in the first instance may be something to be added to the surrounding situation, not something found in it: the act to be done, not some property of the world by virtue of which it demands action. And the emotion may be at some remove from the situation – like an allergic reaction to a food enjoyed at the time but

producing hives a few hours later. ... To assign the feeling a specifically moral content ... so that it might seem to count as the perception of a moral property, we need to see it as directed toward an abstract thought: that the act in question is forbidden, say. (Greenspan 1995: 195–96)

Here Greenspan has identified a difference between the kind of perception that emotions are and sense perception. It is true that sense perception is of the sort of thing that can be sensorily perceived, and paradigmatically of what is physically present. (I ignore cases like long-ago burned out stars whose light, still arriving, enables us to see "them," and the more pedestrian cases of "seeing" someone on television.) Since emotions are often about things that meet neither of these qualifications, they cannot be sense perceptions. Fear is often about events anticipated rather than present, and regret is about things no longer present. Further, it is essential to some such "perceptions" that the subject grasp the situation in such terms as *possibility* and *lost past,* and these are concepts rather than percepts.

It is characteristic of construals, even ones that have some sensory content, that they involve non-sensory content as well. Take the example from *Emotions,* section 2.3b, of construing the word "table" as a verb. Here we have some sensory content (the sound or look of the word "table"), but the character of the "perception" (the "sound" or "look") of the word is given by the concept of *verb,* which is not sensory. And what I mean by calling the experience of hearing the word "table" as a verb a *perceptual* experience is not that it has this sensory content, but that it has the character of an experience, that it strikes one in a certain way that is analogous to the sensory quality of a sound, and that we experience a certain passivity in the way it comes upon us that is also characteristic of sense perception. The strictly *sensory* perception of the word does not change as the construal changes, yet the word "table" *sounds* different, we are inclined to say, when you hear it as a verb, even though the "as a verb" is purely conceptual. Greenspan correctly points out that if moral qualities are "perceived" via emotions, they must be qualities that cannot be given in sense perception; but it doesn't follow that they can't be given in any kind of perception at all.

Evaluative properties differ significantly from secondary properties

Simon Blackburn chides David Wiggins for marveling that philosophers have "dwelt nearly exclusively on *differences* between 'good' and 'red' or 'yellow'" (Wiggins 1987: 107; italics added; I quote from Wiggins, rather than Blackburn, who misquotes him). Then Blackburn says "it is very easy to rattle off significant differences between secondary properties and those involved in value and obligation" (Blackburn 1985: 13) and quickly lists several significant differences: (1) you don't show incompetence in ascription of secondary qualities by being ignorant of the primary qualities on which they supervene, but you are incompetent in ascribing moral properties if you are unaware of the factual properties on which *they* supervene; (2) defective perception of secondary qualities results from damage to receptors like retina or taste buds, but defective moral perception results from character defects, which are very different from organ damage; (3) we know immediately when our secondary quality perception fails, but when our moral perception fails (as a result of moral corruption) we typically do not notice it; (4) if all humans ceased to see blue, blue would *ipso facto* no longer exist; but everyone's coming to think it permissible to maltreat animals would not make this permissible; it would just mean "that everybody has deteriorated" (14); (5) secondary properties vary in salience cross-culturally depending on the qualities' importance to a society, but, once a predicate is found for such a property, "there is no prospect of finding that [the predicate] has a radically different extension" (14); by contrast, value predicates are applied very differently in different groups or at different times; (6) it is possible to perceive a secondary quality perfectly well, yet not care about it, but this is not possible with moral qualities; (7) value predicates are attributive: a single action may be good *as* action of a commander-in-chief but bad *as* an action of a father, but secondary qualities "just sit there: a red tomato is a red fruit and a red object just bought at the grocer's" (15).

But Wiggins and McDowell never denied the significant differences between secondary quality perception and moral perception; they only asserted some significant similarities. Among the similarities are: (1) moral properties can present themselves to consciousness in a way that is experientially similar to the presentation of secondary qualities in sense perception; that is, moral perception stands in contrast with (merely) inferring the property, thinking of the property, imagining the property, believing the property to be present, knowing the property to be present (this is unsurprising given the reality of conceptual perception); (2) people can vary in their competence to perceive moral qualities, just as they can vary in their competence to perceive secondary qualities; (3) the variation of competence is in each case due to the condition of the perceiver (the variance in competence in the moral case being made by differences in (a) moral conceptual competence and (b) moral caring); (4) moral and secondary qualities are alike "subjective" (species-relative) in depending ontologically on features of the human condition, in contrast with radically objective qualities like molecular structure; and (5) perceptions of moral qualities and perceptions of secondary qualities are alike in being capable of grounding beliefs that are either true or false.

But the analogies that I exploit with sense perception are not limited to the perception of secondary qualities, since I tend to the more natural examples of perception of situated objects, and not just of their sensory properties. Both the differences from perception of secondary properties that Blackburn sketches above and the similarities that I sketch turn on the fact that moral perception is *conceptual concern-based* perception rather than merely sensory perception. If conceptual concern-based perception is a reality, then Blackburn's points help to clarify how moral perception works, rather than show that it doesn't exist.

A phenomenological argument

Ronald de Sousa, who himself defends a perceptual account of emotions, raises this objection:

> For perception, as recently pointed out by Alva Noë, is "transparent" in the sense that when you attempt to depict your visual field you just end up drawing a picture of the room you are in (Noë 2000: 124–26). The effect of passion is precisely the reverse: when the angry man, or the joyful bride, or the jealous husband attempt to describe the world, they succeed only in describing their own state of mind, or perhaps even just the hormonal (or as it used to be said the *humoral*) balance in their body. (de Sousa 2011: 29)

This is not true. The person in an emotional state, like the person describing what he sees, largely describes the part of the world that, in her emotion, she is attending to. She says, "The dirty bastard took me for all I had" or "This is a wonderful day!" or "He's always gazing at other women with that famished look" or "Look out, the train is coming!" We can, of course, *imagine* someone saying, "My blood pressure is up" or "My body feels light as a feather!" "I have this creepy feeling all over my skin" or "My heart is racing!" But such ways of talking are both less common and less informative. Just as the person who is reporting on his visual impressions most often tells you what he sees, the person reporting on his emotions most often tells you how the world appears to him.

The phenomenal content (occasion) objection

Even if we accept the idea of conceptual perception, it might be thought, it will need some kind of phenomenal vehicle to get it moving. The construal will need an *occasion* such as the duck–rabbit drawing or the fish sentence (either its sound, or its look, or its "sound" as we rehearse the sentence in thought) – something that can be perceived *non*-conceptually. An advocate of the construal approach to emotions who interpreted sympathetically the Jamesian idea that emotions are bodily feelings might be inclined to assign to the visceral, tactile, and muscular sensations that are often associated with emotions the role of supplying the phenomenal occasion for the construal. Jesse Prinz's theory (2004: chap. 3) can be read in such a light. We can display thus the schema it suggests:

1	2	3	4	5	6
Eliciting event (optional) (ARROWS INDICATE CAUSATION)	Mental state (perception, thought, judgment, imagining)	Bodily reaction	Perception of the bodily reaction (the **EMOTION** itself)	Construal of the bodily reaction in terms of, or as indicating, a core relational theme	Action in response to the core relational theme (optional)
→	→	→	→	→	

Here follows a case that could illustrate this six-part schema. First, perhaps an eliciting event occurs. Maybe you hear on the radio that a tornado has wiped out the small town in Kansas where your parents live. The report makes you think, second, that maybe your parents have been killed or injured. Third, this thought makes your body react in certain ways: your heart beats more rapidly, your blood pressure rises, the muscles in your abdomen and shoulders tighten, etc. etc. Fourth, you perceive (feel) this medley of bodily changes. Fifth, you "read" (construe, perceive) the bodily sensations *as* saying *my dear parents may be dead or in big trouble!* (The emotion would seem to be fear or anxiety about your parents' safety.) Sixth, you respond to the fifth stage of the process by calling your parents on the phone. On Prinz's schema, interpreted as a kind of construal view, the sensations of bodily changes play the role of phenomenal content occasion that seems required if the theory is to be a perceptual one.

Let's note some differences between the above kind of construal view and mine. On Prinz's view, the emotion proper doesn't occur until stage 4 of the process – the subject's perception of his bodily changes. The construal of the situation "in the world" as threatening (which presumably Prinz doesn't regard as a perception) is apparently not itself the emotion; the emotion is the medley of bodily sensations, that is then *interpreted* or *read* as *indicating* the threat in the situation. This is a difference from my view, which is that the emotion is a construal of the situation "in the world" as containing the threat. We might wonder, too, how the mental state at stage 2 can give rise to the bodily changes characteristic of anxiety if it's not itself already an emotion. Surely there's a difference between hearing a radio report of a tornado that elicits all that bodily commotion and hearing a nearly identical one (say, about a different town in the Midwest) that elicits none. What's the difference between these two ways of registering the information? On my view it's the difference between registering with anxiety and registering without. That is, the mental state at stage 2 has to be already a recognition of the emotional import of the object to which it is responding. In my terms, it must already be a concern-based construal. Or, in Prinz's terms, the core relational theme has to have been detected already before the bodily change kicks in. So, I'm inclined to locate the emotion at stage 2 and to think of the bodily changes as concomitants or accompaniments of the emotion that supply part of its familiar phenomenology, rather than as the emotion itself. The occasion for the construal (what corresponds to the duck–rabbit *figure*) is the situation "in the world." It is the *situation*, not the sensation of bodily changes, that lends itself to construal as an instantiation of a "core relational theme" (I call this the instantiation of the formal object of an emotion type).

In Chapter 3 I noted that construals require that what is construed in a certain way lend itself to such construal. I noted that the duck–rabbit was impossible, or nearly impossible, to construe as a bowl of gerberas and the fish sentence impossible to construe according to schemas other than two propitious ones. This fact may raise a problem for the interpretation of Prinz's theory as a construal view. The situation in the world – that a tornado has ripped through Leavenworth, Kansas – lends itself to a construal in terms of a threat to something cherished, but it is far from clear that the medley of sensations of fluid releases and muscular contractions can supply a plausible occasion for such a construal. Again, it seems that we have to go back to stage 2 to explain how the corporeal sensations get construed in terms of the relevant core relational theme. That is in fact what Prinz does in explaining how a pattern of gut reaction that may be shared by several emotion types gets "read" in the particular terms of anxiety (say), rather than of shame or disappointment (say): the subject construes his gut in terms of *the situation* (see Prinz 2007: 65–66).

Ordinarily, we experience our emotions as directly about situations, and not as about situations as indicated by the states of our bodies. But in some cases, our emotional experience does fit the Prinz schema. On some occasions I feel a churning in my gut, wonder what it's about, perhaps cast about among interpretations using my situation as a key, and come to realize that in fact I'm anxious, and, furthermore, anxious about the wellbeing of my parents. On the view of emotions that I'm promoting, I was already construing my parents as in some kind of jeopardy, though I was not initially aware of it, and so was already in a state of emotion, before I was aware of being aware of the situation in the way characteristic of anxiety. I felt my bodily reaction before I felt the emotion, and came to feel *the emotion* only upon interpreting my bodily reaction. But, on my view, construal doesn't require awareness *of* construal; and if I was concernfully construing my dear parents as in some kind of jeopardy in such a way as to cause the churning in my gut, then I was already in a state of anxiety at stage 2, even though I didn't become aware of it until stage 5.

Remember: the phenomenal content objection is that emotions can't be perceptual because perception requires phenomenal content, but the evaluative predicates that would be the content of emotional perception are dispositional and thus not phenomenally representable. William P. Alston (1991: 43–48) seeks to answer the phenomenal content objection, or what I would rather call the phenomenal occasion objection. The heading of the present section is *The Phenomenal Content Objection*, but Prinz (on my interpretation) and Alston conceive phenomenal content differently than I do. They think of it as the *occasion* for the construal, the perception of *what is construed* in a certain manner (say, the perception of the *figure* of the duck–rabbit) whereas I think of the conceptual content of the construal as informing the phenomenal content (the perception of, say, the duck in the duck–rabbit). If we think of construal as having the form, *perceive X in terms of Y*, then the phenomenal content of the experience, as Alston and Prinz have it, is only *X*, while on my understanding of phenomenal content it is *X in terms of Y*; the phenomenal content is not the perception of the occasion, but the perception of the occasion *in certain terms*.

Alston credits Tom Downing with bringing the argument to his attention. Alston is concerned to defend the proposition that certain rather widely reported experiences of God are generically perceptual (not sense perceptual) experiences and thus may be actual perceptions of God, despite the impossibility of representing God in sense experience. His conclusion is thus analogous to one of my corollaries, namely, that people may perceive qualities like injustice, culpability, praiseworthiness, admirableness, goodness, and badness. Like me, he takes sense perception as the paradigm case of perception, and, like many of the objections to my proposal, the phenomenal content (read: occasion) objection trades on a feature of sense perception. The objection is that perception essentially depends on phenomenal content – in sense perception, such presentations as the visual quality of red, the auditory quality of middle C, the flavor quality of saltiness. Predicates that cannot be so presented cannot be perceived. For example, one can visually perceive that a man has brownish skin, but not that he is a physicist. There is no phenomenal content for being a physicist because this is a dispositional predicate. Similarly, in experiences of God, God is purportedly presented as having certain predicates – e.g., goodness, power, love, compassion. But this cannot be perception, says the objector, because these predicates are dispositional. A precisely analogous objection can be raised to my claim that injustice is perceived in indignation. Injustice is a relational (and historical) predicate, and consequently is not the kind for which there can be phenomenal content.

Alston's solution is to admit that dispositional predicates, which are predicates of objects, cannot be perceived, and to posit a special non-sensory phenomenal content for perceptions of God. Persons who have the religious experiences in question do not literally perceive God's goodness, etc.; they perceive instead qualia of God that are analogous to sensory qualia (these are what I'm calling the phenomenal occasions or vehicles), and they take these as *indications* of such dispositional predicates as goodness, compassion, etc. Then they *describe* their experience in objective terms. They say, for example, that they perceive God's grace, whereas really they experienced a phenomenal quality such as seemed to them to *indicate* a being that was gracious. But, Alston suggests, this situation is formally similar to that of sense perception.

> Our discussion has reflected the fact that in both areas of perception [mystical and sensory] we typically attribute to external objects, on the basis of perceptual experience, objective properties that go beyond anything that is displayed in that experience, for example, being a dog or being very powerful. In both areas we are, at least tacitly, assuming that the phenomenal complex in question is a reliable indication of the presence of the objective property being attributed. (Alston 1991: 48; italics added)

In this quotation Alston supposes that only the phenomenal properties – these being "intrinsic," "atomic," "basic" (see 44 n. 33) – *display* anything (his more usual word is "presents"). The rest seems to be something other than presentation – perhaps inference, belief, interpretation, or conceptualization. This solution does not seem to be applicable to my problem of apparent perception of moral properties in emotions. God himself is not a relational or dispositional predicate, but a substance, a personal being who *has* such predicates. So that even if no phenomenal presentation of God's dispositional predicates is possible, a phenomenal presentation of *God himself* might be. But, at least in my example from Dostoevsky, there seems to be no such phenomenally presentable subject of the predicate of injustice. In that case the only thing phenomenally presented to you is the words of the narrative (seen on paper or heard); and I don't suppose we want to invest the printed text or the voiced narration with the power to effect a phenomenal presentation of the Underground Man himself; for this would have to be non-sensory, like the presentation of God. But I would not be very much tempted by this solution anyway, because it does not seem to represent perceptual experience accurately.

How odd to say that in the visual experience of a dog, the object's *being a dog* is not presented! This seems to undermine one of the dearest desiderata of Alston's theory, namely, that the thing that is perceived is directly presented to consciousness (supposedly something in the "real world"). Oliver Sacks recounts an amusing and poignant incident that represents more or less the phenomenal presentation-as-indication scenario.

> I had stopped at a florist on my way to [Dr P.'s] apartment and bought myself an extravagant red rose for my buttonhole. Now I removed this and handed it to him. He took it like a botanist or morphologist given a specimen, not like a person given a flower.
> "About six inches in length," he commented, "A convoluted red form with a linear green attachment."
> "Yes," I said encouragingly, "and what do you think it *is*, Dr. P.?"
> "Not easy to say." He seemed perplexed. "It lacks the simple symmetry of the Platonic solids, although it may have a higher symmetry of its own. . . . I think this could be an inflorescence or flower."
> "Could be?" I queried.
> "Could be," he confirmed. (Sacks 1970: 13–14)

Dr. P's neurological affliction deprives him of an ability that is basic to normal human perception: the ability to *see* whole things. The spirit of the construal view is to suppose that most of the things that are presented perceptually in experience are whole and complex, not atomic phenomenal bits or aspects of things, from which the things themselves can be grasped only by "going beyond" the experience, taking it as an "indication" of what is beyond it. What Alston calls the "phenomenal qualities" that are presented in perception I prefer to call the "phenomenal occasion" of the perception, since the synthesizing and organizing power that I call construal operates in virtually all perception.

Several times Alston admits as much. He says, for example, that things have "whole-looks" (47), and says that we could in principle even form phenomenal concepts of such complexes (analogous to the concept of the sheer appearance of redness):

> I could correctly report that X looked like a house or a Porsche or a bald eagle or tasted like a white Burgundy or sounded like Handel, or, to switch to the particular, that something looked like Susie's house or Jason's Porsche, thereby giving you an idea of how it looked, tasted, or sounded. Yet I am using objective, nonphenomenal concepts in doing so. No doubt, in each case some complex pattern of visual, gustatory, or auditory qualia is being presented by virtue of the awareness of which I can tell that the object looks like a house, Jason's Porsche, or whatever. And no doubt, it is in principle possible to form and use a phenomenal concept of just that phenomenal pattern. (Alston 1991: 46)

He also admits that belief-systems can affect the phenomenal character of experience, though he insists that they do not do so in every case, and goes on to say:

> Although I recognize [that] the subject's conceptual scheme and belief tendencies can affect the *way* something appears to her, I do *not* acknowledge that it can affect *what it is* that appears to her. When I look at my living room, the same objects present themselves to my visual awareness as on the first occasion I saw it (with that furniture in place), even though they look differently to me on the two occasions. It is essential not to confuse what object(s) is appearing to my experience and what it appears as. This distinction has also succumbed to the current obsession with the omnipotence of conceptualization. (Alston 1991: 39; italics original)

I agree that one can often distinguish what is perceived from what it is perceived as, and I agree that Alston's experience of his living room is a case in point. However, this distinction is not so easily preserved in other cases. When the medical pathologist looks through her microscope at the slide of skin tissue and identifies some of the cells as basal cell cancer, her conceptual scheme is essential not merely to the *way* the slide appears to her, but to *what* appears to her. The uninformed layman, looking through the microscope at the same slide, does not experience a presentation of basal cell cancer. If he has been informed by the pathologist that some of the cells on the slide are basal cell cancer, he may believe and know that basal cell cancer is before him; but if the conceptual scheme has not begun to shape his perception, he will still not experience a visual presentation of basal cell cancer. He will not see the cells for himself, and his visual deficiency is at the same time a conceptual deficiency.

Construals, of which I take emotions to be a sub-class, are perceptions in which things are recognized as having a character and situations are grasped as belonging to types. Thus they involve just the kind of phenomenal presentation that we have in recognizing a house as a house or Jason's Porsche as Jason's Porsche. Alston's opposition to the view that perception is essentially conceptual seems to be behind his insistence on the perception-as-indication scenario and his stress on the kind of phenomenal presentation that I call the phenomenal occasion. But if it were true that our perceptual experience is limited to what Alston regards as properly phenomenal, we would not have perceptual recognition of the vast majority of things that we in fact can see and hear and taste.

I suggest that the person who hears the story of Liza with indignation and compassion perceives the injustice in the situation in an especially forceful, immediate, and basic way. Here one can, if one wishes, say that it is one thing to perceive the situation and another to perceive it as being unjust. But, assuming a sensitive reader, why not also say that the injustice of the situation is something "seen"? As indignation arises in the hearer or reader of the narrative, the injustice emerges as a new quality of the situation. It is arguable that redness is not a substance, but a quality of things. But, on Alston's view, if I am not mistaken, redness can be a "what it is that appears . . ." And, similarly, the injustice of the situation with Liza can be "what it is that appears . . ." Even clearer cases are the old woman in the figure (see Roberts 2003: 70) and the meaning of the fish sentence. It is true that one sees the *figure* as a picture of an old woman, hears the *fish word string* as a sentence; but this does not exclude one's seeing *the old woman* (or the picture of the old woman) in the figure, and hearing *the sentence* in the word string. These two cases are especially instructive and can carry us closer to the moral cases precisely because what I'm calling the occasion of the construal is so minimal, and the contribution of the conceptual so comparatively great.

The phenomenal content objection rests on a narrow picture of perception in which sensory qualia are given too large a role and are treated as like building blocks out of which anything that is to count as perception proper must be constructed. This picture underrates the integrated or "construct-ive" or holistic character of perception that is highlighted by attention to the phenomena of construal. It underrates the place of concepts and language in perception and the power of thought and imagination (as it operates, for example, in the hearing and appreciation of a narrative and the many "impressions" that a narrative may make). It underrates the potential of human "impressions" – and potentially veridical ones at that – to cut loose from sensory data or at any rate to make much impressional content out of meager sensory input. Strong impressions of situations may, in the human being, have little more sensory content than that of the visible signs or audible voicings of the language in which they are described; and they may not even have that, if they are not communicated in language but only mulled over in thought. Human perception is "constructed" out of much more than sensory qualia – or, to acknowledge the possibility that Alston proposes – their non-sensory analogs. Experien-tially, constructions *are* qualia and qualia are almost always constructions. I see no reason to suppose, a priori, that there must be qualia analogous to pure redness or pure middle-C-ness (if there is such a thing) for the presentation of either God or injustice. I do not see why relational properties cannot be presented perceptually. Indeed, they are presented perceptually as a matter of common experience.

Human impressions (experiences, perceptions) fall on a continuum of what we may call sensory significance. The case of a stick in a bucket of water appearing bent is an impression with high sensory significance. Here the sensory impression itself carries a great deal of "information," and in a way that does not depend very much on cultural variables, though it does probably depend in part on memory and the kind of experiences of straight and bent things that everybody can be counted on to have had by some date fairly early in childhood. The "impression" made by this visual experience is rigid in a way that the "impression" made by the visual or auditory experience of the word "table" as a noun is not. One can see or hear "table" as a verb more or less on command, but one has great difficulty in seeing the stick as straight, even though one *knows* that it *is* straight. It persists in looking bent, even to the best informed and trained of us. By contrast, the visual and auditory impressions made by human languages have virtually no sensory significance, but acquire their power to make impressions from convention and linguistic and cultural context. Given two equally mature readers of the Dostoevsky story, one reading in Russian, the other in a good English translation, nearly the same *moral* impressions will be made by the dissimilar *visual* and *auditory* impressions of the English and Russian texts.

Human emotions range over this whole continuum. On the maximal end there is a kind of simple reflexive fear that most people experience when they look down into an unprotected precipice. But most adult human emotions are towards the other end of the continuum, depending in significant part on background experience, social placement, and moral development. One might initially think that the example of reading or hearing a narrative is unfair (even though it's pretty typical as an emotional "stimulus"), since the visual or auditory impression is of a "symbol" and not of what the experience itself is about. But much the same analysis would have to be made if you did not read, but experienced the episode between the man and Liza as an eyewitness and ear-witness of the very events that the written narrative recounts. The sensory impressions here – of heard words that they speak in conversation, of seen movements of their bodies in the settings of their interaction – are still radically in need of support by memory (to put together what is going on now with what has gone before), linguistic ability (to understand what they are saying to one another), and moral and psychological understanding (to "see" what they are doing by penetrating the meaning of their actions). The moral qualities of the situation, as perceived in your indignation and compassion, are vastly underdetermined by even the most explicit sensory access to the situation. A corollary of this fact is that eyewitnesses, with their richer sensory experiences, are often inferior, in their grasp of narrative facts, to non-eyewitnesses who have a deeper understanding of morality and human psychology. The difference between the heard narrative and the eyewitness cases is that the sense impressions involved in hearing the narrative are not part of the intentional content of the experience of the narrative, including any emotions that may be experienced; while the sense impressions involved in the eyewitness case *are* part of that intentional content. The moral of this paragraph and the preceding two is that where the intentional contents of our experiences are concerned, no sharp division exists between sensory impressions and the conceptual, imaginative, and memorial contributions that our minds make to them. Our experiences are never, or hardly ever, purely sensory impressions, and some of our richest experiences feed on a very slight diet of present sensory input.

Jesse Prinz's Jamesian idea is that the phenomenal vehicle of all emotions is the same kind of thing, and that that vehicle is bodily sensations. According to his theory, every emotion is (so to speak) a construal of one's own gut in terms of some personally significant theme, something about which one is concerned. The theoretical impulse leading to this generalization is like the one that leads Alston to assign a special (non-sensory) phenomenal vehicle to experiences of God: unless there is some distinctive characteristic phenomenal vehicle, these experiences can't have either the perceptual quality that they seem to have, or the class unity (as emotions, or as experiences of God) that they have. It seems to me that neither Prinz's nor Alston's theory is borne out by experience, and about both theories I propose that we reject the presupposition.

As to Prinz's in particular, not only does he want his theory to make emotions perceptions; he also belongs to a tradition according to which feelings in the gut are what distinguish emotions from other types of mental events. But Prinz is very clear that for the gut feeling to become an emotion of any particular type it has to be read as about something that concerns the subject. I have pointed out that he can't explain why the gut reaction arises without presupposing that the subject already has construed the situational object of the emotion as something about which the subject is concerned. I propose that such a concernful apprehension of the situation is enough to make the mental event an emotion.

What then shall we say about the phenomenal vehicle? If emotions are concern-based construals, then what matters is that the subject construes the situational object in some way that impinges on the subject's concerns. A great many kinds of phenomenal vehicles can bear such a construal: the visual or auditory impressions of a text, sensory perception of a situation, mental images (memory, imagination – often fleeting and fragmentary), and sensations in the gut. As to the last, it seems clear that once we feel sensations in the gut as part of emotional experience, these sensations feed back into the perception of the overall situation and become part of the phenomenology of emotion. Seldom is the bodily sensation the focus or vehicle of the construal; ordinarily the situation is center stage and the bodily sensations are periphery or background, though panic attacks in which the subject's construal of himself as threatened is initiated by the feeling of a rapid heart rate or some other bodily event would be a counterexample. Some construals are mode-specific: construals of the duck–rabbit are visual; construals of a melodic fragment in terms of a larger setting are auditory; there are olfactory construals and tactile construals. Prinz's theory makes emotions mode-specific: they are all gut-sensational. As concern-based construals, emotions are not mode-specific; they are cross modal, or mode-indifferent.

The belief-justifying character of perception

Another argument against the perceptual character of emotions trades on the epistemic character of perception: real perception can provide a reason for believing because perception itself doesn't depend on reasons. It thus provides a reasons-independent basis for something that does need reasons, namely, beliefs (see Brady 2011). In requiring reasons for their justification, emotions are more like beliefs than like perceptions. If I say, "There's a flower in Sacks's lapel," and you say, "How do you know?" my saying, "I can see it from this window" usually settles the matter. You won't say, "How's *that* relevant?" But if I say, "Bob's firing Scott was unjust," and you say, "Why do you say so?" and I respond, "I'm indignant at Bob for firing Scott," that doesn't settle the matter. You want to know *why* I'm indignant. You want non-emotional evidence (reasons) – something factual about the circumstances of the firing. Perceptions put us directly in touch with the facts, and that's what makes them the kind of thing that can justify both emotions and beliefs. So, in this regard, emotions are very different from perceptions.

This argument's plausibility depends on limiting both perception and emotion to simple cases. It is true that we don't generally ask for reasons to justify someone's report of a simple perception like that of a flower, and we do generally want to know what justifies an ordinary person's fit of anger. But both perception and emotion can be complex and sophisticated, and when we think of examples on that end of the spectrum, more similarities emerge. To take an example of sensory perception that is just a little bit sophisticated, think of seeing the old woman / young woman figure as a young woman. I, being a little slow in the understanding department, had to be taught to do this by my wife, and she did it by giving me reasons, as you might say, for seeing the figure as a young woman. She told me how to make the role-assignments and, following her instructions, I eventually came to see for myself that the figure was a picture of a young woman. So, here, something very much like reasons makes perception possible (our earlier example of the rabbit in the underbrush is another case: "see – there's his eye!"). Similarly, but at a much more sophisticated level, the tissue pathologist can see things on a microscope slide that untrained people can't see because of her training in a rather elaborate explanatory conceptual system. Her perceptions have been justified, and have come into existence, through a system of reasons – reasons that she in turn will give to her students in training them to see what a pathologist is able to see on a slide ("How do you know that's basal cell cancer?" – "Well, look at this characteristic shape of the cell"). So, perception is not always unjustified by reasons, and starting with these more complex kinds of perception we can return to the apparently simple perception of the flower in Oliver Sacks's lapel and see that it too is a construal in which the parts of the sensory manifold (the convoluted red form with a linear green attachment) are assigned their proper roles in the whole. Each of the features of the manifold functions as a kind of "reason" for construing the thing as a flower. The features that for Dr. P functioned as reasons for thinking that the thing was an inflorescence or flower are, for neurologically normal people who have been normally trained by their experience with flowers, automatically incorporated into our seeing of the flower.

So, reasons are less foreign to standard perception than might appear after a review of simple cases. What about emotions? Are they ever straightaway justifiedly trusted the way standard perceptions so often are? The seasoned tissue pathologist comes to make judgments automatically after seeing certain things on the slide, and her students treat her perceptions as authoritative. So, sophisticated perceptions are sometimes straightaway trusted as justifying judgments. Similarly, Aristotle pictures the virtuous man as one whose emotions get their objects "right" in a variety of ways (the gentle [*praos*] person gets angry at the right person for the right reason with the right degree of affect, etc.). If this is possible, and if emotions are perceptions, as I have been arguing they are, then the virtuous person is the moral counterpart of the expert in some field such as tissue pathology. And the story about how the virtuous person comes to be someone whose emotions are epistemically trustworthy is this: he or she combines a proper concern for, say, just states of affairs with conceptual mastery of justice *in situ*: she distinguishes with adequate subtlety the shades of difference among cases, the pragmatics of situations in which justice must be compromised, the degrees and kinds of responsibility of individuals in the cases, and thus emotionally perceives actions and situations with reliable accuracy. These personal characteristics (of care and conceptual skill) give rise to a wide range of emotions about justice in situations: joy, sadness, gratitude, anger, relief, disappointment, hope, despair, regret, retrospective satisfaction, and more. Her emotional perceptions are reliable (not infallible) belief producers about justice situations, just as the tissue pathologist's sense-perceptual dispositions are reliable (not infallible) belief producers about the states of tissue.

The causal condition of perception and epistemic justification

A related objection to the perceptual thesis is that sense perception has a causal condition (Searle 1983: chap. 2) that construal, and in particular emotion, lacks. For me to be seeing a purple gerbil, it is not enough that I am having a visual experience of a purple gerbil and that there is a purple gerbil before me. Also required is that the purple gerbil be causing my visual experience. Because of the causal condition on sense perception, my having a visual experience of a purple gerbil before me is prima facie grounding for the belief that there is a purple gerbil before me, in a way that the mere belief that there is a purple gerbil before me is not. After all, if the gerbil's being before me and being purple is in fact causing me to have the visual experience, then in normal, non-Gettierized cases, there *is* a purple gerbil before me. Of course, one may have visual experiences of purple gerbils when no such thing is causing the experience. Because the causal condition can go unsatisfied, the justification provided by sensory experience is only prima facie.

Do emotions make an implicit claim about their own causation analogous to the one that sense perceptions make about theirs? And, if emotions do make such a claim, can it be the basis of a justificatory function analogous to the one that sense perception's causal claim can have? Might your indignation at the Underground Man thus have a tendency to show that he treated Liza abominably?

I have noted that the propositional content of emotions is not necessarily mediated by *sensory* experience, and that by far the more important contribution to the perceptual content of sophisticated human emotions is imaginal, memorial, and conceptual. So, it is clear that the causal mode, if emotions have such, is not primarily one in which environmental events impinge on the sensory receptors, as presumably they do in the gerbil case. The causation in question, if there is such, is going to have to be less the sort of thing that can be explained in physics terms, and more the sort of thing that is explained in terms of intentional states. Nevertheless, emotions are responses in some broad sense – responses to environmental occurrences, to narratives, to memories, to arguments, reflections, and processes of association. Just as the intentional content of sense perception claims implicitly that the thing seen, heard, etc. is impinging causally on the sensory receptors, so the intentional content of emotions claims implicitly that whatever the emotion is about is causing the emotion, or at least that the emotion would not be as it is were not the situation, including its moral properties, as *it* is (or was, or would be, or might be, or will be). This is because the emotion, when felt, is experienced as a sensitivity to the situation. Thus, your felt indignation at the Underground Man makes the following claims:

- The man's actions towards Liza are culpably unjust.
- My indignation towards the man is to be explained by the culpable injustice of his actions.

In both cases, as we have seen, the subject of the mental state may not believe this implicit causal claim (just as a person may not believe his eyes, for example, when looking at a stick in water that appears to be bent). The causal claim differentiates both sense perception and emotion from mere belief or mere judgment. My comments here apply to felt emotions, which, according to Roberts 2003: 323–28, are reflexive in the sense that the subject is aware not only of the object of the emotion, but aware of himself as the subject of the emotion, and thus aware of the emotion. The causal claim would seem to be absent in the case of unconscious emotions, inasmuch as the emotion in that case is not an intentional object, and thus could have neither causal nor other properties ascribed to it.

The extent to which the content tends to justify the belief depends, in each case, on the history of correlations between the experience-type in a given type of subject and the type of the event or object that it implicitly claims to have caused it. Simple reflex emotions in animals seem to be fairly reliable indicators of the existence of what they are about. For example, fright responses in mice that have not been tampered with by artificial conditioning and are situated in their natural environment are pretty reliable indicators that there is some threat in the environment, just as in human beings the visual experience of redness is a pretty reliable indicator that something red is impinging on their visual receptors. When it comes to more sophisticated cases, reliability varies quite a lot among individuals and can depend on expertise or other excellence. The auditory impression of an embedded augmented fourth is a more reliable indicator of an augmented fourth in a well-trained musician than it is in a beginning student of music theory. And, similarly, intense anger in a morally mature person is a more reliable indicator that some serious offense has been committed than it is in a silly or irascible person.

To suppose that perception is justificatory, whether it be sense percep-tion or emotional perception, and whether it be primitive or sophisticated, is to presuppose some conception of proper function. Even the simplest sort of color perception is not to be relied on if we cannot presuppose that the subject's visual apparatus is working properly in an appropriate environment, and we cannot rely on the mouse's fear responses if we suspect that it has been subjected to artificial fear conditioning or if someone has placed little bowls of artificial fox urine around its habitat. Similarly, we may not rely on the visual impressions of a microscopist who is the product of a perverse or outdated conceptual training, and if we are Nietzscheans we will not take Malcolm Muggeridge's (1986) emotional responses to the work of Mother Teresa to be a good indicator of the value of that woman's work, because we will think that his emotional responses presuppose a false world view. If you have undergone a moral development that desensitizes you to justice and injustice, we cannot expect the story of Liza and the Underground Man to cause you to have veridical emotional perceptions. In all these cases we reject the deliverances of the perceptual powers in question because we don't take those powers to be functioning properly in a suitable environment – we take it that because of some malfunction of reception, either in the faculties or in the character of the subject, or some oddity in the environment in which they are operating, the object is not causing the proper and veridical response.

Even though the simple kind of causal connection present in the purple gerbil perception is absent from the tissue pathologist's perception of what's on the microscope slide (the latter depending on a potentially controversial mediation by theory and specialized training), still, if someone asks, "What makes her think that what's on the slide is basal cell cancer?" the natural answer is, "She looked and saw it." And we assume that what was on the slide caused her to see what was on the slide. We *could*, of course, ask for a detailed account of the particular visible features of basal cell cancer, and the theoretical background that justifies the relevance of those visible marks, that she was unanalytically going by in seeing what she saw on the slide. But we don't ordinarily require that. If the expert saw it, that's good enough, because what she saw caused her – because of her expert sensitivity – to have the visual experience she had.

And, similarly, if someone asks, "What makes this reader think that Underground Man treated Liza unjustly?" one natural answer is, "When he read about the situation, he became indignant." And we assume that it was the story that caused him to feel indignation. We could, of course, ask for a detailed account of the particular narrative features that would justify the judgment that Underground Man treated Liza unjustly, along with the moral outlook that lies behind such justificatory relevance, and we might be especially inclined to ask for them if we have some doubt about this particular reader's sensitivity to justice-issues (so we're worrying about the nature of the causal connection between the story and the reaction to it). But if we think the reader is properly sensitive to such issues, we may just accept his judgment as deriving properly from his affective response to the story, much as we accept the testimony of the tissue pathologist as deriving properly from her sensory response to the slide. One way the cases are disanalogous is that often all we want from a pathologist's report is a trustworthy verdict, whereas in the moral case we usually want more understanding of the judgment. So, even where we don't distrust the reader's judgment, we usually want to know the story for ourselves, and to feel the emotional force thereof. But this disanalogy doesn't seem to affect the present issue.

The simpler cases of sense perception raise little or no controversy about the proper functioning of the relevant sense organs. Answers to the question, did a sound occur just now? or is the field in front of you black or white? will raise little controversy about what it is for the organs to be functioning properly. Thus, if two people with equally good eyesight and vantage point spot what the one sees as a coyote and the other as a young wolf, deciding which one saw rightly may involve deciding which one has the more refined concepts in this field. But it seems unlikely that disagreements about such concepts will run very deep or be very intractable. By contrast, the distinctively moral emotions' reliability as perceptions is relative to a deeply contestable conception of proper function, because the proper functioning in question is not just that of an organ, but of a person, and not just of a concept, but of a conceptual scheme or world view which itself seems to be partly presupposed by the experiences that most powerfully justify it. Mikko Salmela (2011) thinks "the epistemic analogy between perception and emotion fails" (20) because of the greater role of normativity in the standard of the truth for emotions as compared with that of sense perceptions. But analogies are by nature incomplete. Limitations noted, the analogy survives. See Blackburn's similar dispute with McDowell and Wiggins, discussed above. The perceptual experiences involved in the daily emotional life of Mother Teresa and Friedrich Nietzsche diverge radically, and yet each may represent proper or nearly proper functioning by the standards of his and her own outlook.

I remind the reader that the existence of deeply different moral outlooks, combined with the impossibility of rationally resolving the disagreements, does not imply that partisans of the opposing viewpoints who are aware of their rivals' views are thereby unjustified in holding their own views to be correct and the emotionally best formed exemplars of their outlooks to be reliable perceivers of the moral values in situations. To admit irresolvable moral pluralism does not commit one to moral relativism. Nietzsche and Mother Teresa can't both be right about the values of the things on which they centrally disagree.

The beasts and babies objection

The final objection that I'll consider in this chapter is not strictly an objection to the thesis that emotions are perceptual states, but an objection to my claim that they have a conceptual or propositional structure. I have answered this objection more fully elsewhere (Roberts 2003: 107–09; 2009b: 221–24; 2010: 569–74), but, since it persists, and may occur to some readers, I will here briefly reiterate my reply.

The objection (Deigh 1994: 2004; D'Arms and Jacobson 2003; Tappolet 2010) is that my notion of emotions as concern-based construals makes them too sophisticated for some of the beings to whom just about everybody wants to attribute them. Hardly anyone will deny that dogs, squirrels, horses, chimpanzees, and many other species of animals experience at least some of fear, anger, jealousy, joy, hope (eager expectation), and grief. And human children well below the age of understanding or speaking a language can experience at least some of these emotions. Therefore, emotions cannot be concern-based construals.

One feature of my account that makes such objectors especially suspicious is my use of "defining propositions" to characterize emotion types. Take, for example, the defining proposition for jealousy:

> *It is very important that B have a special personal attachment to me, but R is taking (has taken, may take) B's special attachment away from me with B's responsible collusion or consent, with a result of R's having B's special attachment for himself.* (Roberts 2003: 261)

The defining proposition identifies schematically a way of "seeing" (construing) a situation. The situation contains various conceptual elements: three individuals (A, B, and R), a relationship called "special personal attachment," and a transaction or potential transaction called "taking the special personal attachment and transferring it away from me (A) and towards R." The propositional form of the defining proposition specifies how these elements in the situation have to be arranged in the subject's construal so that the construal amounts to jealousy. Now the objector looks at all this complexity and thinks, "It's impossible that a dog have all those concepts, and deploy them in that propositional way in his perception of the situation."

Now, of course, I'm not saying that the dog speaks English and so is able to rehearse all of this in the reflective form of independent thoughts as I have just done. On my view, emotions are perceptions, not thoughts, as critics (for example, Tappolet 2010: 329 n.) sometimes claim. So, consider an ordinary dog feeling jealousy, as people ordinarily attribute it to her. It's your dog Hilde, and you've just arrived at your place with the boy you've been out with. You go to the kitchen and get a Coke for each of you. Hilde's curled up in her corner, apparently not paying much attention to you. You sit down on the sofa in front of the TV and start snuggling with your new friend. Before you know it, Hilde is on the sofa between you, licking your face enthusiastically. You say, "Hilde's jealous." Right. And what's going on in her mind? Well, Hilde is A, the emotional subject. You're B, the beloved whose special personal attachment is important for her to have. The boyfriend is R, the rival who seems to Hilde to be having that special personal attachment transferred to himself from Hilde.

What does Hilde have to do conceptually to be in this state of emotion? She has to be able to distinguish the individuals in the scenario: herself, the beloved, and the rival. She seems to be perfectly clear about the difference between the roles, and who's playing which one. She has to cherish the special relationship she has with you, and to see that relationship as being alienated by the boyfriend. It seems pretty obvious that she doesn't have perception-independent *thoughts* corresponding to the roles. She's probably not capable of *reflecting* on her relationship and on the idea of its being alienated from her. But she's capable of making the needed distinctions among the roles and identifying the relational issue that is raised by this stranger's snuggling with you. She doesn't have to be a language-user to construe the situation in the way characteristic of jealousy.

5

Emotional truth

Introduction

In the previous two chapters I have argued that, generically, emotions are perceptions, understanding *perception* as indifferent between true and false. To be a perception in this sense is to be a kind of mental state that *can* be true or false, and I have given several examples of emotions that I take to be true. In this chapter I will address two questions about emotional truth: (1) How can we tell which emotions are true and which false? and (2) What makes some emotions true and others false?

We don't ordinarily call emotions true or false. We don't say "Joe's anger about being passed over for promotion is true (or false)." But we do say, "Joe is right (or wrong) to be angry . . .;" "Jill was right to be afraid of the rabid dog;" "Jamie was wrong to feel ashamed of what she did;" and so forth. And the idea I'm getting at is that if emotions are perceptions, then Joe is right to be angry because the way his anger presents the situation to him represents the situation as it really is; that Jamie was wrong to feel ashamed because there was nothing really shameful in what she did or was, nothing about the situation that justified her shame's representation of the situation.

An emotion can be right or wrong in at least two ways. One of these is the pragmatic way. For example, it might be wrong for Jill to feel fear of the rabid dog not because the dog is harmless (it isn't), but because if she feels afraid she will send signals to the dog that make it more likely to attack. Or it might be wrong for Joe to feel angry about not being promoted, not because his being passed over was perfectly fair (it wasn't), but because Joe has a weak heart and anger increases his susceptibility to a heart attack. These examples of pragmatically right and wrong emotions are not examples of emotional truth and falsity as I will discuss them in this chapter. On the perceptual view that I have been promoting, an emotion is a representation of the situation to which it is directed, and so it can represent that situation correctly or incorrectly, accurately or not accurately. In this sense of "right," Joe is right to be angry only if he has really been treated unjustly, and Jill is right to fear the rabid dog only if the dog is a real threat to her wellbeing. These are the truths (or rather, truth claims) that Joe's and Jill's emotions bring to light.

In Chapter 3 I argued that because our emotions, like other perceptions, present situations to us in ways that can be true or false, they tend to occasion evaluative *beliefs* in us: if I'm angry that I was passed over for promotion, I tend to form the belief that I have been treated unjustly, and, if I'm afraid of a dog, the belief that the dog is a threat to me (in most cases, probably simultaneously with the formation of the emotion). I also noted that we sometimes resist believing what our emotions are telling us. I might be angry about the promotion while thinking that it's really not true that I have been treated unjustly. In my anger it *feels* to me as though I have been wronged, but I realize that in fact I haven't been. This is one of the ways emotions are like sense perceptions: as we don't always believe our eyes or ears, neither do we always believe our regrets and fears. We can resist their claims only because they do present situations to us in ways that can be true or false, and do so in a way that falls short of being beliefs.

According to Aristotle, some virtues are dispositions to have right emotional responses. Gentleness or good temper is a disposition to feel anger "on the right grounds and against the right persons, and also in the right manner and at the right moment and for the right length of time. . . . those who do not get angry at things at which it is right to be angry are considered foolish, and so are those who do not get angry in the right manner, at the right time, and with the right people" (Aristotle 1934 [*Nicomachean Ethics* 4.5, 1125b32–34, 1126a4–6 (Rackham)]). Courage, similarly, is a disposition to feel right fear and confidence: "The courageous man then is he that endures or fears the right things and for the right purpose and in the right manner at the right time, and who shows confidence in a similar way" (*Nicomachean Ethics* 3.7: 1115b18–20 (Rackham)). Some of these formulations of "rightness" may express or allow for a pragmatic criterion of rightness in emotion, but Aristotle's references to getting angry at the right person (presumably the offender, rather than some innocent person onto whom the anger might get diverted) for the right reason (presumably the offense rather than the color of the offender's skin) and fearing the right things (presumably the real dangers) suggest that at least part of rightness is emotional truth. If we follow Aristotle's hint, it will be the *virtuous* person whose emotions tend to get their objects right, the person who has had a good upbringing in a well-formed community, and who has contributed to his own moral development by acting in accordance with the standards of virtue and thus by developing good habits both of action and emotion. It will be the person who has come to care about what is truly good and has learned competently to discern good and evil in the situations of his life. The picture that emerges is that of emotions having to conform to standards that are not themselves emotions. Emotions that are true are ones that conform to such standards. If anybody's emotions are the standard of right emotion for Aristotle, it will be the person of practical wisdom. Thus it is not the emotions as such that are the standard of right emotion, but the standards of an ideally developed person, one who has become practically (or evaluatively) rational. When I speak of a person being evaluatively rational, I mean that he tends to make more or less spontaneous rational evaluations of the situations he encounters. Of course, he also needs to be able to deliberate well, but the aspect of practical rationality that I'm stressing at the moment is the spontaneous one.

An analogy is in order. All normal people have visual experiences. Such experiences can be true or false, veridical or not, accurate or not. But, in certain areas of life, and to some extent in all areas of life, it is not simply visual experiences that we trust to give us visual truth, but *people* whose visual powers have been properly *trained* in one area or another of visual input. Basketball referees become very competent at the rapid visual recognition and classification of fouls on the court, and can see things that ordinary people systematically miss. (With the advent of instant slow-motion playback, we have a more precise and less disputable way to test the truth of such visual experiences.) Coaches and other trained basketball watchers can also see strategies in play (patterns in the movements of the players) to which most of us are more or less blind, even despite our 20 / 20 vision. Art historians can visually discriminate with a pretty high degree of reliability the works of particular painters, distinguishing them from even very good imitations. Bird watchers can see telltale features of bird species to which others, with equally good eyesight and visual access, are blind. Each of these areas of perceptual discrimination belongs to a tradition of some sort in which the perceptually developed person has been "brought up," and to whose evolution he himself may have contributed. In a similar way, we may think, virtues like compassion, justice, and generosity will equip their possessor with emotional sensitivities that allow her to discern the moral features of situations; and these powers of perception, like visual ones, will have resulted from nurture and experience within a moral tradition.

Sometime in the early modern period, moral philosophers started thinking of the task of philosophical ethics in the way that I described in the opening chapter of this book. That is, they started thinking of it less as an *exploration* of ethical values for the sake of cultivating wisdom and more as a *technical search* for the foundations of ethical values. Perhaps they were reacting to a sense that the rough theological and ethical consensus that had prevailed in Europe since the early Middle Ages was breaking up, and that a new foundation had to be laid (discovered) that was not similarly fragile or subject to dispute. One can hardly cultivate wisdom without even knowing for sure what it is, thought they, perhaps, and so the first task of philosophy must be to establish the foundation. The divorce of this task from theological tradition was not immediate or general, but David Hume's version of the project at the height of the Scottish enlightenment aimed to derive ethics almost entirely from natural human emotions.

Hume on emotions and virtues

We might say that for Aristotle a moral emotion is reliably correct only if it arises from a virtuous disposition of the subject. Emotions are evaluative perceptions, and it is the virtuous person whose value-orientation to the world is reliably correct. Wherever the standard for the virtues comes from, it is not from the emotions. Hume inverts this Aristotelian order. For Hume a trait is a virtue only to the extent that it is met by a certain emotion of pleasant approval on the part of an observer, and is a vice only to the extent that it is met with a certain emotion of unpleasant disapproval. "An action, or sentiment, or character is virtuous or vicious; why? Because its view causes a pleasure or uneasiness of a particular kind" (Hume 1896 [*A Treatise of Human Nature*, iii.i.ii: 471]). "The distinction of moral good and evil is founded on the pleasure or pain, which results from the view of any sentiment, or character" (iii.ii.viii: 546–47). The qualification, "of a particular kind" in the earlier passage is important because for Hume the pleasure or discomfort must be a moral kind of emotion – for example, admiration or indignation, rather than the delight one takes in a beautiful landscape or the disgust a polluted river evokes. Hume also goes on to point out that not everyone's emotional self-report is equally reliable in this regard, because some people are subject to the illusion created by confusing an emotion of one kind with that of another. For example, in contemplating one's virtuous rival, one might mistake the non-moral displeasure that one feels about the rival's competitive advantage for a moral contempt or disgust about his bad character. By contrast,

> a man of temper and judgment may preserve himself from these illusions. In like manner tho' 'tis certain a musical voice is nothing but one that naturally gives a particular kind of pleasure; yet 'tis difficult for a man to be sensible, that the voice of an enemy is agreeable, or to allow it to be musical. But a person of a fine ear, who has the command of himself, can separate these feelings, and give praise to what deserves it. (*A Treatise of Human Nature*, III.i.ii: 472)

In the last sentence of this quotation we may discern two rather different constraints on the doctrine that to be a virtue is simply to be a trait that evokes pleasant approbation. To be in command of oneself is presumably to be able to figure out which of the two emotions – the disgust at the enemy or the delight in her warbling – is the one to use in assessing the music. It is to be able to assign the disgust to its proper cause and attend to the enjoyment of the music as the feeling relevant to *its* assessment. The task here is to "separate these feelings." The other, rather different, constraint is the necessity of a "fine ear." A person whose musical para- digms are the Elvis Presley favorites may respond with puzzlement and distaste or boredom when treated to *The Art of the Fugue*. Most "fine ears" are the product of at least an informal education in the Western musical tradition, and the finest are the product of many, many hours of listening reflectively to the best music as decided by the standards of that tradition. Discerning virtue and vice takes more than an ability to separate one's various emotions by their causes and objects; it takes the ability to have the right emotions among which to make the separations.

Analogously, to return to Aristotle's theme, the person whose moral emotions are reliably "right" will be one who has been well formed according to the character-standards of the right moral tradition. Hume is not a relativist, and expresses strong opinions about the paradigmatic characters of moral traditions other than his own. In his second *Enquiry* he expresses a strong sentiment of disapprobation that "Epictetus has scarcely ever mentioned the sentiment of humanity and compassion, but in order to put his disciples on their guard against it" (Hume 1983: 103). With similar disapprobation he points out in "The Standard of Taste" that "the sage Ulysses in the Greek poet seems to delight in lies and fictions, and often employs them without any necessity or even advantage" (Hume 1985: 228). Mohammed, in the Qur'an, "bestows praise on such instances of treachery, inhumanity, cruelty, revenge, bigotry, as are utterly incompatible with civilized society" (229). The sight of compassion, forgiveness, gentleness, and truthfulness warms the cockles of Hume's moral sensibility, while lying, violence, revenge, and religious narrow-mindedness evoke something on the order of contempt, disgust, or outrage. These responses are not surprising in someone who has been well reared in a society saturated with Christian tradition. In Hume's case the Christian background is not the whole story of his formation; he is a figure of the Enlightenment, a new movement within modernity in which human autonomy is especially admired and such "monkish" traits (Hume 1983: 73–74) as humility, obedience, devotion, self-denial, penitence, and trust in God are viewed with repugnance. It is from this Christian-flavored Enlightenment perspective that Hume emotionally beholds and judges sages of other moral traditions. We might well wonder how Hume can have so much confidence that his own emotional responses are the right ones while they are so at variance with those of his apparent moral peers from other traditions. Can it really be that human emotions – even when they arise in a mature moral agent, are properly separated as to type, and are felt from a personally disinterested perspective – are the ultimate standard of moral values? We will return to this question in a few pages when we look at some recent sentimentalisms, but I want first to return briefly to Aristotle.

Aristotle on emotional truth

Aristotle has a neat answer to the question of emotional truth. Indeed, it's a matter of simple calculation. It is called the doctrine of the mean. The trick is to figure out which human traits are virtues; once that is determined, then a person's emotional responses will be true if they express the traits that are virtues. You figure out which traits are virtues by first determining the matter of the continuum that a virtue has to do with, then finding the middle of the continuum; and that's the virtue. Emotions that are outputs of the virtue in question are (likely to be) true. This is Aristotle's apparent answer to our epistemological question: how do we know which emotions are true? It is not his answer to the metaphysical question: what makes emotions true when they are true? In other words, he doesn't think that the fact that a fully virtuous person of practical wisdom's feeling an emotion is what *makes* it true. Here's his story:

> In everything that is continuous and divisible it is possible to take more, less, or an equal amount, and that either in terms of the thing itself or relatively to us; and the equal is an intermediate between excess and defect. By the intermediate in the object I mean that which is equidistant from each of the extremes, which is one and the same for all men; by

the intermediate relatively to us that which is neither too much nor too little – and this is not one, nor the same for all. (Aristotle 1934 [*Nicomachean Ethics* 2.6: 1106a27–34] (Ross))

That is, if one divides the continuum in two *equal* parts, the point of division will be in the *middle* of the continuum. This is the basic mathematical idea of a mean. Take the virtue of gentleness (*praotês*); it is the mean with respect to anger. Anger, then, is what I'm calling the matter of the continuum; it's what the continuum determining the virtue of gentleness is a continuum *of*. Let's say the absolute defect is zero anger, and the absolute excess is the maximum amount of anger that any human being is capable of; the mean between these two extremes will be "the intermediate in the object." Now a virtue is a disposition to *choose* (*Nicomachean Ethics* 2.6), and so gentleness, as an intermediate in the object, will be the disposition to choose the amount of anger that is intermediate between the absolute defect and the absolute excess of anger.

But this can't be gentleness, for at least two reasons. First, a virtue is also a disposition to choose what is fitting *for each situation*, so the amount of anger that is virtuous will be measured to the situation. Offenses of great gravity and culpability call for more anger than minor offenses, so it won't do to hit the absolute mean every time. Second, human gentleness is the mean, not relative to the object, but "relative to us," and the opinion that Aristotle consults seems to be that in human affairs the best disposition involves a certain amount of leniency: rather than be disposed to the intermediate amount of anger simply relative to the severity of the offense, human affairs will go better if we seem to "err rather in the direction of deficiency" (Aristotle 1980 [*Nicomachean Ethics* 4.5: 1126a2 (Ross)]). But things are even more complicated than this.

Anger does come in amounts: it can, for example, be more or less intense, and more or less lasting. But it doesn't vary only in amounts. It also varies along dimensions of non-quantitative appropriateness. One example is anger's target. To be right, your anger about what the boss said to you this afternoon needs to target the offender, and not some innocent bystander like the children or the dog. Another non-quantitative dimension is culpability. The boss may have said something harsh to you this afternoon, but anger at him is appropriate only if you didn't deserve it and he is in the wrong for having said it. The reason for the anger is another such dimension. You might be right that what the boss said to you was unduly harsh, but if the real reason for your anger is the money you lost in the stock market last week, something is still wrong about your anger. Such considerations as these lead Aristotle to formulate the doctrine of the "mean" in partially non-quantitative terms. He seems to be less than fully aware of sliding from a quantitative to a partially qualitative interpretation of the "mean" when he says that moral virtue

> is concerned with passions and actions, and in these there is excess, defect, and the intermediate. For instance, both fear and confidence and appetite and anger and pity and in general pleasure and pain may be felt both too much and too little, and in both cases not well; but to feel them at the right times, with reference to the right objects, towards the right people, with the right motive, and in the right way, is what is both intermediate and best, and this is characteristic of virtue. (Aristotle 1980 [*Nicomachean Ethics* 2.6: 1106b16–25 (Ross)])

But, clearly, to introduce qualitative criteria of rightness of emotion is to abandon the idea of a mean, which is essentially quantitative, as a sufficient criterion of emotional truth. And merely to say that an emotion is true when it gets its object right in various ways is not to give a criterion of emotional truth. In Book 6, in his introduction to the discussion of practical wisdom, Aristotle refers back to passages like the one just quoted, and admits that

> if a man had only this knowledge [of how to determine the states of character that yield emotional truth], he would be none the wiser ... Hence it is necessary with regard to the states of the soul also, not only that this true statement should be made, but also that it should be determined what is the right rule and what is the standard that fixes it. (Aristotle 1980 [*Nicomachean Ethics* 6.1, 1138b29–30, 33–34 (Ross)])

He then promises to tell us what the right rule is.

But he never does so. Or does he? The doctrine of the mean seems to be an effort to give a neat criterion of emotional truth, a formulable "principle" that applies across the board to the virtues that are the dispositions to feel emotions that are "right." It's pretty clearly a dead end. But much of *Nicomachean Ethics* consists of accounts of particular virtues – by a conservative count about four books, and if you count friendship as a virtue (Aristotle says it's "a virtue, or implies virtue" (8.1)), that would make six out of ten books, and if we take continence to be virtue-like the count will mount further. If the doctrine of the mean isn't doing this conceptual work, then what is? What is Aristotle's actual approach to the virtues?

His usual way of sorting out conceptual matters – exemplified by his discussion in *Nicomachean Ethics* 1.4–12 of the nature of human happiness (eudaimonia) – is to survey the diverse opinions of the many and the wise, subject them to critical evaluation, and then formulate his own view of the matter, attempting to find valuable insights among the diverse opinions and to preserve as much as possible from them. Reading Aristotle as applying this dialectical approach, if less overtly, in his accounts of the virtues, we can see that the real "rule" for what constitutes the traits of the person most likely to achieve emotional truth is not the doctrine of the mean, even in its preferable non-quantitative formulation, but is derived by a critical and discriminating acceptance of the best opinions found in one's moral community. In Aristotle's accounts of the virtues and their corresponding vices he refers repeatedly to the doctrine of the mean, and no doubt the model does guide his reflections. The explanatory lists of dimensions of the emotion that need to be got "right" provide guidance for explorations of the virtue-concept. But I think that a careful reading of the accounts of particular virtues will show that the normative work in his accounts is actually accomplished by an application of "Aristotelian dialectic."

Consider the short discussion of gentleness (*praotês*) in *Nicomachean Ethics* 4.5. Aristotle begins by noting that "we" use the word "gentleness" for the virtuous disposition with respect to anger even though it doesn't quite refer to the mean, but to a disposition that "inclines towards the deficiency" (1125b28 (Ross)). He then uses the passive voices of "praise" (*epainô, epainomai*) and "blame" (*psegô, psegomai*) to characterize "our" attitude to right and wrong dispositions, respectively. "The man who is angry for the right reasons and at the right people, and, further, as he ought, when he ought and as long as he ought, is praised" (1125b31–33 (Ross; altered)). In contrast, the person who gets angry for the wrong reasons, in the wrong way, at the wrong time, or at the wrong persons, is "blamed" (1126a5 (Ross)). When Aristotle explains the reasons for thinking that the virtue or vice has the properties he's attributing, he uses "seems" or "is thought" (*dokeô*). As to the vice of deficiency, those who do not get angry for the reasons they should "are thought to be fools" (1126a5 (Ross)) because they don't stand up enough for themselves or their friends when they're insulted, and such an attitude "is thought to be slavish" (1126a9 (Ross)). Then Aristotle divides the vices with respect to anger into kinds according to which mistakes they are most prone to: the hot-tempered, the choleric, the sulky, and the bad tempered, and he evaluates them separately. For example, the hot-tempered become angry too quickly and too intensely, as well as for the wrong reasons and at the wrong people, but they have the mitigating grace that they get over their anger quickly.

The sulky, by contrast, are grudge-bearers and so "are most troublesome to themselves and to their dearest friends" (1126a26–27 (Ross)). He ends the chapter by commenting that we don't blame people who deviate just a little bit from the "mean," and sometimes we even praise people who fall nearer the deficiency as gentle, and people who fall nearer the excess as manly, and that "it is not easy to define how, with whom, for what reason, and how long one should be angry" (1126a34–35 Ross; altered); "it is not easy to state in words; for the decision depends on the particular facts and on perception" (1126b4–5 (Ross)).

Aristotle sounds a little frustrated. True, he hasn't given us a rule in the sense of a concise and precise formula such as we might ideally prefer. But the discussion we've just witnessed, guided by his philosophical and psychological skill with reference to what "we" think and praise and blame and what "seems to us" to be so, is not without guiding value. In the passage I quoted earlier from Book 6 about the right rule and the standard that fixes it, Aristotle seems to be hoping for something more principle-like than the reflections we've just reviewed. But, if it's true that the decision depends on the particular facts and on the discernment of the one who must make the judgment about, e.g., whether a particular instance of anger is right or wrong, and if so, how, then perhaps we should expect nothing more precise. As Aristotle himself notes, ethics is not rocket science (*Nicomachean Ethics* 1.3, 1094b13–16 (Ross)). I propose that the "right rule" that Aristotle refers to at the beginning of Book 6 is, in rough outline, supplied by the discussions of the virtues that occupy such a large part of *Nicomachean Ethics*.

Aristotle's analytic dependence on the fact that "we" praise the virtues and blame the vices may remind us of Hume. But Aristotle would not, like Hume, say that a trait is a virtue or vice *because* it evokes approval or disapproval in the observer. The observer's response to a trait is not *constitutive* of its value-status nor does it *cause* that status. Instead, it gives epistemic *access* to the trait's value-status; it allows the observer to *appreciate* the trait *as* a virtue or a vice. Epistemic access will not, on Aristotle's view, be equally distributed in the human population. Barbarians are not likely to have good judgment here, nor are slaves and uneducated people. The people whose discernment can be trusted in this matter will be intelligent people who have been properly brought up in a well-ordered city state. They will be people who at least prima facie qualify as virtuous. In the final chapter of *Nicomachean Ethics*, which effects a transition to Aristotle's treatise on politics, he argues that we can expect very little moral education to be accomplished through philosophical arguments, and that, for argument even to be helpful, "the soul of the student must first have been cultivated by means of habits for noble joy and noble hatred" (10.9, 1179b24–26 (Ross)). Such habits will be shaped by legislation devised by people of practical wisdom, and presumably one kind of object of such well-cultivated taste will be the traits and sentiments of the student's fellow citizens. Indeed, we might add that the noble joy that the student experiences in response to the virtues of her fellow citizens, and the repugnance she feels at their vices, is a social legacy of the legislator's emotions of approval of the traits his legislation is designed to form. But the kind of order that we see in Aristotle's city state – customs of judgment, of taste, of belief, of procedure, of emotional responsiveness – does not come from nowhere, but is a product of a long historical evolution, of experience, of conceptualization, of discussion and debate. Homer, the Greek playwrights and other poets, Solon and Pericles, and countless other legislators, leaders, and philosophers contribute to this tradition. In this, morality is like science and philosophy and the arts and crafts: it is a product of historical development, and especially of great moments in that history. It also has strands and variants that correspond to different historical trajectories.

Before leaving Aristotle I want to consider how to generalize the Aristotelian approach to emotional truth that I have been developing. The virtues that he discusses are structurally diverse, despite his efforts to bring them all under the control of the doctrine of the mean. Of the eleven or so moral virtues that he discusses in *Nicomachean Ethics*, only two (courage and gentleness) are analyzed as means with respect to a type of emotion (and courage is analyzed in terms of two complementary emotions: fear and confidence). Liberality is a mean in amounts of material goods freely given (neither too much nor too little, on the right occasions to the right people in the right way, etc.) and distributive justice is a mean only in the sense of a proportional equality in the distribution of some good to some parties. Aristotle does say about both liberality and justice that a person can be said to have the virtue only if he takes joy in performing the characteristic actions, but he does not suggest that these virtues are a mean with respect to joy.

Still, I think we can get an Aristotelian account of emotional truth by generalizing from the model of gentleness. Only a few emotions, according to Aristotle, are evil by type. Envy would be an example, and *Schadenfreude*, if we take that to be a distinct type of emotion and not just a bad variant of joy. In many of Aristotle's discussions of virtues and vices he countenances ones that lack names. So there seems to be no reason in principle why we shouldn't suppose that there is a virtuous disposition with respect to most of the emotion types that have both good and bad instances: a "mean" with respect to hope, another with respect to joy, and so on for respect, jealousy, disappointment, grief, pride, compassion, and all the others. I say "most," because Aristotle will not allow emotions that ascribe fault to the subject to be virtuous even when they get the situations right; the quasi-virtue of shame is a disposition to feel proper shame (*Nicomachean Ethics* 4.9), but a person who feels it properly is by that very token defective in virtue. For each qualifying emotion type the Aristotelian virtue will be the disposition to feel the emotion in the "mean," that is, at the right time, towards the right thing, for the right reason, in the right intensity, for the right length of time, and so forth. The person who feels any such emotion in the "mean" will have attained that bit of emotional truth.

One gets the impression that Hume would like to think of his emotional observer of agents as plumbing only the affective resources of a bare human being, though, as I have indicated, Hume's own value judgments bear the marks of Christianity as well as of the Enlightenment. In a similarly ahistorical aspiration, Aristotle, in one of his philosophical moods, would like to think that we can determine whose emotions are reliable belief-forming perceptions by seeing whether the disposition from which they arise falls in the middle of an emotional continuum. I have tried to show that this is not actually Aristotle's procedure, and that in fact he approaches the question of emotional propriety (which includes truth) with something like Aristotelian dialectic. But Aristotelian dialectic is essentially a culture-dependent, and thus tradition-dependent, method. The inquirer starts with his tradition (perhaps in comparison and interaction with other traditions), critically questions the claims, and thus forms a conception of the disposition to emotional truth. All claims to evaluative truth, no matter how thorough and rigorous the investigations may be that support them, are historically situated and in principle subject to revision. If we think there is such a thing as emotional truth, then it will in this respect parallel scientific truth, which, though in one sense never absolute and final, is nevertheless justifiedly taken by its advocates to be truth.

Sentimentalism again

In Chapters 3 and 4 I argued for a conception of emotion according to which emotions could be perceptions of value in situations, and thus could be a basis for true moral judgments. So far in the present chapter I have been discussing the first of our two questions about emotional truth: how can we *tell* which emotions are true and which false? The answer I sketched is a kind of Aristotelian one, according to which we do so by consulting the best of our moral tradition and other relevant data, suitably processed by critical reflection. I turn now to our second question, what *makes* some emotions true and others false? This question is about the *nature* of emotional truth. What sort of thing are the truths that emotions put us in touch with, if there are such truths?

Officially, Hume may be thought to deny the existence of emotional truths because of his commitment to a "non-cognitivist" understanding of emotions. Truth is a kind of correspondence between experience, on the subjective side, and a reality that is objective; truth occurs when this correspondence is one of accurate representation, that is, where the subjective experience (say, perceptual experience) represents the objective reality as it actually is (at least approximately). If emotions are pure projections, mere colorings imposed on a reality that doesn't have the properties that the projections seem to suggest, then there can be no such thing as emotional truth. However, we've seen that Hume doesn't allow that just any emotional response to a state of affairs is equally appropriate, and lays down the two (or three) constraints that I mentioned earlier: (1) the subject's ability to distinguish morally relevant from morally irrelevant emotions, and (2) the good moral taste that enables one to have appropriate moral emotions, which, I argued, is essentially to have the moral dispositions of a sage, and, moreover, (3?) of the right kind of sage. Furthermore, an examination of Hume's accounts of emotions will show them not to be consistently non-cognitive. The objects of emotions are sometimes said to "cause" them, whereas, on a purely non-cognitivist view, we would expect emotions only to cause their objects (to appear as they do), and not vice versa.

Hume's metaphysical view of emotional truth is elusive and appears to be muddled. However, its logic – at least one side of it – comes clearly into view in the work of Jesse Prinz, an avowed Humean. In Chapter 4 we saw that, according to Prinz's theory of emotion, even though emotions are perceptions of certain states of the body, they come to be about "core relational themes" – or, better, instantiations of core relational themes. Such instantiations are objective, or at least quasi-objective. A core relational theme is a kind of matter about which a person may be concerned, such as demeaning offense (anger), danger (fear), irrevocable loss (sadness, grief), or the subject's transgression of a moral requirement (guilt) (for a chart, see Prinz 2004: 16). Groups and individuals may differ considerably in what instantiates such core themes, triggering the relevant gut reaction and its interpretation in terms of the theme. For example, many people of our acquaintance are reliably horrified or disgusted by the thought of eating human flesh, but there are cannibal groups who are not horrified by this (Prinz gives a rundown of some of the many cannibalistic peoples in the world at Prinz 2007: 224), but may be horrified by other things, such as sacrificing a chicken with the wrong ritual invocations, or having intercourse with a menstruating woman.

Prinz calls himself a moral realist – that is, a person who thinks that moral emotions can be objectively true or false, and we might think that such strongly contrasting patterns of emotional response as those just mentioned could not possibly all be true. However, Prinz is also a self-described moral relativist, and thus thinks that such contrasting horror responses (or lack thereof) *can* be compatibly true. The eating of people can evoke in me a feeling of horror that gets reality right, while the cannibal rejoices in the eating of people and her joy similarly gets reality right. How can this be? The key is Prinz's notion of a *sentiment*. In his vocabulary a sentiment is a well-established disposition to feel a range of emotions of different types. For example, the cannibal *likes* eating human flesh and hearing about the activity, so she will *enjoy* herself at a cannibal feast, and be *disappointed* if she misses one because of illness or a conflict in her schedule, and feel *resentful* of someone who prevents her from attending for no good reason. I, by contrast, *dislike* (to put it mildly) the eating of human flesh, and so will feel *horror* and *disgust* if forced to attend the feast, and will feel *joyful relief* at hearing that the missionaries have managed to put a stop to the practice. If my sentiment about cannibalism is a well-established part of my emotional repertoire, then when I feel these emotions in situations of mental lucidity and adequate information, my emotions are authentic, or *true to my emotional constitution*. And, likewise, the cannibal's strongly contrasting emotions can be true to *her* sentiments. Thus, there is such a thing as emotional truth and falsity. An emotion is false when it fails to correspond to the subject's sentiments, say, because the subject is under- or misinformed about the situation or in an abnormal emotional condition (say, under the influence of drugs).

Prinz's relativistic theory clearly does not capture what moral realists have insisted on. He thinks that moral judgments are objective in the sense that they are about the dispositions of objects to cause certain emotions in the judgment's subject. That is, they are about response-dependent properties, where the responder is whoever is doing the responding (as long as he is responding out of a well-established sentiment). As response-dependent properties, either of two things can be emphasized: (1) the object, which, as response-dependent, gets its evaluative status from the responding subject, or (2) the subject, which, through its stability as expressing a sentiment, gives the evaluative status to the object. The response-dependent property can be characterized either as the O's property of being disposed to cause E in S, or S's property of being disposed to feel E in response to O. Richard Joyce complains about the subject-relativity of Prinz's theory that

> the domain of "observer" [the subject that I have designated "S"] is left entirely open, it can include saints and sociopaths, Gandhi and Jack the Ripper, Fred in a good mood and Fred on drugs, Cro-Magnons and Martians. Given this openness, any given action could instantiate the full complement of moral properties: Hitler's Final Solution could be good, bad, permissible, evil, blameworthy, praiseworthy, obligatory, unfair, reasonable, and supererogatory – *all at the same time.* (Joyce 2009: 512; italics original)

(Joyce probably shouldn't have mentioned Fred.) This is very different from Aristotle, who trusts only the emotions of the person of practical wisdom to be reliably correct, and thinks that these emotions will *be* correct, not because they are about properties that metaphysically depend on the response of the person of practical wisdom, but because they provide access to the truth about what is good or bad. Prinz also differs from Hume, whose position seems inconsistent since on the one hand he wants moral properties to be response-dependent, but on the other does not want just anybody's response to be right (as long as the person is self-consistent in his sentiments).

Prinz is willing to rest satisfied with relativism: many rival evaluations of the Final Solution are potentially true, given the possibility that they express the sentiments of the individuals and societies making the judgments. Ronald de Sousa (2011) appears to disagree with Prinz, in the interest of something a little closer to emotional truth. He thinks that even though our emotions are the source of all values, "we want them to be more than a mere projection of self, precisely because they are so important. We want them to be correct, or adequate, or *true*" (xv). He puts his confidence in the open interaction of emotions within the individual and open interaction among individuals and cultures: moral views will eventually converge under the pressures of open discussion and debate.

> the best hope of emotional rationality lies in the broadest possible assessment of our emotions, *in the light of our emotional responses themselves,* providing that these are dictated by a comprehensively educated range

of emotional capacities. The heart of both rationality and morality lies in a holistic assessment of one's emotional dispositions, constantly tested against one another. (de Sousa 2011: 24; italics original)

On the level of the individual, we often have emotions about emotions: we feel envy, say, but then we feel guilty or ashamed about our envy. But in other contexts we may feel that our guilt or shame are infantile or a holdover from our past, and feel contempt for or regret about our guilt and shame. De Sousa's advice here is to let this inter-emotional testing work itself out until something like equilibrium is achieved. That should put us closer to emotional truth. He calls this policy "axiological holism" because it involves taking our emotions not singly but in packages that include all our emotions – and all our interlocutors' emotions. On the level of culture, free and close interactions among cultures should similarly sort out true from false emotional dispositions. For example, extended and deep cultural exchange between a modern and a cannibal society can be expected to result in emotional convergence favoring the modern: eventually the cannibals (or at any rate their descendants?) will come to feel as we do about eating people.

It seems obvious that "axiological holism" does, over time, foster convergence. But I think it's overoptimistic to think that all deep emotional disagreement can be overcome in this way. People have reasons for adhering unwaveringly in the face of confident disagreement to parts of their moral outlook, some more than others, and some questions may not be rationally decidable, if we mean by "rational" that both sides to a debate can appreciate the views of the other side adequately to bring about agreement. Differences that are not due to difference of intelligence or understanding of the others' views are ones that openness and dialog will not resolve. Philosophers know from their own dialogs how elusive convergence can sometimes be. Think of de Sousa's (2011) commitment to naturalism and Alvin Plantinga's (2011) equally aggressive and confident commitment to theism. These are certainly "emotional," as well as intellectual, commitments. (I invite anyone who doubts either the emotionality or the intellectuality of these two philosophers' commitments to read the books just cited.) The difference is profound and it's possible and even likely that no amount of discussion will lead to a resolution. If Plantinga were allowed to rear de Sousa's children, or vice versa, there would probably be some crossover between the camps, at least; but mere open, rigorous discussion is not guaranteed, or even likely, to lead to such crossing over on issues of fundamental disagreement.

Even if open dialog could be expected to yield perfect emotional convergence in a given generation, the problem of outlook-pluralism arises cross-generationally. We know that our emotional responses differ from those of our ancestors and can easily believe that they will differ also from those of our distant descendants. So, if our emotions are somehow the metaphysical foundation of all values, it looks as though there can be no such thing as emotional truth, but only, as Prinz thinks, emotional "truth" *for* me, *for* you, *for* us, and *for* them and, we could add, *for* now. Emotional "truth" is a historically, culturally, and, perhaps even individually, local phenomenon.

J. L. Mackie (1977) has a name for such truth: "error." But isn't that a little harsh? Don't we talk about truth and falsity within the bounds of fiction? Isn't it *true* that Fanny Price never marries Henry Crawford? Don't we say, within the bounds of a game, that this is allowed and that is not, and claim to be uttering truths in saying so? Don't we say, within the bounds of a local custom, "It's done this way, not that way," and speak the truth? Moral "truths" may be bounded historically, culturally, or perhaps even individually; but isn't there still room for speaking of truth and error? Prinz and de Sousa think so, but Mackie thinks not, because he thinks that when we make moral claims we don't think of ourselves as speaking within the bounds of a fiction or a game or a custom. If I think that slavery is outrageously unjust, I take myself to be saying something objectively and absolutely true *about slavery* and *without regard to my emotional dispositions*, and not to be doing anything like participating in fiction or a game or custom. As a moral person, I think that slavery would be unjust even if every human being in the world thought it permissible (say, because, by enslaving a small minority a vast majority could have a significantly better life).

So, it looks as though morality, as an institution, demands that values be objective – metaphysically independent of any individual or communal valuer. They are what the right-minded valuer values, but they don't get their value from our valuing them. Mackie takes Plato to be paradigmatic of the western tradition of philosophical ethics in this regard:

> Values themselves have been seen as at once prescriptive and objective. In Plato's theory the Forms, and in particular the Form of the Good, are eternal, extra-mental, realities. . . . But it is held also that just knowing them or "seeing" them will not merely tell men what to do but will ensure that they do it, overruling any contrary inclinations. . . . Being acquainted with the Forms of the Good and Justice and Beauty and the rest they will, by this knowledge alone, without any further motivation, be impelled to pursue and promote these ideals. (Mackie 1977: chap. 1, sect. 4)

This statement contains a significant historical omission. It is true that Plato's Forms are both objective (independent of any valuer) and "prescriptive" (such as to motivate valuers). It is also true that being acquainted with the Forms is sufficient to motivate the beholder. But by omitting to tell us about the arduous task of becoming the kind of soul that is epistemically and morally *capable* of being acquainted with the Forms, Mackie makes Plato sound crazier than he is. Books 3 and 7 of *Republic* are devoted to outlining this moral education. Book 3 describes the "music" – literature, drama, and music in our sense of the word – in which the young leaders-to-be are formed to love what is good and noble and fine. From childhood on, these souls are to be formed for "resemblance, friendship, and harmony with the beauty of reason" (401d). Plato ends the discussion by having Socrates say that "it has ended where it ought to end, for it ought to end in the *love* of the fine and the beautiful" (403c; italics added). Books 6 and 7 are about the later, more-conceptual part of this same education that fits the student to behold the Good and other Forms with high-level appreciative acquaintance. Here Plato's view is very much like that of Aristotle as I described it earlier: only by being formed in virtue does one become able to perceive moral truth, and the education that forms one thus is a "sentimental" education, an education in the emotions (Plato speaks of love).

This response on Plato's behalf is important, but it doesn't rescue him from Mackie's primary criticism of moral realism. As I noted, Mackie thinks that realists describe the moral attitude correctly, as in contrast with sentimentalists and expressivists who think they can explain the logic of moral judgments in subjectivist terms. When we say, in a moral attitude, that an action is good or obligatory or impermissible, or that a trait is a virtue or a vice, we are not merely expressing our approval or disapproval, nor are we referring to some property that depends essentially on our approval or disapproval. Instead, we are claiming that the action or trait has a property that is at the same time objective *and* "prescriptive" or motivating or choiceworthy. To say that the property is objective is to say that it's metaphysically independent of our prescribing or desiring or choosing it, but to say that it's prescriptive is to say that it is *in itself* "prescribed." On Plato's view, says Mackie, "an objective good would be sought by anyone who was acquainted with it, not because of any contingent fact that this person, or every person, is so constituted that he desires this end, but just because the end has to-be-pursuedness somehow built into it" (Mackie 1977: chap. 1, sect. 9). This paradoxical property, says Mackie, suffers from "queerness." In its simultaneous desirability and independence of anybody's desiring it, it is unlike anything we come across in the universe. Since moral judgments by their very nature posit such a weird kind of property, we must become moral skeptics.

A way out that some may find attractive

But maybe not. In an article defending Peter Strawson's "Freedom and Resentment" against interpreters eager to read rich moral conceptual content into such natural human reactive attitudes as gratitude for intentional benefits and resentment for intentional harms, John Deigh comments,

> it would ill serve [Strawson's] program to put forward, as an alternative set of facts providing an adequate basis of praise and punishment, facts about, say, there being a government of the universe to which all humans are subject and in view of whose laws one can identify morally worthy actions as well as morally wrong ones. (Deigh 2011: 200)

Let us agree that positing such facts would ill serve Strawson's program, which we may regard as a cousin of sentimentalism. It might, nevertheless, well serve a program of explaining the objective prescriptivity that Mackie finds metaphysically queer. If the government of the universe takes something like the same attitudes towards the facts that arouse gratitude and resentment in wise human beings, the very status of this government as the ungoverned government of the universe would seem capable of conveying to or justifying the analogous attitudes on the part of human creatures. The government's status as sovereign supplies the objectivity of the values of what it values, and its valuing those values provides their "prescriptive" force, that is, their status as *values*. Because the government is itself a valuing agency, what it values does not have the Platonic oddity of being a value, like the Form of the Good, that has its value in itself, without essential reference to any valuing subject; for the government *is* itself such a valuing subject.

Supposing such a government, how would the "governing" proceed? That is, how would the directives, policies, rules, laws, or will of the government get passed on to or become effective in the lives of the governed – the human subjects who are subject to the government? Here are two alternatives, one psychologically external, the other internal. (1) The government governs by sanctions: penalties for nonconformity and rewards for conformity; so that the primary emotional mediation of the norms to the governed is by fear and hope. Here the governor is best conceived as commander, and the commander's will (rules, directives) remains to some extent alien to or external from the ends of his subjects, who are motivationally more or less "unruly" as measured by the conformity of their wills, desires, and ends to those of the government. (2) The government governs as a loving parent governs his or her household, by guiding, modeling, cajoling, and *occasionally* by commanding – but above all by caring for the governed, loving them and thus giving them a sense of personally belonging to him. Here the model is benevolent kingship. The government governs in such a way that the hearts of the governed can grow into affective conformity to the heart of the king. Thus the government nurtures loyalty in the governed, a participatory insight into the goodness of what the government loves that is born of loving that same thing. The government loves the good and presupposes in its way of governing that the subjects are capable of loving it and even disposed to love it, and induces its subjects to love it by loving them. It is possible to subsume something like (1) under (2). In that case, the government of the universe uses commands and punishments on occasion, but its aim is ultimately to govern in the way of (2); and when it does issue decrees, it issues them out of benevolence for the governed, and with the aim that the hearts of the governed should come to reflect the values of the government.

John Hare (2005) points out that such attunement of the hearts of the governed to that of the government shouldn't be thought of, across the board, as imitation of the government's emotions. Such analogical imitation will sometimes occur, as in the recommendation of the parable:

> Suppose one of you has a hundred sheep and loses one of them. Doesn't he leave the ninety-nine in the open country and go after the lost sheep until he finds it? And when he finds it, he joyfully puts it on his shoulders and goes home. Then he calls his friends and neighbors together and says, "Rejoice with me; I have found my lost sheep." I tell you that in the same way there will be more rejoicing in heaven over one sinner who repents than over ninety-nine righteous persons who do not need to repent. (Luke 15:4–7 *New International Version*)

But the government of the universe will not have, in its repertoire, some of the emotions that are appropriate for human beings and reflect objective values. The reason, says Hare, is that emotions are situational and the government of the universe never finds itself in some of the situations where human beings typically find themselves. For example, the government of the universe, being morally perfect, will never be in the kind of situation in which the right-valued human being feels contrition.

The same is perhaps true of fear and hope. How then shall we think of emotional imitation in this case?

On the view of emotions that I have defended in this book and in Roberts 2003, emotions are concern-based construals. Values, and the affect and motivation that reflect values, come into emotions by way of the concerns on which the emotions are based. Emotions, then, are first-personal construals of situations in terms of subjects' concerns. The government of the universe no doubt has concerns of which human beings have no idea and that would be utterly inappropriate for us to have. But, assuming, as the parable does, that the government and the governed have some concerns appropriately in common, this will be enough to make moral imitation of the government by the governed a way to secure the objectivity of the values of the governed. In the case of contrition, the contrite will construe themselves as having followed too much the devices and desires of their own hearts, in opposition to the devices and desires of the government. This is a construal that the government couldn't have. But the contrition is based on a concern that the human subjects share with the government. In thus feeling sorry for their deviation, they express solidarity with the purposes of the King, and thus access emotional truth.

On the view sketched above, then, to say that *you should respect your neighbor* is to say that you should respect your neighbor; it is not to say: respecting your neighbor makes me feel good, nor that respecting your neighbor has a property such that I respond to it with positive affect out of a well-established sentiment, nor that those who are most reflective feel it to be true. But neither is it to say that the government of the universe is concerned that you respect your neighbor; that may be true, but it isn't what the proposition *you should respect your neighbor* means. (Many people who think that *you should respect your neighbor* is true don't even think there *is* a government of the universe.) However, if you believe there is such a government, then a good answer to the question, how can it be that *you should respect your neighbor* is an objective truth? is that the government of the universe is concerned that you respect your neighbor. Mackie and the sentimentalists are right, against Plato, that the idea of a value that is so objective that it has no subjective correlate is "queer." But I think Mackie is also right about the phenomenology of ordinary moral consciousness, at least that of many people: it takes its most central and serious moral beliefs to be true.

Given the variety and rivalry of views about what the government of the universe, if there is one, is like (that is, what concerns it has), the metaphysical proposal of this section doesn't solve the problem of moral pluralism. But for those who accept its type of solution, it does show how fully objective emotional truth is possible. And, in doing so, for those who accept it, it prevents the undeniable empirical observation of emotional pluralism from degenerating into moral relativism.

Conclusion

In the last three chapters I have argued that emotions can play an epistemic role in the moral life. They can do that because, as I argue in Chapter 3, they are a kind of perceptual state that I call concern-based construals. They are evaluative impressions of the various situations of our lives, based in our concerns or cares, and as such they have the potential to be the perceptual basis of our moral judgments. In Chapter 4 I answer a number of objections to the perceptual thesis, and in doing so further develop our understanding of it. In the present chapter I address two questions. First, how can we determine which emotions to trust to deliver evaluative truth? I answer this question in a way reminiscent of Aristotle: we can do so by considering the *endoxa* of our moral tradition, the common opinions of the many and the wise, as well as alternative and rival views from outside our tradition, subjecting these to critical philosophical and psychological examination, and coming to the most reasonable conclusions within our ken. The second question is about the metaphysical status of any purported emotional truth, such that it can actually be an objective emotional truth. I argue that the most plausible account I can think of is theological: emotional truths will be concern-based construals that are factually accurate and based on concerns concernfully endorsed by the sovereign personal government of the universe.

The chapters that follow give considerably briefer treatments of other moral aspects of human emotions. In Chapter 6 I examine emotions' practical role in the motivation and moral identity of actions. In Chapter 7 I look at emotions' constitutive role in both good and evil personal relationships. Chapter 8 examines the complex ways emotions enter into the happiness and thriving, or, as may be, the unhappiness and dysfunction, of human lives. Finally, Chapter 9 anticipates the goal for which this book and its predecessor (Roberts 2003) are preparatory, with a discussion of the various ways that emotions and emotion dispositions are involved in the moral personal traits that we call virtues.

6

Emotions and actions

Introduction

We sometimes explain actions by reference to emotions. Some of those actions are deliberate and others are not. I don't mean by "deliberate" to suggest extensive deliberation, but I do mean to stress the agent's thoughtfulness and awareness of what he or she is doing. I'm especially interested in actions that are deliberate in this sense because most actions that are characteristic of virtues are deliberate. Just as many emotions have an epistemic dimension that provides for excellence in moral perception and judgment, many also have a motivational dimension that contributes to excellence of action. In Chapter 3 I pictured a simple case of motivation by fear as follows.

Basic concern	Construal	Consequent concern
I care about this child's wellbeing →	I construe X as threatening the child's wellbeing →	That the child be protected against the threat

The general rational structure of fear can be represented in a defining proposition thus:

> **Fear of X for Y**: *X presents a threat to Y of a significant degree of probability; may X or its threatened consequences for Y be avoided.* (Roberts 2003: 195; modified)

Let us say that *I call to the child to come to me*. The explanation of this action is that I fear for the child's wellbeing. More specifically, I see his wellbeing as threatened by his proximity to the edge of the wall he is walking on, and my construal of the situation is infused with my concern for his wellbeing (my caring about him). We could say that my reason for calling to him is that he was getting too close to the edge of the wall for safety. My reason for acting in this way is given by, because it is embedded in, the emotion. It is clear that my action, as emerging from my emotion, is "logical"; it makes rational sense: I desire the child's wellbeing and see his proximity to the precipice as a threat to his wellbeing. From this combination it "follows" that I will desire that the threat be avoided or that the child be protected against the threat. A variety of actions or other events might satisfy the consequent desire (jumping up and walking between him and the edge, calling to someone else to get him away from the wall, etc.), but whatever action I undertake from fear for him will have the character of such avoidance or protection. The actions that follow from this fear may be more or less adroit, more or less effective, more or less well chosen for their purpose; but any of them will be broadly rational in being responsive to the emotion: the situational perception with integrated concern (fear).

In the previous paragraph I write "logical" and "follows" in scare-quotes to avoid the implication that the consequent concern (desire) emerges from the construal by active inference. Rather, the emotion, as a concern-based construal, just yields the desire. Once the desire is in place, my settling on a means to achieve its end (in the example, the child's safety from the danger of the precipice) may well proceed by means-end reasoning, fast or slow.

Affect and motivation

In Chapter 3 I distinguished two consequences of the concern basic to an emotion – affect and motivation – and there I focused on affect because it was more relevant to the epistemic function of emotions that was under discussion in that chapter. Let me now expand that discussion so as to clarify more thoroughly the difference between affect and motivation.

What is affect? In most usage by psychologists and philosophers, it is a vague concept, meaning something like, "having to do with the likes of emotion and emotional feeling." I try to give "affect" a more definite sense, in an effort to distinguish it from emotional motivation proper. Most basically, perhaps, I want to say that affect is the way an emotion *feels*, where the feeling of the emotion has a valence (positive or negative, pleasant or unpleasant). Some emotions "feel good" (joy, triumph, gratitude, pride, hope, etc.) and others "feel bad" (grief, despair, frustration, fear, anxiety, sadness). Affect has implications for preferences: we prefer feeling good to feeling bad. But it follows from the characterization of affect as the feeling *of an emotion* that it is not just a blank feeling good or bad (maybe the way a mood feels), but a feeling good or bad *about* whatever the emotion is about. See Peter Goldie's discussion of "feeling towards" in Goldie 2000. If Goldie thinks of feeling towards as a characteristic of emotions as a class (all emotions), then he must be committed to the claim that all emotions have affect; I think that is contradicted by the existence of unfelt emotions. If an emotion is fully unfelt, there is no way that it feels. Affect is feeling good about the healthy birth of one's child or uncomfortable about the child being dangerously close to the precipice. Affect can attach to other things than emotions, for example, moods: good moods feel good, and bad ones bad. Zajonc (1980, 1984) speaks of affect in connection with feeling better when seeing something familiar than when seeing something unfamiliar, or when seeing something primed with a smiley face as compared with something primed with a frowning face. But "affect" is not used with just any experience that has positive or negative valence: one doesn't normally speak of affect in connection with bodily pains and pleasures. To be motivated by affect to do something would be to do that thing as a way of getting or sustaining positive affect, or as a way of avoiding or escaping negative affect. For a view of emotional motivation as "escape from discomfort," see Greenspan 1988: 53, 75, 153; and for critical discussion of the view, see Roberts 2003: 162–67.

Crudely, an emotion is a construal of a situation as *good* or *bad*, and it is the emotion's affect that registers consciously such value qualities of the situation. In connection with emotions, then, affect is the pleasant or uncomfortable character of the construal that constitutes the emotion, and so provides a perceptual experience of the situation's "evaluative" aspect. This is only a crude characterization of emotional affect, because the goodness or badness is always more concretely qualified by the construal as the goodness of this or that good prospect on this or that basis (hope), this or that benefit from this or that benefactor (gratitude), this or that excellence of this or that person or thing (admiration), or the badness of this or that loss (grief or sadness), or of this or that offense committed by this or that person (anger, resentment), etc. In our present example, affect is the discomfort that registers the badness of the threat to the wellbeing of the child I love. On the account I'm proposing, the pleasure or discomfort that an emotion carries is due to the way the subject's construal of the situation satisfies or frustrates the concern on which it is based. Because it is a perceptual registration of the goodness or badness of the situation it is about, affect is important, as I argued in Chapter 3, for the epistemic function of emotions in the moral life.

Both the affective dimension of the construal and the consequent concern that are yielded by the uptake of the basic concern in the construal are "logical." It stands to reason that if my concern for my child's wellbeing is integrated into my perception of him as threatened with injury, this perception will be uncomfortable. Likewise, if my dispositional concern for my child's wellbeing is triggered into an episode of actual desire by my construal of him as threatened with injury, it stands to reason that the construal will transform the more general and dispositional concern into the more specific and active concern to protect him from the injury that threatens.

Affect and motivation must be distinguished. One is a *feature* of the construal, the other a *product*. Also, it is possible for an emotion to be *felt without being motivating*. Boredom and some kinds of joy – a happy nostalgia, for example – may be loaded with affect but not attended by the desire to do anything in particular (except, perhaps, to continue, or stop, feeling the emotion; but, then, this is not the essential kind of emotional motivation; see below). A third difference is that you can be unaware of your motivation, but you cannot be unaware of what you feel. (You can, of course, be unaware of what you are *disposed* to feel.)

Besides these differences, an emotion's affect and its consequent concern have, in the cases of most emotions, significantly *different proper functions*. Some theorists think of emotional affect as the motivating dimension of the emotion (Greenspan 1988; Tappolet 2002: 159 [but see Tappolet 2010]; Döring 2003: 224; Zagzebski 2003: 116), and therefore the key to explaining actions that are motivated by emotions. It is true, as Zagzebski says, that affect is "pushy" (2003: 116). If the affect of an emotion is the pleasant or uncomfortable feel (experience) of seeing the situation as it is seen by way of the emotion, then affect gets its pushiness in virtue of a pleasure principle: *seek pleasure, avoid pain*. In particular, the pushiness of affect is *either* pushiness away (repulsion) from the pain *or* pulliness (attraction) towards the pleasure. The pain or pleasure – of what? – of the situation that the emotion presents, or of the seeing of the situation in the way characteristic of the emotion? It seems to me that the natural way to think of affect's "pushiness," as pain or pleasure, is of its pull towards the pleasure *of the emotion*, or the push away from the discomfort *of the emotion*.

If we think of it this way, then motivation by affect has a moral problem. Consider how ethically inappropriate would be the action of the parent in our opening example, were he motivated by the discomfort of his fear for his child's wellbeing. If fear moved us simply by providing a discomfort from which, as agents, we would seek relief, a parent might achieve this end by taking a tranquilizer that would dispel his anxiety whenever his child was in danger. Most parents would reject *such* a way of assuaging their anxiety because in fact they are motivated not by the prospect of relief from the pain of fear but by the prospect of their child's safety from the threat. If, as his *way* of avoiding the pain of fear, a parent chose securing the safety of his child (rather than the tranquilizer), the presumed outward aim of parents' fear for their children's safety would be secured, but the relation of the parent to the child would still be askew. (See Chapter 7 for an account of emotions' function in constituting proper interpersonal relations.) Fear for the child's safety, in a well-formed parent, is an expression of his concern *for the child* – an expression of his love for the child – and the action that in fact dispels his anxiety is thus also an expression of his love, not an expression of his concern for his own emotional comfort. (As is suggested by the last sentence, when we are motivated by affect, it is by way of a *desire* to have or escape the affect in question.)

But perhaps this is not the only way to think of affect as motivating. If we think of the pleasure or discomfort of the emotion as a way of seeing the goodness or badness of *the situational object* – that is, thinking of it as a mode of value-perception – then we would be thinking of the emotional *object* as being attractive or repulsive, rather than the emotion. On this interpretation we would be seeing the (painful to us) threat to the child as something to take action against, or the hopeful (pleasant to us) prospect of a rectification of injustice as something we may take action to promote. But this second interpretation of "affect" turns out to be none other than the evaluative core of the desire that I have called the emotion's consequent concern. To desire that the threat to the child's wellbeing be avoided is to see the situation as prospectively bad *with respect to the child's wellbeing* and as *open to correction*. If affect is to differ from motivation, it seems that it must be the good or bad feel *of the emotion*.

We are, of course, familiar with cases of emotional motivation by affect. We may give to Oxfam to assuage our guilt; we may hide truths from ourselves to escape anxiety; we may reread a novel with a happy ending to experience again the emotional uplift it first yielded, or not reread a depressing story to avoid the emotional suffering it would bring us. In morally significant cases, we may be so afraid of negative affect that it may take courage to resist its motivational pull. In morally trivial cases, motivation by affect can be harmless enough, and in Chapter 8 I'll note that in extreme cases it can even be prudent. Furthermore, in one emotion type that I can think of, the emotion's intrinsic motivation and its motivation by affect coincide. When nostalgia (Roberts 2003: 280–81) has a consequent concern, it seems to be a desire to relive the experience

in question for its pleasant affect. But, as a general account of emotional
motivation, the idea that emotions motivate us by their affect is a corrupt
view. (For a similar critique, see Blum 2011: 177.)

I conclude, then, that it is by way of satisfying the emotion's consequent
concern, and not by way of escaping from the emotional discomfort of
negative affect or procuring the emotional pleasure of positive affect, that
emotions most properly function as moral explanations of action.

Less rational cases

Not all actions stemming from emotions are rational in aiming to satisfy
a desire that is generated according to the internal logic of the emotion as a
concern-based construal. For example, when I am alone at home, sometimes when I walk by one or another of the many photographs of my
grown and absent children that are strewn throughout the house, I pause
before the picture and tell the child how much I love him or her and
perhaps give him or her a little kiss (right on the glass that covers the
picture). Such a gesture is normally directed to the child in his presence,
and plausibly serves the aim of communicating affection to the child and
maintaining an affectionate relationship with him or her. Since I am not so
crazy as to confuse the picture for the child, the present action doesn't
seem to have *that* point. If not, then what point does it have? It does seem
to express the desire to communicate affection and maintain an affectionate relationship, but the action is almost totally useless for that end. So,
this action, while intentional, is not exactly deliberate (at least not if we
take "deliberate" to imply aiming at some outcome; of course, it *might* be
deliberate – if, say, I'm aiming to cultivate my love for my children by this
exercise). If, with the Stoics, we think of the content of emotions
as necessarily believed, this kind of case seems paradoxical, since I clearly
don't believe that my words and kisses will communicate affection
and maintain an affectionate relationship. But it makes perfectly good
sense on the supposition that emotions are concern-based construals:
I imaginatively construe the picture as my child and myself as in his or
her presence (which is easy enough, since the picture is a photo of my child
and I'm in its presence), and by this little fantasizing ritual get a certain
satisfaction of my desire to communicate my love.

Rosalind Hursthouse (1991) discusses an analogous case, of a woman
Jane who out of hatred scratches the eyes out of a photograph of her rival
Joan. Hursthouse presents the case as part of an argument against the
belief-desire model of action explanation. She concludes that Jane scratches

out the eyes in the photo simply because she desires to, not because she believes that doing so will fulfill any desire of hers. So, Hursthouse concludes, we have an intentional action whose motivation does not involve any belief of the kind that would be posited by the belief-desire model.

Michael Smith (1998), in an effort to rescue the belief-desire model, points out that Jane scratches out the eyes in the photo of Joan because she desires to scratch out the eyes in the photo and believes she can do so by performing certain scratching movements. Smith admits that this explanation is not very satisfactory, since we want to know why Jane would want to do such an odd thing in the first place, and he answers that it's just a fact that hate or anger makes people want to do things like scratch out eyes in photographs.

Peter Goldie (2000: 128–36), responding to both Hursthouse and Smith, points out that while it is not "primitively intelligible" that a person would scratch out the eyes in the photograph of someone she is angry with, it *is* "primitively intelligible" that she would scratch out the eyes of that very person. Hatred of the kind that arises from anger gives rise to desires for revenge. Jane scratches out the eyes in the *photo* because she desires to scratch out *Joan's* eyes but is too civilized to want to harm Joan so brutally, and so gets satisfaction from performing this *symbolic substitute* action. These "primitively intelligible" desires are the ones that I identify as the consequent concerns generated by emotions of a given type.

Sabine Döring (2003) finds a common error in the discussions of Hursthouse, Smith, and Goldie: they all suppose that emotional motivation involves *desire*. Döring appeals to behaviors that occur quite automatically with emotion, such as gripping one's purse more tightly in anxiety or (this is my example, not Döring's) shedding tears when sad. Such behaviors are not intentional actions at all and so are not to be explained by desires to "perform" them. Döring claims that these behaviors are motivated not by desire but by affect; and then she generalizes this explanation to all emotional motivation. Although she thinks an emotion can sometimes supply a reason for acting, "it does so only in a mediated way" (228), and "the motivational force of an emotion has to be explained by reference to the emotion's affect. ... emotional motivation is independent of desire" (215).

If emotions are concerned construals – concernful ways of "seeing" the emotion's object – whose content is not necessarily believed by the emotion's subject, then it seems natural to interpret Jane's response to the photograph of Joan as a construal of Joan, "loaded" with all the historical background of Joan's identity and offenses against Jane. Hursthouse is right that Jane's action is to be explained in terms of desire without recourse to belief. But her account is unsatisfying insofar as without *any* reference to the "cognitive" content of the emotion, the desire to mutilate the photograph is opaque. Clearly, Jane doesn't *believe* that the photograph is Joan, or that mutilating it will harm Joan; but, surely, making sense of the action requires that *something* in Jane's mental state connects Joan with the photograph. Her explanation would be richer and more satisfying if it included consideration of the internal "logic" of an emotion type and the way the basic concern generates the consequent concern by filtering it through the construal. I think Goldie is right that Jane's hatred of Joan yields an ambivalent desire to mutilate *Joan*. Since she is construing the photograph as a representation of or stand-in for Joan, it is also natural for her to express her hatred of Joan by mutilating the photo. Her desire is not to express her emotion, or to gain the satisfaction (emotional pleasure) that her expressive action will possibly yield, but *to harm Joan*. If, as I have proposed, we need not believe the propositional content of our emotion, then neither, perhaps, need we believe our action will achieve the aim of the desire that such a construal generates. Smith is right to stress the emotion as the key to the explanation, but in straining for a belief-desire explanation of the action he lands on one that is not to the point, and appeals rather blankly to the emotion as the source of the desire. Goldie comes closest to having a satisfying explanation: the idea of symbolic substitute action probably works for some cases, and is a nice way of backing off from the belief-desire model without giving up on cognitivity altogether. In the same vein, his idea that the desire to mutilate is "primitively intelligible" given intense anger could be made more intelligible and less primitive by attending to the logical structure of emotion types. Finally, I agree with Döring that affect is not the same as desire, but she doesn't make clear how affect is supposed to motivate either actions or the automatic behaviors that are characteristic of some emotions. My view is that affect doesn't motivate either kind of behavior. Sadness *gives rise* to tears, but doesn't *motivate* them. For motivation, desire is needed. Even in the cases where affect explains action, it explains it by reference to a desire to gain, sustain, stop, or avoid affect.

Emotions as defining actions

If I want to have a dermatologist check out the blotch on my nose because I am afraid it may be skin cancer, the desire may not be adequately characterized by saying that it is a desire to visit the dermatologist. As a desire consequent upon this particular fear, it has a special character or definition: it is defined by my fear of skin cancer, which is to say, by such considerations as *this blotch might be skin cancer* and *skin cancer is dangerous to my wellbeing*. We can see the point by comparing this desire with other desires to visit a dermatologist, desires defined by other reasons, perhaps consequent upon other emotions. For example (to take a case of motivation by affect), I might desire to visit a dermatologist from nostalgia: the thought of a dermatologist I dated twenty years ago fills me with sweet reminiscences that trigger a desire for more of the same, and I know that the office and paraphernalia will evoke such memories. The two desires may coexist, or one may be a "front" for the other. But they are clearly different, even though both are desires to visit the dermatologist. They differ in reasons that affect the more particular description of what is desired, and the difference of reasons derives from a difference of emotions. But the reasons generated in the emotion define not only the desires that may be consequent on the emotion, but also actions that are motivated by the emotion (via the desire).

My thesis, then, is that emotions are not just external origins (causal factors) of actions. Let us say that I act by making an appointment with the dermatologist. One answer to the question, "What are you doing?" is "Making an appointment with the dermatologist." But a more definite characterization of my action is possible. It can still be asked, "What are you *doing in* making an appointment with the dermatologist?" and to that the answer may be either "Protecting my health" or "Getting myself some pleasant memories." These quite diverse actions are differentiated by the emotions that motivate them. They are typically related semantically to the actions to which they contribute causally: the reasons that define the emotion, and thus the emotion's consequent desire, also define the actions that are motivated by the emotion. *What* one is doing is affected by whether one is acting out of fear, anger, embarrassment, nostalgia, or envy, and, of course, by what particular fear, anger or envy one is acting out of. This fact has implications for the moral value of actions.

Emotions and the moral value of actions

Emotions often have important consequences, and this fact makes room for a consequentialist kind of value that emotions can have. (A) A father's anger leads him to do verbal and physical violence to his wife and children, which, of course, makes everybody unhappy, including him. Seeing that anger is at the root of these misery-producing actions, he evaluates it as bad and goes into therapy to mitigate the emotion or rid himself of it, or at least learn to control the behavior to which it tends. (B) A mother tries to inculcate in her son a disposition to feel gratitude for benefits received. Her thinking is this: when he feels gratitude for benefits, rather than indifference or even resentment, he will tend to act in ways that bring further benefits to himself; and, being happier, he will tend to spread felicity among his fellows. In these cases, the consequences of the emotions are mediated by actions they motivate. But emotions can have consequential value even without generating actions, by way of expressions that fall short of action. Facial and gestural expressions of emotion can have an uplifting or depressing effect on conversation, and this in turn can have far-reaching consequences for good or evil. I mention *consequential value of emotions* for the sake of completeness and to highlight the more important and interesting *intrinsic practical value of emotions*.

Jeremy builds a fine badminton court in his backyard. In a flat area of the lawn, carefully rolled and shrouded on three sides by giant lilacs to protect it from the wind, it has two-inch galvanized iron poles set in concrete and a hand-crocheted net of the finest nylon. In consequentialist terms Jeremy's act is excellent. The family enjoys the court many days of spring, summer, and fall; it gives rise to visits from the neighbors and fosters friendships. But we can ask other evaluative questions about his act, that carry us back into its origins and its internal character.

Imagine that Jeremy has long resented his father for spending weeks on end away from home when he was a child, cutting his deals and making his millions and neglecting his family. In the back of Jeremy's mind, as he digs his postholes and rolls the lawn, he is saying to himself, "Take this, Daddy. By the power of invidious contrast, this court will be a silent witness to the miserableness of your contemptible paternity." Such are the thoughts that sing in his joy as he contemplates, from his lawn chair, his children's shuttlecocking of a summer evening. Now let us say that Jeremy's resentment misrepresents his father and the father's relation to his children. It is true that his father was away from home a lot and was overly concerned with making money; but his culpability is not as Jeremy's emotion depicts it. He was socially inept vis-à-vis the family, but his concern with money was strongly, if misguidedly, tied to his concern for Jeremy and his sisters. In fact, the father was neither malicious, indifferent, nor negligent towards his children. The moral objection to Jeremy's resentment, then, is that it is unfair, and the part of that unfairness that we are stressing at the moment is that the resentment is a misrepresentation of his father's actions.

From another moral point of view, it may be thought that Jeremy's resentment is improper because it is so passive and underhanded and involves a self-construal as impotent; he cannot forthrightly punish his father, so he builds toys for his children that "testify" to his father's failings. If Jeremy is good, on this Nietzschean view, he needs to give up such passive self-construals, affirming himself, his agency, his power, forgetting what lies behind, lightly brushing off his "oppressors" and pressing on to his own glory. The Nietzschean assumption would be that people who have the potential to be good are never passive in the way that their resentment would show them to be. And the people whose resentment does fit them are bad people precisely *because* it fits them. Using my terminology, in people of the first kind, resentment is always intrinsically bad, while in people of the second kind the emotion may be intrinsically good, but is always expressively bad: it expresses a bad character. These Nietzschean judgments are a condemnation of resentment generally – as an emotion type (see the discussion of the logic of resentment in Roberts 2003: 214–16).

But non-Nietzscheans may well think that resentment, even in good people, sometimes gets its situational objects right. If one's father was indeed culpably negligent or maliciously disregardful of his family, and his concern with making money really didn't have one in benevolent view, then one's resentment of him may not misrepresent him; it may be completely fitting and fair. This is not to commend it all-things-considered, since the emotion can be morally evaluated in several other more or less independent ways. In some moral outlook it may be thought that even a father who in one sense deserves to be resented ought not to be resented by his son, since a son has a filial duty to love and respect his father. (Since the father's behavior does constitute an emotional problem for such a son, the prescription may be forgiveness.) Here a son's fitting resentment of his father would be rejected on relational and expressive considerations. Or the fitting resentment of a really bad father might be criticized on eudaimonistic considerations: it should be mitigated or dispelled because it is "eating up" the son. Or, again, consequential considerations might tell against it: it may be in some way harmful to the development of the son's children, or to the wellbeing of his marriage.

But if, as I am suggesting, actions are defined in part by their motives, and thus by the emotions that define the motives, then Jeremy's building of the badminton court is defined by his resentment. His resentment is its meaning, as an act of this particular agent, and the moral value of his resentment is a significant part of the action's moral value. If, as he digs the postholes, we ask, "What is he doing?" one answer, of course, is that he is making a badminton court. But if we are interested in the intrinsic moral value of that action, this answer is insufficient. We want to know what he is doing it *for*, what he is doing it *as*. If the request for further specification is met with the answer, "For his children's enjoyment," the inquirer will still be in the dark about an important kind of moral value of the action, unless he is told about Jeremy's resentment of his father. This information makes possible the special moral assessment of the action as an action *of this agent*. Then alone does it become reasonably clear what *he* is *doing*. The moral identity of an action that is motivated by an emotion is intrinsically or semantically tied to the emotion as a concern-based construal. If the resentment that motivates Jeremy's building the badminton court is fair, then to that extent the action is good; and, to the extent that it is unfair, the action is unjust.

We tend to be morally suspicious of resentment as an emotion type. Let us now consider an emotion we tend to trust. Are acts of gratitude ever intrinsically morally evil? Let us say that I badly need a kidney transplant, and my doctor, who is a friend, is willing to falsify some documents to make it appear that I should be given priority over other patients who have been waiting longer than me and whose medical condition is more desperate. I feel deeply grateful to her for this favor, which I know to be criminal; indeed, I am quite explicitly grateful *that she was willing to commit this criminal injustice for me*. Out of gratitude to her I thank her profusely and take her and her husband out for an expensive French dinner. This act itself, taken apart from its defining motive, would hardly be considered morally bad. But it is not what it appears to the casual onlooker to be; its moral definition is *an act of gratitude for a crime*. The gratitude is immoral because it ascribes overall goodness to an act that is bad; and the entertainment at dinner is intrinsically bad because it is defined by the motive of this gratitude.

In a discussion of this point David Solomon pointed out that we might approve of the patient's gratitude if, say, he was known for his ingratitude or we had some worry that he might let the doctor take this great risk for his sake and then add insult to crime by not even being grateful. This shows that while the patient's gratitude is seriously bad, it has aspects that can be appreciated morally. In particular, gratitude attributes good will to the benefactor, and if this part of the gratitude is intrinsically warranted, the benefactor must have good will. (Let us assume that the doctor commits her crime out of good will to the patient.) It seems good, or at least permissible, that the beneficiary's state of mind should acknowledge the benefactor's good will, even if this good will towards the beneficiary is expressed immorally, as in the present case. So, Solomon's point can be seen as trading on the intrinsic evaluation of an emotion, but analytically, so to speak – evaluating in virtue of an aspect rather than the whole emotion. His cases also seem to trade on the expressive dimension of the morality of emotions: the emotion of gratitude is good, however intrinsically wayward it may be, in expressing a character capable of it. And the goodness of a character capable of gratitude is no doubt connected to the relational and eudaimonistic potentials of gratitude. Even if it is impossible to find any instance of gratitude that is absolutely bad, the instance in our example *is* clearly intrinsically bad, and Solomon does not deny this. The considerations in this paragraph show why we are inclined to think that gratitude, as an emotion type, is good.

Similar considerations show why we are inclined to think that resentment is bad. Even though resentment is intrinsically praiseworthy in some circumstances, it can never be an all-things-considered ideal emotion to feel. It is warranted only in morally compromised situations and partakes of unhappiness and social antipathy. There won't be any in Heaven. Asymmetrically with gratitude, however, it does not always express a bad character – at least not in the moral outlooks of which we are most likely to be partisans.

Actions can and typically do derive from more than one emotion. A man who builds a badminton court for his children out of unfair resentment of his father's neglect may also be doing it out of love for his children. Assuming that love of his children is a morally praiseworthy emotion, then the action is defined by both a good and a bad motive, and so turns out to be both good and bad. Or, alternatively, the same action (building a badminton court) is two actions, spiting his father and blessing his children, one good and one bad. (It may be more actions than that.) These results are not problematic, but are normal consequences of the fact that actions are defined in part by their motives and that multiple motives can be in play. Most of our actions are morally ambivalent because in doing what we do we are performing so many different actions, with different and sometimes opposite moral qualities.

Lawrence Blum makes a point similar to the one I've been pressing in this section. "The action of helping someone out of compassion or concern has quite a different significance from helping someone as a way to relieve a cause of the [helper's] own distress. It feels like, and is, a different action . . ." But then in a footnote he says, "This is not always so, because in some situations we may care only that a certain result ensues from an action, not what sentiment or emotion the action expresses" (Blum 2011: 189). I've been arguing that the emotion that motivates the action determines the action's moral identity. This is unaffected by what someone other than the agent cares about with respect to the action. I may be so glad to have been rescued from terrorist kidnappers that I don't care whether my rescuer acted out of concern for my wellbeing or because my family paid him handsomely for his work. The moral status of the rescuer's action depends not on what I care about, but on what *he* cares about.

Intrinsic value of actions: subject's relation to his emotion

Our discussion so far has passed over two crucial possibilities. The first is that an agent is epistemically justified in having and acting on an intrinsically bad emotion. The second is that the agent acts on an emotion that he or she does not endorse. I begin with the first possibility.

Let us return to our example of Jeremy building a badminton court out of unfair resentment against his father. The action's disvalue is conveyed to it from the unfairness of the emotion, which consists in the emotion's misrepresenting the subject's father's neglect of the family. A question that we did not raise earlier is that of the subject's epistemic relation to his emotion. A subject may be justified in feeling a false or unfitting emotion if he had no reasonable opportunity to gain a correct view of his emotion's situation. If, for example, the father was very much out of communication with the son, and the mother was not forthcoming about the father's concerns and understanding, the son might be justified in resenting his father's neglect, even though the resentment is unfair. In this case I think we should say that as regards the evaluation of the son as a moral subject, it is as though his resentment is morally correct. Still, the emotion is – we might say "objectively" – unfair. This distinction between the subjective and objective intrinsic value of an emotion seems to carry right over to the action that the emotion motivates. Thus we need to distinguish the question whether the *subject* is justified in building the badminton court out of resentment of his father, from the question whether the *action*, thought of independently of the subject's responsibility, is good or bad in virtue of its origin in the subject's emotion. The distinction will no doubt be difficult to apply in many cases, due to the vagueness of the concept of having had a reasonable opportunity to gain a correct view and the complexity of the psychological and historical factors affecting such opportunity. Let us look at the second possibility.

I have often pointed out that the adult human subject of an emotion may endorse or withhold endorsement of his own emotion. He may think his emotion silly, irrational, morally substandard, shocking, consequentially regrettable, wrongheaded, sinful, self-serving, the result of chemical or environmental influences, etc. The kind of endorsement by which emotions are made into value judgments is that in which the subject takes to be true the impression of the situation that constitutes the emotion; that is, the subject takes his emotion to have the kind of value that I have been calling "intrinsic." Sometimes people act from emotions that they don't endorse in this sense. We may ask whether such repudiated emotions convey their intrinsic moral value to actions that they motivate, in the way that I have been discussing.

Let us say that Huckleberry Finn's friendly compassion for Jim is intrinsically good; that is, he sees Jim as worthy to be helped to escape and in need of such help, and Jim *is* worthy and in need of help. Huck does finally help him to escape, and does so from this motive; so, if this were the whole story about the action, we would say, following the account given in the last section, that the intrinsic moral goodness of the emotion is conveyed to the action. But the story says that Huck does not endorse his compassion, but acts akratically. This repudiation seems to cut the line of conveyance, but, as in the justification case, here also we need to see the conveyance as being between three things, not just two: not just between the emotion and the action, but between the agent, the emotion, and the action. The connection between emotion and action seems secure enough, but the agent is cut off from the other two by his failure to endorse either one. It is as though he just lets the emotion take over, and have its natural outcome in action. This description is an exaggeration: The emotion *does* still belong to Huck, even though in a sense he refuses to own it. The reader admires *Huck* for his love and commitment to Jim, and thinks he is confused about himself: his friendly compassion belongs to Huck's true self, but Huck doesn't know it. His repudiation of his compassion compromises the attributability of the moral worth of the emotion and action *to the agent*, but it only compromises it, does not completely cut it off. We might say that the value is attributable to Huck as an emotional being, but not as a full rational agent. Nevertheless, the akratic mitigation of the tie between Huck and his action affects the action's status as action: it becomes more like a mere event and less like an *action*. An action, after all, is essentially an event *performed by an agent*, and akrasia weakens this origin. I am grateful to John Hare for helpful discussion here.

Huck's is a case of a repudiated intrinsically good emotion leading to action. Do our observations hold also for repudiated intrinsically bad ones?

Consider a mother who strikes her child in anger while knowing that the child does not deserve the punishment and that her anger is caused by frustrations at work. Immediately after, she regrets hitting the child, and sobs in remorse. The anger is unjust, and conveys its injustice to the action. (The action would not be unjust in the same way had she hit the child inadvertently in an effort to reach something off a shelf; because of the anger, she does *intend* to hit the child, and to hit him *as a punishment*.) Symmetrically with Huck's case, I judge that her unwillingness to stand behind her emotion and action weakens the attribution of evil to her agency. Just as we attribute another kind of goodness than full agentic goodness to Huck, we attribute another kind of badness to her, namely, weakness as an agent – lack of "control" or "practical rationality." Like Huck, she is a semi-agent carried into action by her emotion, in spite of her better judgment.

Are all actions motivated by emotion?

Another way to put the question of this heading is to ask whether all desires that motivate actions are consequent concerns of emotions. Actions can be individuated in more or less fine-grained, more or less global terms. Drilling a hole in one's badminton pole can count as an action, and, if someone asks, "Why is Jeremy drilling that hole?" it would usually be pretty silly to say, "Out of resentment against his father." The question is probably looking for an answer like, "To attach a device that holds the net." It is the more global, life-significant, action of building the badminton court that takes the explanation in terms of the emotion. But many small actions of everyday life are not part of any such larger, significant action. If I reach for the salt at the table, my doing so need not be explicable in terms of any emotion, nor need the action be part of any larger one that can be explained in terms of an emotion. Of course, I *might* be eating, not out of hunger, but out of fear that I won't have another meal for the next two days; and I *might* reach for the salt, not because I want to salt my food but because I want to spite somebody else who wants the salt. But these are special cases; many actions, both more global ones (like eating a meal) and more micro-level ones (like picking up one's fork), are not plausibly explained as deriving from any emotion. So, my topic in recent sections – actions' derivation of intrinsic moral value from emotions – is not about all actions, but only about those that do happen to be motivated by emotion. The thesis is that the moral value of the motivating emotion is conveyed to the action it motivates. But we might also ask whether all actions that *can* be intrinsically morally assessed are motivated by emotion. Are some morally assessable actions motivated by desires that are not consequent concerns of any emotion?

Acts of negligence are morally assessed, but some of them are not very plausibly construed as motivated by emotion. For example, if a worker on a nuclear power plant neglects, from inattention, to tighten completely some of the nuts he has been installing, he may be held culpable, yet it is possible that no emotion moved him to this neglect. He is culpable because he should have paid closer attention; but we need not say that he neglected his duty out of resentment or anxiety or any other emotion. Some emotion *might* have caused the negligence. Perhaps it did so without motivating it. Perhaps he is angry with his wife or anxious about a sick child, and his emotion distracts him from his work. Here, because the emotion causes the neglect without motivating it, it doesn't supply the purpose of the neglect. Indeed, the neglect seems to have no purpose. We might call this unmotivated neglect. But "acts" of negligence in this sense are perhaps best thought to be acts only in an extended sense; such "acts" are really failures to act properly rather than improper actions. On the other hand, motivated neglect – neglect that is action in a robust sense – *will* probably arise from some emotion: perhaps the worker consciously or unconsciously resents his boss, or the government, or his wife, and the negligence is a case of revenge; or maybe the "negligence" is motivated by impatience. But motivated negligence does not seem to be quite negligence proper; we are inclined to say that vengeful or impatient negligence is "negligence."

Another kind of actions that are morally assessable yet perhaps not motivated by emotion are those that are motivated purely by duty, if such exist. Let us say that, out of anxiety, our nuclear plant worker is beset with the desire to return home to his sick child, but pays careful attention to tighten all the nuts, and, knowing that he may have been distracted, carefully checks all of the day's work one extra time even though this delays him further in getting home. He does this not out of fear of the inspector or loss of his reputation as a worker, nor out of fear of guilt or shame or any desire consequent on such emotion, but simply out of a sense of duty: this is what he ought to do in the circumstances, and he wants to do what he ought to do. Is he motivated by any emotion? Kant would say he is motivated by respect for the moral law. But must everybody who is motivated by the consideration that X is what he ought to do be motivated by respect for the moral law? Maybe so. Why would he want to do what he ought to do if he doesn't construe the situation as one on which the moral law impinges and then, besides, regard the moral law as worthy and due to be taken seriously? For this, plausibly, is what respect for the moral law is. So, maybe we have not yet found morally assessable actions that are not motivated by emotion.

Reflections on affective motivation

In psychotherapy, as to a lesser extent in everyday life, people become reflective about their emotions, and want either to promote, or to terminate or mitigate some of them. Our reasons vary for wanting these things as do our methods for accomplishing them. We may regard emotions like invidious pride or malicious joy as ignoble, and wish to dispel them despite the pleasure they bring. We may want to promote an emotion in ourselves – say, anger, guilt, or romantic love – because we feel more "alive" when our emotions are active and intense, even if some of them are rather painful. Sometimes we wish to re-experience an emotion primarily because it was so intensely pleasant, or to rid ourselves of one because it is distressing. In the last category are often such emotions as anxiety, shame, despair, disappointment, regret, grief, and guilt.

We manage our emotions in numerous ways – by shifting our attention, by rethinking our situation, by undertaking behavior inconsistent with our emotion, by dropping our control, and perhaps in other ways. One straightforward way to extinguish an emotion that has a currently satisfiable strong consequent desire is to act in satisfaction of that desire. If in consequence of his anger a man wants to beat his child, he may find that beating the child dispels his anger by satisfying it. If in consequence of her anxiety about nuclear power a woman desires to reduce its threats, she may mitigate her anxiety by joining a protest rally.

But it is one thing to aim, in performing an action characteristic of an emotion, to achieve what the consequent desire aims at, and another to aim, in so acting, at reducing or extinguishing the emotion's pain. The first betokens a personal dwelling in the meaning of the emotion, in the emotion's moral significance, while the second is a dissociation from that meaning – as though the emotion is chiefly a hedonic tone or anyway a hedonic tone with a *background* meaning, a "feeling" that arises out of certain thoughts. Just as a pain in my knee is not a moral viewpoint on anything, so a negative emotion is on this way of thinking chiefly a painful experience, though a complicated one. It is a pain predicated on a construal of the situation that in one sense is my own construal, but in another sense is not, since I treat it as chiefly a source of pain. My personal connection with the emotion, in that case, is not that it is how I see a certain corner of the world, but rather that it is a pain in my soul. Or, perhaps, it is how I see a corner of the world, but I dissociate from the "I" who so sees the world by adopting an ironic distance from that "part" of myself. The emotion is not so much an expression of my central self, as a problem for that self. If I can get rid of it by an injection or some process of psychotherapy, that may be fine, because morally speaking it has become, through reflection of a certain sort, a more or less alien state of mind anyway.

Many emotions, I have been arguing in this chapter, are moral viewpoints on things, taking "moral" in a broad sense. If I am angry at my congressman for voting to cut federal funding for a program that provides nourishment and health care for poor children, my anger expresses a moral viewpoint: the congressman's action is culpably wrong, and he deserves to "pay" for his delinquency. If I am anxious about the wellbeing of the many poor children in our country, it is because I construe their wellbeing as important and threatened. In both cases, my emotion may be an expression of my moral character, and may be a right perception of the situation to which it is directed.

Let us say that I am suffering pretty significantly from these emotions. I find them disrupting my sleep and causing me general depression. I am a therapeutically minded, reflective, self-managing, dissociative and self-ironic sort of person, and I think to myself, How can I get relief from this emotional misery? It occurs to me that one way to get rid of anxiety is to do something to alleviate the threat, and one way to get rid of anger is to satisfy its consequent desire by doing something punitive to the putative offender. So I say to myself, "I can probably get at least temporary relief by writing an abusive letter to my congressman."

But if this is my motivation for the action, then the moral quality of the action that would normally be transmitted to it by the emotion is undermined. The consequent concern of an anxiety for the wellbeing of poor children is a desire *to alleviate the threat to them*, and the consequent concern of an anger at my congressman for damaging the poor children's prospects is a desire *to punish him for this delinquency*. These are the desires that, if they motivate the action of writing the letter, convey a positive moral status to the action. (I assume for the moment that a desire for a delinquent's punishment can have positive moral status.) But my hedonistic-therapeutic desire to get relief from the discomfort of my anxiety and anger is a very different one, and changes the moral quality of the letter writing. The "reflective" motivation by the emotion does not confer on the action the *same* moral status as the non-"reflective" emotional motivation confers; and we may well think that it confers no moral status *at all*. For we may think that, insofar as an action is performed to relieve the agent's discomfort, it lacks positive moral status.

If, following Chapters 3–5, we think that emotions, rightly felt, can be a source of moral knowledge (a perceptual acquaintance with moral truths), the thought here might be an application of Bernard Williams's famous dictum that "reflection can destroy knowledge" (Williams 1985: 148): the "therapeutic" switch from personal investment *in* the emotion to the ironic perspective *on* the emotion might be thought to deprive the perception of its subjective anchorage. Because of the therapeutic distancing from the emotion's perspective, the connection to the subject has been mitigated in something like the way it is mitigated in the case of Huck Finn discussed earlier. I'm not claiming that Williams would endorse this application of his dictum.

I suggest that, just as dissociating from an emotion because it gets the situation wrong is an action in the service of the moral life (however it may be conceived), expressing proper motivation and proper transcendence of the emotion, so dissociating from an emotion that one takes to get the situation right, because it distresses, or refusing to dissociate from an emotion that one takes to get the situation wrong, because it pleases, is prima facie an action contrary to the moral life, expressing improper motivation and improper transcendence of the emotion (but see Chapter 8 for qualifications). Other possible cases of compromising the moral stance of an emotion by acting out of a desire to relieve its discomfort are the following. • A person is grieving the death of his son and takes the advice of his therapist to undertake certain exercises of memory to hasten the time when his pain will be less. • A person feels guilty about the fact that his affluent lifestyle is lived partially at the expense of people in third world countries, and gives donations for relief work to relieve the discomfort of his guilt. • A person feels pity for a sufferer and takes action to relieve the suffering so as to relieve his own suffering from pity. From the moral point of view that the emotion expresses, all such actions compromise the emotion's moral stance – or, rather, they compromise the moral stance that the *person* would have in virtue of this emotion's being *his*. I repeat that such compromise is not necessarily all-things-considered wrong.

Pleasant emotions can partake of an analogously false structure of motivation, in case a person acts well out of a desire for the emotions' characteristic pleasure. As Aristotle notes (Aristotle 1980, *Nichomachean Ethics* 1.8, 1099a16–17; 2.3, 1104b5–7), a person who is morally well formed will experience delight in performing good actions – just, liberal, truthful – at least under "normal" circumstances. If the joy or hope with which the action is performed has positive intrinsic moral status, then the emotion confers this status as well on the action in which the pleasure is taken. It is characteristic of the well-formed person that he or she takes pleasure in certain actions *because of their moral character*. For example, he takes pleasure in giving aid *because it helps someone*, or in correcting a calumny *because it restores justice* or *because it brings out the truth*. Such joy is an expression of a moral concern. Perhaps we can imagine a person who finds such actions pleasant beginning to perform some of them *because they are pleasant*. If this becomes a pattern, extensive or deeply ingrained, and especially if increasingly exclusive of the normal moral motivation, it undermines the moral life. The person's concerns have shifted from the objects of the moral life to emotional pleasure. But since the pleasure she seeks at the beginning of the degeneration process is conditioned on her being concerned for the moral objects, she will, if the process continues, become less capable of the emotional pleasures characteristic of the moral life. Now instead of taking pleasure in justice, truth, and the wellbeing of other people, she must find her emotional pleasures elsewhere, perhaps in the laudation she receives for her deeds.

The distinction on which the argument of this section has turned – that between an emotion's *having* a hedonic character and its *motivating by* its hedonic character – is often neglected by philosophers. A standard argument for psychological egoism is that since moral actions by a well-developed moral agent gratify the agent (relieve his emotional discomfort or give him emotional pleasure), moral actions are egoistically motivated – that is, are done *for the sake of* emotional relief or pleasure. This account of motivation is thought by many to be an attack on morality itself. I agree, for reasons that I have given.

Conclusion

In the present chapter I have explored the thesis that one of the ways emotions can have moral value is by motivating actions with moral value. The discussion has shown that, as long as we are considering the intrinsic moral value of actions – their value simply as acts of an agent and not as events with certain consequences – their moral value is derived in large part from the emotions that motivated them. The implication might seem to be that actions *as actions* contribute nothing in the way of intrinsic moral value, and that all intrinsic moral value resides in emotions or in other kinds of motives, if such there be. This conclusion would be false. The moral world is a world of actions, and not just of mental states. Gratitude that generates acts of gratitude has a moral dimension that merely felt gratitude lacks, because human beings are agents who live in a public world. Acts motivated by the emotions are essential to the fabric of a shared life, that very life to which the moral categories apply and which it is their business to shape. So, the point of the discussion is not the unimportance of actions, but the importance of emotions, and the point of this chapter in particular is that to a large extent the moral value and character of actions is defined by the emotions from which their motivation springs.

We have seen how emotions give moral significance to actions. Do actions give moral significance to emotions? They often confer a consequential value on emotions, either by being or by mediating consequences with utility or disutility. But actions don't confer on emotions the kind of semantic or defining significance that I have been at pains to explain during most of this chapter, though they do complete emotions essentially. It is not accidental or incidental that people *act* out of gratitude, anger, and fear. Individual episodes of emotion can be disconnected from action, but it is impossible to imagine emotion that is systematically or essentially disconnected from a public world, and from emotion subjects' character as agents in that world. Emotions, as concern-based construals, are conceptually particularized ways of caring about states of affairs, dividing into two broad types: positive or approving ones, and negative or disapproving ones. Both categories of emotions are, in the majority of cases, responses to more or less public situations and aim, in their motivation, at similarly public states of affairs. As agents, we are not just in the business of evaluatively construing those situations in one way or another, but of acting on them, to modify them into other situations or to maintain them.

7

Personal relationships

Introduction

We have examined how emotions have moral value by perceptually fitting their objects and so contributing to moral knowledge (Chapters 3–5) and by contributing to moral action (Chapter 6). In the present chapter we look at how they have value and disvalue by contributing to the moral status of our personal relationships. I will argue that while it is generally good for our relationships that our emotions fit their objects and generate morally good actions, this kind of value of emotions is detachable, in particular instances, from the other two kinds. In the second section I argue that the value (positive or negative) that an emotion has for some relationship is not wholly explainable in terms of the emotion's fittingness or power to generate action. Indeed, an emotion can be relationally good while not perfectly fitting its situational object, or relationally bad despite fitting it; and emotions can be good or bad in this way where they have not even a chance of issuing in any action. Then in the third section I sketch a general account of how emotions constitute personal relationships, and ask what is the significance, if any, of the fact that a variety of types of emotions – envy, admiration, pride, gratitude, fear, contempt, respect, anger – contribute to the moral shape of our personal relationships. After this, looking at two different sets of emotions, I defend and elaborate, with reference to examples, the sketch in the third section by describing the emotional "logic" of friendship and enmity, civility and incivility. In the sixth section I distinguish positive from good relational value and negative from bad relational value (morally bad friendships are positive but not good) and roughly sketch what makes the difference between good and bad positive relationships. In the penultimate section I note the variety of the modes of endorsement of emotions for their relational value.

A value different from perceptual fit and action motivation

Gareth Matthews offers the following examples, which he says are puzzling on the assumption that emotions are (in St. Augustine's phrase) "an invisible inner motion" (perhaps like the sensation of a skipped heartbeat?):

> Suppose my sister has foregone a chance to hear a concert so that I could hear it. Suppose ... it is important to her that I be at least minimally grateful to her for what she has done. What exactly is ... important to her? That I have a certain feeling, a certain mental datum? And how can that be seriously important to her? Or is what is important to her that I act toward her in a grateful way? But acting toward her in a grateful way may not please her at all, may even upset or annoy her, if she discovers that no feeling of gratitude accompanies my actions. So we are back to the feeling of gratitude. And how can it be important to her that I have a certain feeling?
>
> Or take ... feeling sorry for having done someone a wrong. Suppose my friend is prepared to forgive me a grave injustice I have done him if he knows I am sorry. How can it be so important to him that I have a certain feeling? Or is what is important to him that I behave in a contrite manner? But if he discovers that I behave as if appropriately contrite, but do not really feel sorry, he may be even more upset than before. So it is, after all, my feeling sorry that counts. (Matthews 1980: 345)

Matthews goes on to say that to explain the importance of these emotions in these contexts, we must get beyond thinking of them as mere "inner motions" and notice that they involve ascriptions, evaluations, and motivations of various sorts: gratitude "carries with it the recognition of what one takes to be a benefaction and a disposition to look favorably on one's putative benefactor" (345) and contrition "carries with it the recognition that one has wronged another and the disposition to behave toward that person in a compensatory way" (346).

To put the explanation in terms of my account of emotions (Roberts 2003), the importance that the one person's emotion has for the other is a function of how the one person is perceiving the situation, including both himself and the other, with certain concerns. In wanting Matthews to be grateful to her, his sister wants him to construe her as his benefactor in this particular matter and so to see her and what she has done for him as good – and not merely to construe her and it in these terms, but to do so in a heartfelt (concerned) way. In both cases an action could issue from the emotion, but in both cases Matthews points out that the other person desires the action only if it is an expression of the emotion; his merely "going through the motions" of saying "thank you" or "I'm sorry" is not adequate, and may even be offensive. Furthermore, in such cases, it is often not necessary to perform the action at all, if the other person knows how one feels. The emotion might be expressed in an inflection of voice or a look; or the other might be satisfied that it is there just by knowing Matthews. In such cases of personal interaction, it seems that the really crucial thing is the emotion itself and the consciousness of it on the part of both parties. The action often functions as a token or expression of the emotion.

The relational character of the emotion is indicated by the relations that are identified in the sentence in which we describe the subject's emotion, especially by the prepositions. We say "Matthews is grateful *to* his sister *for* giving up her concert seat *for* him, and because he appreciates her *for* what she did, he desires to make some return *to* her *for* the gift." His emotion is about her as the agent with certain definite attitudes and about the gift *she* has given to *him*. It is a concerned acknowledgment of the relations among these three things: himself (his indebtedness), his sister (her benevolence), and her gift (something good). She responds to his gratitude by acknowledging his acknowledgment and his desire. She is gratified by his gratitude. His gratitude fulfils her concern that he be gratified by what she has given him and that he acknowledge her as his benefactor. And he may in turn be gratified that she is gratified by his gratitude. This brother–sister relationship seems to be going on swimmingly.

The contrition example is similar except that the relationship has been disrupted by Matthews's "grave injustice." But the friend wants Matthews to feel as the friend feels about the injustice – to find it ugly and bad and himself as bad insofar as he is its perpetrator – and the friend will feel gratified, or at least less offended, upon seeing that Matthews feels this way about the offense – and so the relationship goes on, if not swimmingly, at least better than before the contrition set in.

In both of Matthews's examples, the relationship-constituting emotion on Matthews's side is emotionally acknowledged by the other person, completing the relationship through communication of emotion. Some authors stress the communicative function of emotions in morality (see Sherman: 1997: 40–42, 152–53), and I agree that communication is characteristic of the most paradigmatic cases. But I think the examples show that the communicative function is subordinate to the relational one: the substance of the relationship is in the emotions, and the communication is typically but not always required for the emotion to be deployed in this substantive role. I have been assuming, in accordance with the account in Chapters 3–5, that Matthews's two emotions fit the situations they are about and so yield true impressions. I turn now to a couple of cases in which these features are absent or compromised.

The old Prince Bolkonski lies paralyzed, semi-conscious, and on the verge of death for three weeks, during which time his daughter Princess Maria begins to dream of the freedom that will be hers when he is gone. When she looks in on him she finds herself, to her horror, hoping to see signs of decline (Tolstoy, *War and Peace*, Book 10, chap. 8). She is horrified at her hope, but not because it is inaccurate. Her father has been beastly to her, despite an underlying love for her of which she is aware, and his continued existence does restrict her freedom. Furthermore, her freedom would be a good thing for her – she later finds happiness in marriage. Nor is she horrified because of any action that her hope might move her to perform; she is not at all inclined, for example, to do something to hasten his death. She is horrified at her hope because of its meaning for her relationship with her father. Her hope is a spiritual betrayal of him, a degradation of her love and loyalty to him, a rupture of the bond between them.

Consider now an emotion that is relationally good while failing to fit perfectly its object. Grandma has lived happily with her son's family for the past three years, but now she is failing and needs constant care and her behavior is beginning to take a serious toll on the family's wellbeing. She wants very badly to stay rather than go to a nursing home, where she will feel abandoned no matter how many visits she receives from the family, and she points out to her son that *she* took care of *him* when he was dependent, and didn't "dump" him among strangers to be cared for. As the teenagers in the family avoid home more and more, and the son's wife verges on a mental breakdown, the dutiful and loving son decides that, despite Grandma's wishes, she must go to a nursing home (see D'Arms and Jacobson 1994: 743).

This case suggests that the relational value of an emotion can diverge from its fit- or truth-value and practical value. It seems morally (relationally) valuable to feel guilty about putting mother in the nursing home, yet not all of the propositional content of that emotion is true, and it would be wrong to refrain from putting her in the nursing home, as the emotion seems to dictate. I think the content of the emotion must be *largely* true, however, if it is to be relationally right to feel guilty. To feel guilty in this case is to construe the situation somewhat as follows:

> For the sake of our own comfort and wellbeing we are choosing to do something contrary to the strongest wish of Grandma, to whom we owe honor and nurture; in putting her in the nursing home, we are knowingly bringing her to suffer an injustice.

This much is true, let us say; if something like it is not true, it is hard to see how the emotion can be relationally good. But the son's guilt also ascribes blameworthiness and moral disfigurement to himself (see Roberts 2003: 222–25 for an account of the conceptual structure of guilt), on account of putting mother in the nursing home; and this is false, since he is making the best of an unavoidable bad situation.

Now, we might say, why not just suppose that he simply *ought not* to feel guilty about this? Why shouldn't he try to make himself feel good about it, since it's the overall right thing to do? He could emphasize the positive, and rejoice that the family has been spared the degeneration that Grandma's continued presence would have occasioned. That, after all, is indisputably a good thing. Or, at least, he might feel neither good nor bad about it, but just do coldly what he takes to be right. Why should he feel guilty? Why do we endorse this emotion (if we do), while knowing that it neither fully fits the situation nor should be acted on? The answer must refer to the son's *relationship* with Grandma and his own *moral character*.

As to his relationship with Grandma, simply to rejoice and feel relief that the best thing overall has been done is to neglect seeing the situation from Grandma's point of view. She is *angry*. Her anger is, admittedly, not fully fitting, since anger, like guilt, ascribes blameworthiness to its object (see Roberts 2003: 202–04), and in the case he is doing his best, even though his best is an injustice. So, Grandma's anger is a partial misconstrual of the situation; but there it is, for him to respond to. We might say: "Her anger is wrong; she shouldn't be angry, but only sad and disappointed; and so he should feel not guilt, but regret." But even this seems calloused. One way that it seems preferable for him to feel guilt, and not merely regret, is that guilt on his side more accurately reflects and thus respects Grandma's point of view. If he refuses to feel guilty when she feels angry, he creates a disharmony in the relationship. His refusal is supercilious, alienating, hyper-individualistic. (I acknowledge the existence of moral outlooks in which such individualism would be endorsed as right; my point is just to illustrate the possibility that the relational value of an emotion is partially independent of its intrinsic value.) Furthermore, his motives may be questionable. Is his refusal ungenerously self-protective? Does it perhaps express epistemic fastidiousness at mother's expense? Is he in fact trying to ignore the enormous debt of kindness that he owes her?

Such fastidiousness seems ill placed, anyway. The epistemic badness of slightly inaccurate guilt in such a situation is mitigated by the fact that the subject does not necessarily believe its propositional content. On the construal view of emotions it is a way that he is "seeing" and feeling himself, and he may be clear that, though he feels guilty for putting Grandma in the home, he is not guilty of wronging her. If he is thus clear about himself and the situation, he may endorse the guilty feeling as supporting his relationship with Grandma, while withholding endorsement of it as completely fitting the situation.

As to his guilt's expressing his character, despite its lack of fit, he may endorse the emotion, on reflection, because it expresses his sensitivity to what he is doing, to the injustice, and to the irony of putting her away when she has done so much for him and his. I am grateful to Ryan West for helping me formulate the discussion of the Grandma case.

How emotions constitute personal relationships

Types of personal relationships in my sense of the word are friendship, enmity, collegiality, romantic love, marital love, marital strife, partnership, filiality, parenthood, and siblinghood. Some of these relationships (e.g., parenthood) may seem not to fit in this list since they lack a normative character, but I intend them all to be normative, and think that the words have a naturally normative sense: "collegial," "fatherly," and "filial," for example, mean *characteristic of a good colleague, good father, good son or daughter*, etc. The cases I'll consider are friendship and enmity and relationships of "civility" – positive and negative collegiality and acquaintanceship. It should be clear that by "personal relationship" I don't mean to include relationships such as that of a fan to a celebrity or that of a citizen to a president or other government official. Such relationships are not sufficiently reciprocal to be "personal relationships" in my sense of the expression, even though they are characterized by emotions.

As a first approximation let us say that *a personal relationship is a disposition of both parties to think, act, and feel in ways characteristic of the (good or bad) relationship*. I will now qualify one aspect of this remark and comment on a second and third. The qualifier is that it is not quite right to say that a personal relationship is a disposition. A simple disposition can be characterized by a merely potential narrative: to say that a seed is fertile is to say that *if* it is planted under auspicious conditions it will germinate. Similarly, to say that two persons are friends is to say that if one of them has a significant success, the other will under specifiable conditions feel gratified and if one of them is in need of help the other will under specifiable conditions come to her aid. But an actual friendship cannot be characterized by a merely potential narrative. The fertility of the seed may be an actual fertility without its ever germinating, but the friendship of two friends cannot be an actual friendship without their ever having displayed episodes of thought, feeling, and action characteristic of friendship. Thus, while it is true that friendship is a disposition on the part of two people to act, think, and feel with respect to one another in ways characteristic of friendship, and the friendship is expressed in these episodes, these episodes are also *constitutive* of the friendship, in the way that an episode in a story is partially constitutive of the story. An episode of germinating expresses or shows the seed's fertility, but is not constitutive of it. In this respect, friendship is more like a game of baseball, which is constituted of various acts of hitting, running, catching, etc. A friendship has a temporal extension and is partially made up of its episodes. Among the episodes constitutive of friendship at its best will be felt awareness of such emotions as joy in the other's successes, delight in the other's presence, sadness over the other's pains and losses, and indignation at injustices perpetrated against the friend; and felt awareness on the part of the friend of these emotions in the other.

The first of my two comments on the formula at the head of the preceding paragraph is about the relations among the three kinds of episodes: actions, thoughts, and emotions. The emotions are essential to the actions and thoughts. Without the right emotions, neither the thoughts nor the actions would constitute a friendship. Consider actions. A friendship has a history of actions: doing this and that together, doing this and that for one another. These actions will be aimed typically at the benefit of the two persons involved or the benefit of some third party or cause in which the two, or at least one of the two, have some interest. But it seems that however mutually beneficial these actions may have been for the two, they will not contribute to a friendship unless they are performed with "good will," a non-instrumental interest in spending time together, concern for one another's wellbeing and the wellbeing of the friendship.

Imagine an unusually mercenary business partnership. For each action the partners perform, either for one another or for the sake of the business, it is clear that neither partner performs it out of good will to the partner, nor would he perform it if he didn't believe that doing so would serve his own eventual gain. Such partners may perform thousands of acts, over the years, that benefit one another, and these may benefit one another splendidly, but the parties will never become friends. Or consider a variant of the above, perhaps more usual for businesses. The scenario is the same except that the partners make a show of good will to one another. They play golf together, sometimes without discussing business; they exchange gifts at Christmas. But each is aware that both he and the other do this for

the sake of business, and not really out of good will to the other. This
shows up in some of the emotions. When one partner is sick, it is clear that
the other's worry about him is really about who will bear his workload;
when the one is rejoicing over his newborn child, the other's congratu-
lations are less than heartfelt because he is wondering how this will affect
the output. This relationship will have the feel of a friendship sometimes,
because, under the impression of the show, the partners frequently construe one another as having good will towards one another; but since they
do not really believe this of each other, the feelings and thus the "friendship" will be shallow. Another possibility is that the show of good will
towards one another will be so taking that the two drift, as it were, into a
true friendship. Their motivations change as time goes by, under the
pressure of one another's shows and their own. The play-acting fades into
real living. My first comment, then, is that actions are not constitutive
of a friendship proper unless they express the emotions characteristic of
friendship.

The formula that "a personal relationship is a disposition of both parties
to think, act, and feel in ways characteristic of the relationship" also invites
a second comment, this time on the phrase *both parties*. In paradigm cases
of friendship and enmity both parties perform the actions and have the
feelings characteristic of the relationship, and each recognizes at least a
portion of the actions, thoughts, and emotions of the other in their
significance for himself and the relationship. Personal relationships are
symbiotic, with each of the partners "feeding" emotionally and actively
on the others' emotions and actions.

These are features of the paradigm cases, but not all cases are paradigmatic. Friendships and enmities are usually unparadigmatic at the
beginning. One of the parties begins by expressing emotion and performing actions to which the other responds. One might well say that at this
early, non-reciprocal, stage the relationship is not fully friendship or
enmity. But also there are friendships and enmities that deviate significantly from perfect reciprocity, ones in which most of the emotional
and active work is done by one of the parties. One could argue, again, that
this is not in the fullest sense friendship or enmity: Slobodan Milošević,
when he was alive, could not really be my "personal" enemy in the
required sense because, though I felt emotions towards him that approximate ones I would feel towards an enemy, his actions and emotions
were not at all directed at me. On the other hand, given my attitudes,
if I had become important for him and had he become aware of my
attitudes, he *would* almost certainly have had the attitudes of an enemy

towards me, and our relationship would have been an enmity even if he paid less attention to me than I to him.

So far, I have claimed that personal relationships are constituted in large part by emotions, and in doing so I have clarified in a general way what personal relationships are. But now we must try to penetrate a little deeper into their emotional nature. What is it about them that makes emotions so crucial to them? Why does it make such a difference to a friendship what the friends feel about one another? Why is it crucial for them to respect one another, to rejoice in one another's successes and be disappointed at one another's losses and failures, and not to be too often or too intensely angry with one another? Why do friendships deteriorate when one of the parties begins to feel contempt for the other? Why do friendships suffer when one party fails to feel remorse for his offenses against the other, or gratitude for benefits conferred by the other? Why is it important to enmity that the parties to the relationship do not begin to sympathize with one another, to share one another's concerns, to be angry for the same reasons at the same offenses? Why does enmity deteriorate when the enemies start forgiving one another, rejoicing in one another's successes and feeling respect or compassion for one another? Why is it disastrous for enmity when the parties begin feeling gratitude to one another?

In the next two sections I will argue that emotions constitute positive relationships by embodying certain concerns about what the other cares about, and certain aversions to what the other is averse to, and / or by construing the other person in some way that he wants to be construed or refraining from construing him in a way that he is averse to being construed. Emotions constitute negative relationships by embodying concerns for what the other is deeply averse to, or aversions to what the other deeply cares about, and / or by construing the other person in some way that he is deeply averse to being construed or failing to construe him in a way that he deeply wants to be construed. As social beings, humans are characteristically concerned with how certain others are concerned, especially about themselves and the things they most deeply care about. The interactions (mutual awareness) of these concerns are a large part of what personal relationships are made of. Obviously, we sometimes go against our friend's wishes, just as we sometimes go against our own. This may create little tension in the friendship if the wish we oppose is not terribly important to him, or if our friend understands that we have some deeper interest of his at heart. The construals based on such central concerns, along with the mutual felt awareness or possible awareness of them by a relevantly concerned other, are the major constituent of personal relationships.

These concerns and aversions belong in a variety of contexts and are processed in terms of a variety of kinds of reasons (construals), and this variety is reflected in the distinct emotion types. These reasons or issues are ones that bear on personal relationships; that is, they refer to matters that people care about and care about other people's caring about. Examples are successes and failures (envy / pride, joy / sadness), grounds of personal worth (admiration / pride, contempt / shame, pity / respect), and offenses and blessings (anger / gratitude). Not just any intense concern needs to be shared by both parties to a friendship (to take one example). My friend may be a tennis enthusiast while I find the game uninteresting, but if he wins the Davis cup I will probably need to be enthusiastic that this success is *his*, because in doing so I show my care for *him*. Similarly, our friendship can survive my *opposing* something that he cares deeply about, if in opposing it I manage to make it clear to him that I care about his wellbeing. I will illustrate and explore these phenomena by looking at particular emotion types in the next two sections. I can examine only a selection of emotion types here, but I think the ones I've selected are representative.

Envy and pride

I have formulated the defining proposition for invidious envy as *it is important for me to have the personal worth that would be established by my being or appearing to be equal or superior to R in respect X; however, I am or appear to be inferior to R in respect X; may R be or appear to be degraded in respect X* (Roberts 2003: 262). A counterpart emotion that we might call invidious pride is defined by a similar content: *it is important for me to have the personal worth that is established by my being or appearing to be equal or superior to R in respect X; I have that personal worth in some abundance because I am or appear to be superior to R in respect X.* So, envy and invidious pride are about issues of success and failure construed in competitive terms and as bearing on comparative personal status or worth. People care about their own successes and failures, and care about other people's concerned views of these; and, if they are envious or invidiously proud, they care about their own successes and failures in competitive terms – that is, in *comparison* with other people's similar successes and failures. These emotions undermine friendship because they involve caring for what the other person is averse to, and they involve construing the other in ways the other wants not to be construed. Envy and invidious pride have a number of friendship-promoting counterparts: admiration, altruistic joy, gratitude, inclusive pride, etc.

Roger and Mike have been friends and philosophy colleagues at a middling regional state university for fifteen years. Both have been active in the profession, but heretofore neither has succeeded at what both cherish as a fading professional goal – to teach at one of the Big Ten. Then Mike has the good fortune of growing friendship with a couple of philosophers at the University of Wisconsin and some of his papers begin to receive attention; Harvard University Press signs with him to fashion a book out of some of his published work, and negotiates with him for a book-length monograph. His star is rising; the offer comes from Wisconsin. When he tells Roger of his good fortune, Roger succeeds, but just barely, in covering up his envy; and Mike barely succeeds in covering up his invidious pride. Though neither speaks of his feeling, each feels guilty about having it, sensing that their friendship is compromised. Supposing they're right, how do these emotions undermine friendship?

In envying Mike, Roger painfully construes himself as demeaned. He becomes smaller in his own sight for Mike's becoming larger. He likes himself less because of Mike's success, though this does not at all mean that he likes Mike more. Indeed not, for he construes Mike as an enemy of his personal worth. So, despite their friendship, he wishes Mike ill. (Typically such wishes are not fully conscious. For purposes of the discussion I make Roger and Mike unusually self-transparent.) Roger knows he would be relieved to hear that some of Mike's papers were discovered to be plagiarized and Harvard had cancelled the contract; he even notices background fantasies with this theme. To his irritation he is preoccupied with Mike's success, and finds himself looking for ways to minimize it in his own sight, though he is careful not to speak of it minimizingly with others.

Mike's feeling mirrors Roger's. He construes himself as enlarged and improved, not just by his accomplishment (that would not undermine the friendship), but by his position relative to Roger's. He looks better to himself *for Roger's looking worse*. The emotion shows him to be basically concerned that Roger be less, so that he may be more; and its consequent concern is that Roger acknowledge that he is less, even if without acknowledging the acknowledgment. One reason the envier tries to suppress both telltale signs of his envy and his own awareness of being envious is that envy signals defeat in the competition for self-respect. For the same reason the invidiously prideful person looks for signs of envy in his rival. Thus does Mike search in Roger's responses for signs of envy, and if he finds none he is either disappointed or hypothesizes circumstantially about Roger's envy.

The mutual construal, in situations of envy / invidious pride, as serious rivals (not playful rivals, as in a thoroughly friendly game) so that A's failing to get what A wants is a condition of B's getting what B wants, is the contrary of the construal that characterizes friendship, based on A's and B's mutual well-wishing so that A's failing to get what is good for A occasions discomfort (sadness, regret, disappointment, and the like) for B, and vice versa. We can put the point also in terms of self-perception, which on my analysis is crucial to this kind of envy and pride. A's invidious construal of himself as diminished by B's enhancement, and B's construal of himself as enhanced by A's diminishment, is the opposite of friendship, in which A is gladdened by B's enhancement and B is saddened by A's diminishment. The point can also be put in terms of goodness and badness of success. Each of the rivals sees the other's (actual or potential) success as bad and the other's failure as good, so that, when B succeeds, A sees B as bad because B's success diminishes A, and B sees A as good insofar as A fails and thus enhances B. This is the opposite of friendship, in which each sees the other as good regardless of success or failure, and sees success as especially good because it belongs to the friend, and failure as especially bad because it is the friend's failure.

Envy and invidious pride undermine friendship in contexts of success and failure. Other emotions maintain or enhance friendship in such contexts. Where the success is an achievement of some significance, friendship-enhancing emotions of the non-succeeding friend are admiration, whose defining proposition shows some kinship with envy (see Roberts 2003: 264–65) and inclusive pride (pride in the friend's achievement and in the friend). It may also be triumph (think of celebrations of a friend's victory). Where the success is more fortuitous, admiration is not in order and the friendship-enhancing emotion will be joy in the friend's success / good fortune. Such joy will also be relationally appropriate where the success is an achievement, if it is also some kind of gain for the admired one.

What is the friendship-enhancing emotion for the succeeding friend? If the non-succeeding friend has contributed to his friend's success, then gratitude for this contribution can powerfully reach out to the other and include him in the success. In a similar vein, a feeling of triumph, pride, or joy that includes the friend (construing him as having some share in the achievement) can bond the friends. In the healthiest friendships the achieving friend will look generously for ways to credit his friend's contribution or share in the success, and may even be prone to exaggeration in this regard. Just as the material generosity of a friend is not condemned for its variance from strict justice, so her emotional generosity may be justified despite a small departure from strict truth.

As to emotional truth, by the standards of some moral outlooks, the envious and invidiously prideful offend against their own dignity and one another's, selling themselves short. On such a moral outlook both Roger's envy and Mike's pride embody a standard of self-assessment that demeans them. Both emotions falsely represent Roger as personally demeaned by Mike's relative success and Mike as personally exalted by Roger's failure to match up in these terms. As demeaning, the representation in each case is not just false, but insulting. If friendship requires proper respect for persons – self-respect and respect for the other – then envy undermines friendships in this subtle way as well.

Emotions can constitute morally good or bad human relationships because they are representations of self and other and such relationships are constituted, in large part, of representations (including representations of one another's representations). What kind of representations? Friends and enemies no doubt believe things about one another, including about the other's goodness or badness, but beliefs are not themselves constitutive of such relationships. Roger may believe Mike a fine philosopher and admirable person, and even believe him to be no threat to Roger's value as a person, and yet see him as a threat and so in this sense be his enemy. So the representation is a construal and not just a belief. But mere construal is not enough, either. The central mode of representation in morally significant relationships incorporates caring. Roger and Mike have the same basic concern, namely, to enhance themselves by their superiority to the other. If this concern did not enter into their construals of self and other as rival, winner, loser, enhanced, diminished, etc., the construals would not be emotions and would not undermine friendship. Like enmity, friendship is "passionate": its construals of self and other are based on concern for the relationship and for the other – in the case of friendship, a concern or family of concerns that I have called "good will."

Contempt

I have discussed friendship as undermined by envy and invidious pride, and promoted by their emotional opposites. I turn now to a less intense kind of personal relationship that I call "civil," as undermined by contempt and promoted by respect. By "civil" I indicate a positive relationship promoting the good life of persons not particularly attached to one another as individuals, yet bound together in some kind of interactions. When civil relationships obtain, it is typically between co-workers, neighbors, social acquaintances, and persons interacting in collegial, business, and official contexts.

I have said that contempt has the propositional form, *S is markedly inferior and unworthy in X important way, yet he (it) obtrudes, pretending to equal status and worth; may he (it) be put in his (its) place,* and it is based on a concern for excellence of the kind in question and for people lacking that excellence to stay in their place (Roberts 2003: 256). To put the matter simply and crudely, the contemptuous person concernedly construes somebody as an uppity inferior. I have described a kind of respect that partially mirrors such contempt. Its defining proposition is *X is worthy in Y important way and deserves benign attention and good treatment on account of Y; may he (it) be so treated,* and it is based on a concern for worthiness of the kind in question and for people having that excellence to be recognized as such (Roberts 2003: 266). The "Ys" – the "important ways" in which a person can be construed as worthy or unworthy in these emotions – are various and subject to ideological, situational, and cultural variation. A person may be respected for his beauty, dress, race, possessions, prowess, skills, intelligence, quality of work, social standing, accomplishments, virtues, or inherent dignity as a human being, etc., or be contemned for lacking any of the above or having their opposites.

Most people are concerned to have personal worth and to be construed by some others as having it. Again, people are not merely concerned to be believed to have the personal worth in question, but to be appreciated for it; the individual wants the other to care about him in a certain way, and really to see his worth, and to do this in the way characteristic of respect is for the subject to care about the "Y." Similarly, people are concerned, perhaps even more strongly concerned, *not* to become objects of others' contempt. People are concerned to be respected neither by everyone nor only by their friends, but rather by everyone whose opinion matters. So, a person might not be concerned with whether foreigners construe him as having personal worth; perhaps he thinks *they* have no personal worth, or they are ignorant of what personal worth is; or, for some other reason, or no reason, it does not appear to him that their opinion counts. Also, people tend to be concerned to be respected or not to be contemned for matters that they themselves regard as important. One might not mind too much being an object of contempt for one's dress, if one doesn't care about dress; although if one cares to be respected by the person who contemns one for one's dress, then one may start caring about one's dress *because* it matters to this other person. But, this said, it seems that most people, if not all, have a generic concern to be respected. So, if they are not respected in one area in which they are concerned to be respected, this shortfall may be compensated by their being respected in another area; and if they are not respected by one person or group of persons it may not matter too much, as long as they are confident that *some* person or group respects them. Respects are to this extent fungible, but people for whom respects are completely fungible are immature; we expect people's concern to be respected to be qualified.

One might think that if any personal relationships are free from emotion, it would be civil ones. But civil relationships are not merely composed of the externalities of behavioral exchange – doing what is required to get committee work done, cooperating on a work site, conferring with one another about the school board election at the PTA meeting, giving the new neighbors the requested advice on how to present their trash for pick-up, receiving help from the clerk at the driver's license facility. The behavioral interchange is always emotionally toned; in tone of voice, in phrasing, in glances of the eye, in the alacrity of cooperation, one picks up the other's attitude *towards oneself*, and one responds with feelings about oneself and the other, which in their turn are picked up by the other and reflected back again. Often these subtle emotions are hardly noticed. The quality of these relationships depends to a great extent on whether the emotional expressions on both sides say, as it were, "I find in you a person of worth, who calls forth from me a desire to treat you well," or, rather, "I regard you as of no importance, or less, rather as someone worthy to avoid or treat ill, and if I do treat you 'well,' it is only for expediency." The latter emotion may be expressed and understood even if the required behavioral exchange is "successfully" completed. In Roberts 2003: 250–56 I also mentioned the state that can be called "holding in contempt," which is a lack of respect without any feeling of contempt. It consists in ignoring the other, or noticing her just enough to ascertain that she is of so little importance as not to be noticed as a person at all. In contempt as an emotion, the other is noticed for her offensive obtrusiveness; to hold someone in contempt is to place her below such notice. One often responds to being held in contempt in much the way one responds to being the object of emotional contempt, and this seems to show that the concern that is frustrated is not merely the concern not to be contemned, but the concern to be respected.

How does contempt undermine civil relationships, and how does respect support them? Civil relationships make weaker demands on the good will of the parties than friendship does (we sometimes speak of a person's having respect for another if only she does *not* feel contempt or hold in contempt). Still, personally civil relationships depend on a principle of human nature, namely, that people want to be construed by others – even others not very close to them – as having personal worth. (Here, being respected for one's instrumental worth may be a way of being respected for one's personal worth.) This is a demand of human nature, a demand essential to *relationships* because it is a demand made on the attitudes of other human beings and not to be satisfied in any other way. A's civility to B is thus attitudinally constituted by A's construing B as having personal worth; so, in feeling contempt for B, A is construing B in a way that is inconsistent with civility. Since A's withholding of respect from B frustrates this basic demand of B's nature, B will tend to experience A's lack of civility with one or more of several negative emotions, which in their turn tend to undermine civility.

Shame is the main emotion in which a person construes himself as lacking personal worth or having its negative counterpart (see Roberts 2003: 227–30); it is, so to speak, self-contempt. To react with shame to the contempt of another is to "accept" the other's construal of oneself; to see oneself in the same terms and to evaluate oneself in the same way. Shame is a form of suffering, and expressions of contempt may be intended as punishment. By "accept" I don't mean to imply willing acceptance; the shame may be forced on oneself by the other's negative construal. Indeed, one may feel shame in response to the other's contempt without even believing oneself to be contemptible; such is sometimes the power of another's expression of emotion. Even though shame in response to contempt creates a sort of "agreement" between the parties about the value of the shamed one, it is not a happy agreement, but one in which the shamed person is alienated from himself. But if he is alienated from himself in virtue of his construed lack of worth, he is similarly alienated from the one who feels contempt towards him. Thus the alienation in such a case is bi-directional: A is alienated from B in virtue of A's contempt for B, and B is alienated from A in virtue of A's contempt for B and B's shame. If, in addition to feeling shame in response to A's contempt, B construes A's contempt as unjust (and thus disagrees with it in spite of adopting A's construal of him), then B is alienated from A in virtue of B's anger at A as well. B construes A as doing him an injustice in construing him as of low or negative worth, and on this account wishes for revenge on him. Anger is often combined with shame in response to contempt. Or (though this is less likely) one may feel the anger without feeling the shame. In any case, B's construal of A as blameworthily offensive and deserving punishment (see the analysis of anger at Roberts 2003: 202–04) strongly undermines B's attitudinal civility to A and, if A notices the emotion, is likely to eventuate in further alienating emotions on A's part (say, retaliatory anger and / or further contempt). A fairly common way for B to punish A for shaming B is for B to try to turn the tables by pouring contempt on A: say, by attempting to make A's contempt seem small-minded. If B succeeds in generating a feeling of contempt for A he will "feel better" (while energizing the vortex of incivility), but it seems likely that his contempt will be artificial in the way that was discussed in Roberts 2003: chap. 4. Or he may attempt (probably unsuccessfully) to "hold A in contempt" – which is to say, to be so far above the relational vortex as to feel nothing at all in response to A's contempt. The difficulty of doing this testifies to the strength of the generic human concern to be respected by others, even ones who are not very close to us.

Consider how the relationship goes if A respects B. Respect speaks to the same relational concern of human nature as contempt, except that instead of frustrating it and thus alienating B, respect satisfies it and creates a bond between A and B. The bond may be rather transient, or shallow, if the relationship is merely civil, as we are supposing at the moment. But respect is also a part of deeper relationships like love and friendship. We have seen that A's contempt, when noticed by B, tends to evoke shame in B; similarly A's respect, when noticed by B, tends to evoke self-respect in B. Thus B both likes to be construed by A as having personal worth and finds equilibrium and satisfaction in construing himself as having personal worth; both satisfactions tend to be evoked by A's respecting him. If a typical response to being shamed is anger, a typical response to being respected is gratitude. Tokens of respect (a word of personal affirmation, careful attention to what B is saying, solicitude that B understand one's intentions to be good) tend to elicit a willingness to receive good things from A and to attribute goodness to A, and a desire to pay A back in kind. As a construal of A as good, gratitude is itself somewhat like respect, and so a cycle of positive emotional reciprocity is set up, initiated by respect, just as a cycle of negative emotional reciprocity is initiated by contempt.

I mentioned that people are respected or the opposite *for reasons*. Such reasons range from legitimate to questionable to downright irrational or despicable. People may be respected for their noble accomplishments and virtues or their inalienable dignity (Kant), or they may be respected for their bigotry and the audacity and callousness with which they commit crimes against humanity (Slobodan Milošević). People may feel contempt for someone because he is depraved (Milošević again), or because he is unathletic or dark-skinned. The reasons for which a person is respected or contemned govern (in coordination with the object) whether the emotion is fitting. Here the issue is whether the contempt or respect is warranted by the way the person is. But there are many ways a person *is* that might warrant contempt or respect by way of fit, and we have seen that emotions as construals are selective of attributes. For example, Milošević might be worthy of contempt by reference to his actions and attitudes, but worthy of respect for his Kantian dignity. So, a person might be warranted, as to fit, in feeling either respect or contempt for Milošević, depending on which attribute interested him at the moment. And countless people, if not all, have less strikingly contrasting worthiness-attributes. This latitude in fit-warranted respect or contempt gives scope for endorsement and repudiation of these emotions for relational purposes, without bending emotional truth as in the earlier case of guilt over putting Grandma in the nursing home.

Consider the case of Tamsin and Diane, who work at the same bank. Tamsin has worked for the bank well and loyally for six years and has been hoping for promotion to assistant vice president. She has high standards of banking excellence, and takes joy in doing things right and seeing them done right. But because of family connections with the president Diane is brought in to fill the position for which Tamsin has been longing. Diane is markedly less competent than Tamsin who, working as her subordinate, sees daily Diane's deficiency of knowledge, skill, and basic resourcefulness. Tamsin decides for the time being to endure her trouble in silence, in hope that Diane's blundering will eventually become evident to all. Tamsin feels contempt for Diane. In particular she sees her as an incompetent banker, obtruding where she should disappear, and due to be put in her proper place. If what I wrote earlier in this section is correct, collegiality between Tamsin and Diane will be vitiated. If, as is unlikely, Tamsin manages not to express her contempt in any way that gets picked up by Diane, then her contempt will vitiate the collegiality only from her side.

But now let's suppose that Tamsin sees the collegiality falling apart and sees also that the culprit is her contempt for Diane. She values collegiality as an ideal, but also because she likes to see banking done well, and collegiality promotes it. She will repudiate her contempt, not because it is inaccurate (she believes that Diane is indeed a contemptible banker), but because it constitutes bad collegiality. So far, the repudiation consists in disliking her contempt for what it means for the relationship. Can her repudiation go any further than ruing her emotion? Yes. She may be able to remind herself that, for all Diane's shortcomings, she still has the dignity of a human person and so deserves respect. And, as she *treats* Diane with respect, under the influence of this construal, perhaps Diane puts on a more human, less defensive face and actually appears more respectable to Tamsin. She still makes banking mistakes, but they seem to matter less and have less disastrous consequences once the collegiality is going better. Here the repudiation of contempt goes beyond regretting it, and becomes a matter of taking action against it – making an effort to reconstrue Diane in respectful terms and at the same time to behave respectfully towards her. In managing contempt for relational purposes, it is a great boon to have some general and indefeasible conception of human worth like the Kantian conception of dignity or the Christian conception of creation in the image of God. Elitist outlooks like the Aristotelian or Nietzschean lack such a conception and so may be stuck with contempt in many cases.

The reader may think I have underestimated the power of mere etiquette to foster civil relationships. Is real respect, or the absence of real contempt, necessary? Is it not enough if the parties treat one another politely? Etiquette is a regulation of behavior calculated to show respect or, to use a more cynical formula, to make a show of respect. The latter formula acknowledges that respect is more than mere respectful behavior, but involves inwardness or attitude – that respectful behavior may be hollow. The extent to which hollow respectful behavior can foster relationships of civility depends on some contingencies. People's ability and willingness to "act" what they don't feel varies considerably from person to person. Also, civil relationships vary greatly in their intimacy and duration. A person who is a good actor may be able to have pretty good *transient* civil relationships while feeling contempt or indifference towards the persons he interacts with, but even a good actor may be unable to sustain satisfactory day-in and day-out close interaction with colleagues for whom he feels contempt or indifference. I speak of "satisfactory" interaction rather than about real civility here because throughout this subsection I have supposed that good civil relationships involve the inwardness of respect. On this supposition, the civil relationship of a good actor who lacks respect would be good from at most one direction: in virtue of the good actor's etiquette the other party might feel respected and return respect; but the relationship would still be flawed by the good actor's lack of respect. Finally, it is hard for normal human beings to divorce their emotions from their behavior in the way this challenge suggests. One of the great values of etiquette is that by shaping behavior it also shapes people's feelings. I use the word "feeling" advisedly here, in the way I used it in Roberts 2003: chap. 4. The feelings of respect that polite behavior tends to engender in the one emitting the behavior may not run deep. They may be "superficial" or even "sham" or "false" in the sense that they are not much of an expression of the subject's deepest concerns and understanding; yet they may be genuinely *felt*, and this may be enough. Civil relationships don't make as high demands on depth of concern and understanding as friendship and love, and so superficiality of emotion is not such a defect here.

Bad positive and good negative relationships

I have said that positive relationships like friendship and civility are constituted, in large part, of emotions like admiration of the other, gratitude to her, joy in her success, and respect for her; and that negative ones like enmity and incivility are constituted in large part of emotions like envy, invidious pride, and contempt. The analysis I gave in the last two subsections of how emotions make relationships positive or negative suggests that positive ones are characterized by harmony and agreement and coordination between the parties and negative ones by disharmony and opposition, disagreement and conflict. And I have suggested that a distinct reason for endorsing an emotion is that it is constitutive of a desirable relationship, and a distinct reason for repudiating an emotion is that it is constitutive of an undesirable relationship. What I have written so far suggests the too simple view that positive relationships are good and negative ones bad.

Given what Slobodan Milošević was, and supposing friendship with him to involve admiring him and rejoicing in his successes, it is better not to be his friend. Even civility, if it involves respecting him for anything more than his bare inalienable dignity, may be problematic. Someone might wish him success under a very different conception than he wishes it for himself; and while this might constitute love in the Christian sense of *agape*, it does not satisfy the criteria of friendship. Thus we must be open to the possibility that enmity and incivility may in a few cases be good relationships, and the emotions that constitute them, such as contempt, may be endorsable for that reason even though the relationship is negative. A plausible hypothesis is that when negative relationships are good or positive ones bad, it is because a positive relationship would have to involve *unfitting* emotions. In the present case, it is because Milošević was not *fit* to be admired or respected for the reasons that make admiration characteristic of friendship, or for the reasons that make respect character-istic of civility. We have seen cases in which, for purposes of endorsing emotions, relationship trumps perfect fit; here fit trumps the presumption that positive relationships are good.

Modes of endorsement

Let us review briefly the various endorsements and repudiations of emotion that we have seen in this chapter. Our focus now is not on people's *reasons* for endorsing their emotions (this chapter has focused on cases in which the endorsement or repudiation is for the emotions' implications for relationships), but on what that endorsement *consists in* – by way of what kind of mental or other activity or passivity it takes place.

Gareth Matthews's examples admit of a couple of possibilities. In one kind of case, he feels gratitude for his sister's generous sacrifice and contrition for his injustice against his friend without thinking about these emotions at all. He just goes on, expressing the emotions in gesture and action and judging the things they are about to be as the emotions represent them (thus satisfying the concerns of the relational others). In this very usual sort of scenario the endorsement of the emotions is default; it is implicit in life's drift around the emotions. In another kind of case Matthews is reflective; perhaps his gratitude is a little dim at first and he picks up subtle cues in his sister's face and voice that seem to express disappointment with his response. He thinks, "She wants me to be grateful, and she's right." So, he livens up his emotion by expressing gratitude to her and by dwelling attentively on the benefit she has conferred and her good will in conferring it. Here we have an explicit judgment about the appropriateness of the emotion, and actions undertaken with respect to it; this judgment and these actions are the mode of endorsement of the emotion. In partial contrast with these cases, Maria Bolkonski repudiates her hope for her father's death by feeling a more or less spontaneous horror at it, and then by judging reflectively, but still in this passionate way, that her hope is bad. The son endorses his emotional guilt about putting Grandma in the nursing home by judging, upon reflection, that it is appropriate despite there being some considerations against it and by refraining from undertaking some way to get over it. Roger and Mike both repudiate their envy and invidious pride by feeling guilty about it, without understanding why, at first, but then perhaps with understanding upon analytic reflection. Tamsin's repudiation of her contempt for Diane is at first a dislike of it – not spontaneous like Maria Bolkonski's, but arising out of observing how it affects their collegiality; and then it consists in her fighting it by reminding herself of Diane's human dignity.

Conclusion

I have argued several theses in the present chapter. I have tried to show that emotions have a distinct kind of value by playing a constitutive role in personal relationships, in addition to the values they have by fitting the situations they are about and motivating good actions or otherwise causing good outcomes. Relational value supplies one of the principal kinds of reasons for endorsing or repudiating emotions. Emotions have this value, I argue, because personal relationships are constituted, in large part, of emotions whose situational objects include or are importantly related to the other person in the relationship. And they have this constitutive role because people care about other people's caring about what they care about, and they care about how other people perceive them. A variety of emotion types enter in because of the variety of personal issues that these relationships involve, such as benefits and offenses, the personal worth of the parties, and the parties' successes and failures. I have argued that emotions are constitutive of intense positive and negative relationships (e.g., friendship and enmity) as well as of less intense civil relationships. Generally, positive relationships are good and negative ones bad, but this is not universally so. Lastly, I have pointed out that the modes of endorsement or repudiation of emotions for their relational values are diverse.

8

Emotions and happiness

Introduction

We have noted a variety of interconnected ways that emotions can have value, positive or negative. They can fit or fail to fit the values in the situations they are about, and thus be correct or incorrect, true or false. They can motivate or otherwise contribute causally to good or bad actions and states of affairs and (if they motivate action) contribute to actions' specific goodness or badness. They can partially constitute good or bad personal relationships. Another source of emotions' values, also connected with the aforementioned sources, is their contribution to their own subject's happiness (wellbeing) or the opposite. This contribution, like the contribution to actions, can be either constitutive or causal; that is, the emotions may partially make up a person's happiness or unhappiness, or may bring it about (or both). Since happiness and unhappiness, as I shall understand them here, are dispositional, emotions will often also be symptomatic of the one or the other.

This value contribution can be independent of truth, action, and relationship. For example, one can correctly appraise an emotion as bad to have because it undermines wellbeing, despite its fitting well the values of the situation it is about, or one can appraise an emotion as good to have even though it does not fit its situational object's values. An example of the former possibility is the horror that would fit some of the most horrendous scenes of war as experienced by a participant or near bystander. Even if such horror is perfectly measured to the values in the situations that evoke it, a person might justifiably shield his children (or himself) from such emotion on account of its tremendously negative (painful) character, as well as its possible longer-term consequences for mental health (Sherman 2010). The shielding would most likely take the form of preventing the subject from perceiving the situation, either by preventing perception of the situation altogether or by some method of mitigating the impression the scene makes (e.g., drugs or some dissociative technique). (Prescription of anti-depressants for people in depressing *situations* will involve this kind of assessment / repudiation.) For the same reasons we endorse defense mechanisms against extreme horror, shame, anger, and grief, even though they may prevent us from the richest and most veridical perception of parts of reality. Similarly, we may think that people ought sometimes to have positive emotions that are not valuationally realistic. Perhaps a person whose life-situation does not offer much occasion for fully truthful joy is justified in taking an emotional holiday now and then, losing himself in literary or cinematographic fantasy or maybe even in chemical relief. Again, in endorsing this, we may have in view either just the immediate pleasure of the emotions or longer-term effects on wellbeing. Some therapists let the wellbeing criterion regularly trump ethical relationships and truth, but we needn't be so radical to recognize that such trumping is sometimes legitimate.

But such trumping is the exception; a regular therapeutic policy of emotional unreality must betoken shortsightedness about wellbeing. Far more often happiness is to be found in having emotions that fit the values in their situational objects, and thus express the nature of their subjects in relation to those objects, whether or not such emotions are pleasant. Happiness is more than feeling good. It is a matter of attunement to oneself and to one's world; of acting well whether or not with pleasure; of good personal relationships even if they are sometimes painful and seem unsatisfying.

The meaning of "happiness"

"Happy" and some ancient words we translate by it (*eudaimôn, makarios, beatus*) are subject to at least two kinds of ambiguity: first, the ambiguity between happiness as feeling good (satisfaction) and happiness as wellbeing; and, because happiness refers to wellbeing, they are also subject to variation of concepts of human nature and thus of what is fulfilling for human beings, what our wellbeing consists in. I begin with the first ambiguity; the discussion will naturally draw us to consider the second.

The satisfaction that constitutes one side of happiness is chiefly emotional satisfaction or pleasure, not physical or appetite satisfaction. Mere physical pleasures may be an ornament to the happy life, but it is chiefly meanings that constitute human happiness, the kind of meanings that are embodied in the concern-based construals that I have argued emotions are. A psychologist friend of mine wanted to observe children when they were happy and so instructed his assistant to have candy ready. The "happiness" of the children, even in this trivial example, is the emotional satisfaction of anticipating something good, or the joy involved in possessing something good; and not just the pleasant olfactory sensations afforded by candy. In a similar vein we speak of being happy when our ball team wins or we get a fat raise.

But sometimes "happy" does not mean *experiencing positive emotion*, but something like *faring well* or *in a state of wellbeing*. The unhappiest person may experience emotional pleasure from time to time; if we look at him at such a moment, we may well say, "He is happy for the moment" (he's just come by a bottle), but if asked whether he is a happy *person*, our answer is emphatically "no." We might think these two concepts of happiness are connected in the following simple way: when we speak of a happy *person* (intending his whole life or at least a pretty long period within it), we mean to say that positive or pleasurable emotions strongly predominate in that life or over that period. However, this is only a partial analysis of the concept of a happy person.

Suppose you can be given intense joy by slight electrical stimulation of certain parts of your brain. A surgical implant enables you to plug in to such stimulation and administer it to yourself by depressing a lever. Once you have plugged yourself in and learned to self-stimulate, you overwhelmingly prefer this pastime and slip into a state of radical indifference to all else. You give up other activities – productive and creative work, worship, interaction with family and friends, political activity, self-cultivation through reading and learning of creative skills, etc. Of course, to sustain life one must do other things: eat, sleep, and get exercise. Being reflective enough to realize this and wealthy enough to provide the means, you hire a caretaker who removes you from the pleasure machine periodically and induces you to eat and jog. (Sleep sees to itself, since you periodically doze off while plugged in; you may even have a half-power continuous setting that induces extremely pleasant dreams.) After jogging and dining, you plug in again, maximizing time on the machine. Since the device was invented early in your long life, you are able to put in sixty-five years on it. Would this be a happy life? It might be the most pleasant life possible. It might be the life that everybody would choose after getting a taste of it. But would it be happy?

By hypothesis, you feel very good, almost uninterruptedly. If we ask you whether you're satisfied with your life, your answer is emphatically affirmative. But if we insist that a happy life have wellbeing, we will probably judge you not to be a happy person. The objection would be that such a way of life is unnatural, even if everybody would choose it. It strays beyond the bounds of the normatively human into the territory of emptiness and pathology. Human life (so we may well think) is normatively characterized by work, by interaction with people, by creative activities, and so on. It is part of human nature that fulfillment is found in such activities, well performed in fitting contexts. These are good not merely because and insofar as they result in emotional or other pleasure. To spend sixteen hours a day depressing a lever for mindless pleasure is not just a possible cultural variant of human fulfillment, like nudity or polygamy or skydiving, but a perversion of human nature. No matter how subjectively compelling it may be, it is not within the limits of functioning well as a human being, and so cannot be a happy life. Or to take a much less outlandish example, a life lived entirely without productive work, a life of sheer trivial amusement such as is sometimes available to rich people, seems a good candidate for perverseness and unfulfillment even if, as is unlikely, the subject manages to sustain feelings of amusement.

Or consider Meursault, the "hero" of Albert Camus's *The Stranger*. The reader is struck by the triviality of his emotions. Instead of grieving the death of his mother, he is annoyed by the necessity of going to her burial and takes joy in getting home afterwards. The day he returns from the funeral he amuses himself by beginning a sexual liaison and going to a comic movie. He enjoys his girlfriend's smiles and dresses and body, and is willing to marry her if she wants, but when she asks whether he loves her he says "No." And when she says, in dismay, that marriage is a serious matter, he says "No" again. When his boss offers him an opportunity to advance in the business, he responds with indifference. He is concerned with such things as a dry towel in the washroom at work, a cigarette, a cup of coffee, and the discomfort of intense sunlight. He murders a man seemingly without motivation (he mentions, however, that the sunlight on the beach was making him uncomfortable), and when asked at his trial whether he regrets killing the man, says he feels more annoyance about it than regret.

As the novel indicates, a person like Meursault is a "stranger" to most of the rest of us, and is likely to bring annoyance on himself by getting himself in trouble. He is not well adapted to society. As Camus summarizes the novel, "in our society a man who fails to weep at his mother's burial risks being condemned to death" (Camus 1955: vii, "Avant-propos" dated January 1955; my translation here and below). This might seem to make Meursault's unhappiness an accident of circumstances. We will return to the question of circumstances later in this section. But, for now, let us imagine a Meursault who somehow manages to get through life without any dramatic conflicts with his society. He has a large preponderance of emotional pleasures over pains, but, since he is Meursault after all, his pleasures are all trivial: sex without love, warm sun on one's body, a dry towel in the restroom at work, a boss who demands little, a mother whose death causes minimal inconvenience. Many (though probably not all) will judge such a life to be deeply disordered. No matter how easy and subjectively pleasant it may be, it is not happy in the deeper sense because it is not characterized by concerns for anything important.

Camus is sensitive to this argument. Some early readers judged Meursault to be a wreck (*une épave* – flotsam). Camus denies this, and supports his denial by saying, in effect, that Meursault has a virtue: he is completely candid; he never dissembles. Unlike some people we know, he doesn't pretend to grieve for his mother or love his girlfriend. But such a virtue must be more than the behavioral pattern of readily volunteering the truth about one's inner states. It must be a passion, and Camus says that Meursault has it:

> Far from lacking all sensibility, he is animated by a passion that is profound because tacit, a passion for the absolute and for truth. It's a matter of negative truth, certainly, a truth of being and sensing, but one without which no victory over oneself and the world will ever be possible. (Camus 1955: viii)

Perhaps it is because this passion is "negative" and "tacit" that it does not show up in Meursault's emotions. Maybe our skepticism about this retrospective interpretation can be pardoned because we have in mind cases of a real truthfulness, neither tacit nor negative, such as that of Charlie Marlow in Joseph Conrad's *Heart of Darkness*:

> I would not have gone so far as to fight for Kurtz, but I went for him near enough to a lie. You know I hate, detest, and can't bear a lie, not because I am straighter than the rest of us, but simply because it appalls me. There is a taint of death, a flavor of mortality in lies – which is exactly what I hate and detest in the world – what I want to forget. It makes me miserable and sick, like biting something rotten would do. Temperament, I suppose. (Conrad 1960: 84)

Marlow's concern for truth is manifest in emotions like disgust, horror, hatred, and regret. For Meursault, by contrast, truth seems not so much a matter of concern as something he falls into from lack of motivation to dissemble. One who believes that truthfulness is a virtue, so that this trait is an aspect of good functioning and personal wellbeing, is likely to think that Marlow is happier, in the sense of wellbeing, despite being subject to some pretty intense negative emotions, than even our unrealistically lucky version of Meursault. Significantly, in defending Meursault against the charge of being a human wreck, Camus does not merely appeal to the fact that his life was rather more pleasant than unpleasant, all things considered; but claims (however implausibly) that he was a man of deep and appropriate passion and thus of character.

So, long-term heavy preponderance of pleasure over pain does not qualify a life as happy. By the same token, a life that includes quite a lot of emotional distress may be happy. Consider Ludwig Wittgenstein, of whom Norman Malcolm writes,

> On Friday, April 27 [1951] he took a walk in the afternoon. That night he fell violently ill. He remained conscious and when informed by the doctor that he could live only a few days, he exclaimed "Good!" Before losing consciousness he said to Mrs. Bevan (who was with him throughout the night) "Tell them I've had a wonderful life!" By "them" he undoubtedly meant his close friends. When I think of his profound pessimism, the intensity of his mental and moral suffering, the relentless way in which he drove his intellect, his need for love together with the harshness that repelled love, I am inclined to believe that his life was fiercely unhappy. Yet at the end he himself exclaimed that it had been "wonderful"! To me this seems a mysterious and strangely moving utterance. (Malcolm 1958: 100)

What can make such a painful life happy? Leo Tolstoy's *Anna Karenina* can be read as an essay on happiness, and one that addresses this question. Constantin Levin, a personality in striking ways like Wittgenstein, is the novel's central character and represents the same paradoxical happiness. Two other characters, Anna Karenina and her brother Stepan Arkadyevitch Oblonsky, invite comparison with Levin on the issue of the intersection of emotions and happiness. I will argue that conceiving happiness as *attunement to one's own nature and the nature of the universe* is a key to understanding how both of these characters are unhappy while Levin is happy in the deeper sense of having human wellbeing.

Tolstoy's conception of human nature includes the thesis that faithful family life and a life of work close to the soil are natural for human beings and thus sources of happiness, while deviations such as sexual promiscuity and marital unfaithfulness, avoidance of child-getting, idleness, abstract pleasure-seeking and rootlessness, are misattunements and sources of unhappiness. The central actions of the story are Anna's adultery with Alexei Vronsky and Levin's marriage to Kitty Shtcherbatzky. The two characters are parallel in that at the beginning of the novel they are both basically decent and morally well-formed, though unsure of themselves and thus open to development for better or worse. They are also alike in finding ecstatic, though flawed, emotional pleasure in romantic love (see Part 4, chaps. 9 and 13 for Levin; Part 6, chap. 18 for Anna). In both cases a major form of pain is intense jealousy. Each of these characters is led into crucial actions by choices made in the interaction of circumstances with their personalities. Anna, for example, has contracted a loveless and increasingly unsatisfying marriage at an age too young to reckon with her passionate need for love; while Levin, though isolated by his farm work, is drawn to the Shtcherbatzky family and its daughters by an appreciation of their purity and goodness that is enhanced by his own motherless childhood. Both are "helped" into their marriages by well-meaning relatives. It is clear that for Tolstoy, Anna's life is a profoundly unhappy one (ending in suicide), while Levin's is just as profoundly happy, despite the fact that he has some very low points emotionally, and Anna some very high ones. If one weighed their emotions in a hedonic scale, the ratio of pain to pleasure would probably be greater in Anna's life than in Levin's; but this difference is not enough to account for the difference in their happiness. Despite having some excellent qualities, Anna lives a poor and disfigured life; and despite having some significant defects Levin lives a life that, over all, radiates wellbeing on Tolstoy's conception of human nature and fulfillment.

Oblonsky supplies a different kind of contrast with Levin, since many would spontaneously identify him as a happy person. He is a happy-go-lucky adulterer and general *bon vivant* who neglects his family and is largely without a conscience for the financial and emotional havoc that he works in his wife. For him, work is an occasion for socializing with friends and acquaintances and making a salary; Tolstoy tells us that the most important quality by which Oblonsky gained the universal respect of his colleagues in the government service was "his complete indifference to the business in which he was engaged, in consequence of which he was never carried away and never made mistakes" (Part 1, chap. 5). He is sentimental and so has intense passing feelings of remorse about the pain he causes his wife; he is "touched" by Karenin's suffering when he discusses divorce with him; and feels transient grief after his sister's suicide. But such feelings don't keep him down for long; his good humor and enjoyment of life are irrepressible. He is handsome and generally loved by the members of his set, whose ideas he adopts uncritically. At one point, his wife, reflecting Tolstoy's sentiments, I think, calls him "my disgusting, pitiful, and charming husband."

Compare him with Levin, who suffers from a combination of religious aspiration and religious doubts, who often worries whether he is living justly vis-à-vis his peasants (he is writing a book on agriculture that will revolutionize present thinking about labor), who has deep doubts about his own worth and worthiness (he suffers from what we call low self-esteem), who feels compelled to show his fiancée the diary that recounts his life of debauchery. His main satisfactions are in stark contrast with Oblonsky's: in his wife and child, in the birth of a prize calf, in a day of mowing with his peasants. Unlike the self-stimulator, Oblonsky's pleasures are normal and natural in the ordinary sense; unlike Meursault, Oblonsky is an enthusiast and in a certain sense socially engaged, though by comparison with Levin his relationships with wife, friends, and family are all superficial (perhaps he is in a *hidden* sense a kind of "stranger"); unlike Anna, Oblonsky suffers very little emotional pain. Yet Oblonsky is "pitiful," while in a halting sort of way Levin flourishes. What can be said in explanation of this thesis?

Two kinds of attunement

Hedonic value is no doubt a factor in happiness, but it is only one factor. In the present chapter I am particularly interested in examining features of emotions other than hedonic value (positive or negative affect), by which they contribute to the happiness or unhappiness of their subjects. In particular, I want to think about four happiness-relevant measures on which emotions differ from one another: *depth, import, scope,* and *goodness*. I think that an exposition of how these variable features of emotions affect happiness will go some distance to explain why Levin and Wittgenstein, despite the emotional pain in their lives, can be regarded as unusually happy people, and why Oblonsky, despite his frank, irrepressible good cheer, is "pitiful."

I propose that we conceive happiness in terms of two kinds of attunement, which I will call "metaphysical" attunement (character) and "circumstantial" attunement (satisfaction). Ideal happiness encompasses both kinds, but a person can be judged relatively happy if he has quite a lot of metaphysical attunement, even though he is somewhat badly attuned to his local circumstances. This is the situation of Levin and Wittgenstein. Similarly, a person who is pretty badly adjusted by some metaphysical standard, and yet pretty well adjusted circumstantially, given his poor metaphysical attunement, is often regarded as happy, even by partisans of the metaphysical standard in question. This is Oblonsky's case. On the other hand, if one is abysmally misattuned circumstantially, then even perfect metaphysical attunement may not be possible to regard as happiness. As Aristotle comments, "Those who say that the victim on the rack or the man who falls into great misfortunes is happy if he is good are ... talking nonsense" (Aristotle 1980: 188 [*Nicomachean Ethics* 1153b19] (Ross)), though some moral outlooks (e.g. Stoicism, Christianity) metaphysically accommodate "great misfortunes" in such a way that the sage or saint *can* be happy in the midst of them. And those who are abysmally maladjusted metaphysically will not be regarded as happy by insightful judges like Oblonsky's wife even if they are perfectly adjusted circumstantially.

Metaphysical attunement is attunement to one's real nature and the real nature of the universe. The question about the nature of the self and the universe is a metaphysical-normative question, and is not to be answered merely by observation of how the self and world actually are. Metaphysical-normative views are highly constructive and interpretive, though they typically appeal to commonly observable features of human beings and our universe as a basis for their constructions. An example of such metaphysics would be Camus-Meursault's view of the universe as containing only options and states of affairs that are of no importance, of being a place that is completely indifferent to human concerns, and of humans as beings who can and should recognize this fact about the world and respond to it with perfect honesty and with a corresponding indifference. Another would be Tolstoy-Levin's view of work and family life as natural and thus fulfilling to human beings, and the universe as containing a transcendent dimension that escapes science and objectivity but must be tapped into by human beings if they are to make sense of life. Tolstoy's "metaphysics" is suggested rather richly in his little narrative, *A Confession* (Tolstoy 1996).

Christianity, Marxism, Stoicism, and other metaphysical-ethical systems imply concepts of character-adjustment. This attunement occurs when one cares about what is really important, by the lights of one's metaphysics, and the depth of one's cares is keyed both to the import and to the particular value – goodness or badness – of things. Circumstantial attunement, by contrast, is attunement to the particular circumstances of one's life – e.g. to the fact that my children are healthy and I am loved by my spouse, that my work is important and interesting; or that my children are abusing illegal drugs and my spouse hates me and is having affairs with several others, and that my work is meaningless. A person's circumstantial attunement, or emotional attunement to his circumstances, is to be distinguished from the "fit" of an emotion to its situational object that I discussed in chapters 3–5. A horrendously negative emotion will fit its situational object, in case the object is horrendously bad; but personal attunement to a situation could not have the form of intensely negative emotion. Circumstantial attunement occurs when one's circumstances satisfy one's concerns, yielding positive emotions, or at least do not frustrate them. Levin comes pretty far towards being metaphysically adjusted, but is pretty badly adjusted circumstantially during a good portion of the novel. By Tolstoy's lights, Oblonsky is poorly adjusted metaphysically, but the combination of his character and the local circumstances of his life are such that he is pretty well adjusted circumstantially. His disposition to conceive happiness as pleasure, as getting along with others and having a good time, and his propensity to adapt his views to his social circle, whatever that happens to be at the moment, and to sympathize with whoever happens to be at hand, are traits that make him highly adaptable to his local environment, but by Tolstoy's lights he is without character, badly adjusted to his nature as a human being and the character of the universe. These two aspects of happiness correspond to happiness as satisfaction and happiness as wellbeing. (The fullest wellbeing and the deepest satisfaction are to be had only by having both kinds of attunement.)

Depth and import

One dimension in which emotions differ from one another has *shallow* or *superficial* on one end and *deep* on the other. A second dimension, which interacts with the first, has *trivial* on one end and *weighty* or *important* on the other. The interaction of the dimensions of depth and importance is one determinant of happiness and unhappiness. In general, the person who is happy in the sense of functioning well as a human being (metaphysical attunement) is one who has some deep emotions, and whose trivial emotions are shallow and whose important ones are deep; unhappy people are ones who have only shallow emotions, or whose trivial emotions are relatively deep and whose important emotions are relatively shallow.

The depth of an emotion is the depth of its ingress into the personality. Human emotions are paradigmatically based on or rooted in concerns. But concerns can be more or less masterful, that is, they can be more or less constitutive of the core of someone's personality, or they can be derived from concerns that are in this way central to the person. Some concerns have shallow roots; they are in the personality all right, and emotions occasionally arise out of them, but relatively little about the person can be explained by reference to them. Consider the concern to rise to high relative importance and honor among fellow human beings. Most people have this concern, I suppose, but in some it is shallow and in others deep. In some people this concern shows itself in the joys of winning and the disappointments of losing in small ways – say, at the game of Monopoly – and in the shame they feel upon being exhibited in invidious comparison with others who have better "succeeded" in life; but very little of their behavior and thought is to be explained by reference to this concern; it has shallow ingress in their personality. In others, by contrast, large swatches of their activity derive from their concern for ascendancy over others; it is a central and organizing motive of their lives. Other concerns that may organize a personality are intellectual pursuits (Barbara McClintock's interest in corn genes), athletic ones (Michael Jordan's passion for excellence at basketball), religious and ethical ones (Mother Teresa's love of God and concern for the poor and neglected). Traditional mothers are devoted to their children. Constantin Levin's concerns for family life and agriculture are also examples. Emotions that are based on shallow concerns are shallow: they do not reach very far into the personality; they do not express much about "the depths of the individual's heart." Some people, like Oblonsky, seem not to have much of a passional center of personality. Their lives are "dissipated" in shallow daily concerns for this and that (often pleasures and avoidance of pain). For example, Oblonsky undertakes to persuade both Anna Karenina and her husband to get a divorce, and spends some effort at this; but this concern neither is, nor derives from, any concern very deep in him.

By contrast, an emotion's importance or triviality is the importance or lack of importance of what it is *about*. Trivial anger is anger about some offense that is rather unimportant. Such anger may be deep, despite being trivial, if it is based on a concern central to an individual's personality. For example, a vain person is deeply concerned to be admired by other people, and so may be deeply angered when someone conspicuously fails to admire him. But we may still think the emotion trivial, supposing it is not very important for a person to be admired by others. An emotion can seem to be about something trivial without being so. For example, Levin stares angrily at the elegant long fingernails of a man named Mihail Stanislavitch Grinevitch (Part 1, chap. 5); but this anger is not trivial by Tolstoy's lights, because it is based on Levin's concern for manual labor and is really about the useless and perverse way of life that those nails represent to Levin. (The emotion is also deep, even though it is only passing, because the concern for the laboring life is near to Levin's heart.)

Shallow emotions can be extremely pleasant or unpleasant. For example, ordinary fans sometimes feel intense joy when their ball team wins an "important" game (or disappointment in the other case), but for healthy fans the triviality of the issue is reflected in the shallowness of the emotions. (The outcome may not be trivial for the coach who will lose his job if the game is lost, or the fan who has bet his life savings on the game, but in such cases the emotion is really about losing one's job or life savings, and only mediately about the game.) Psychologically mature people may scream and groan and curse when the opposing team flashes to victory in the last half-second. If we took their blood pressure at the excited moment it might be off the charts, and the feeling of disappointment would be intense indeed. But if they are emotionally mature, they will then go home and have an enjoyable evening with friends, and thoroughly enjoy getting angry at the coach all over again.

Some people, like Oblonsky, have only a shallow disappointment in their children's turning out badly (they "trivialize" this circumstance), and so they are protected by their shallowness from feeling the full impact of their circumstantial misery. Such people may, at least temporarily, seem to themselves to be happy and may *be* happy in an abstractly hedonic sense of the word. But they don't have wellbeing. By the same token, some people may be made genuinely unhappy by the loss of a ball game. I have not heard of an ordinary fan committing suicide because of his team's losing an "important" game, but if it happened it would be an extreme example of this possibility.

So, basic emotional wellbeing consists in proper adjustment of concerns – shallow for trivial things, deep for important ones. But people with this basic emotional wellbeing can be deeply unhappy, if they have negative emotions about really important things. For example, a person who exhibits the metaphysical attunement of caring deeply about the spiritual wellbeing of his children can be made unhappy by construing them as having depraved, disastrous lives. So, it may not be enough to be emotionally well attuned to one's own nature and the nature of the universe. Even if a person is well formed, happiness may depend on some of the circumstances of one's own life, namely, the important ones. Thus happiness in the sense of wellbeing can be missed in several ways. (1) Be undisposed to have deep emotions; (2) be disposed to have deep emotions about trivial matters; (3) be disposed to have shallow emotions about important matters; (4) be well attuned to one's own nature and the nature of the universe, but badly attuned to one's particular circumstances, by having deep negative emotions about important matters.

Let's return to our question about Oblonsky and Levin. How can Oblonsky be less happy than Levin, though he is so far ahead of Levin on purely hedonic measurements? Oblonsky lacks wellbeing because his emotions are overwhelmingly superficial. He and Meursault are alike in lacking deep emotions. Both are human wrecks, with the difference that Oblonsky appears, to a casual observer at least, to have some important emotions – for example, his penitence concerning his adultery; his grief at the death of Anna. And the casual observer may mistake the emotions' importance for depth.

It is not only Levin's positive emotions that tend to be deep; so do negative ones like his anxieties and disappointments about getting married, his guilt, his frustrations with the farming, and anger at his peasants. If Levin's deep concerns were ultimately or predominantly frustrated (as they are not), this would count heavily indeed against his happiness, even though such emotions would show him to be an excellent person, well adapted to his nature and responding in a fitting way to his circumstances. By contrast, Oblonsky's negative emotions (remorse about his adultery, shame at needing to be reconciled to his wife for financial reasons, irritation that the house is in chaos and his children are running wild) don't express or embody any serious misattunement to his circumstances, because these circumstances do not matter very much to him.

But perhaps Oblonsky's emotions are not just shallow versions of emotions that Levin might have. What looks at first glance like a shallow instance of an emotion that in Levin would be deep may in fact be a trivial (or relatively trivial) emotion instead. Compare Oblonsky's remorse about his adultery with Levin's remorse about his premarital unchastity.

> [Oblonsky] could be calm when he thought of his wife, he could hope that she would come around, as Matvey expressed it, and could quietly go on reading his paper and drinking his coffee; but when he saw her tortured, suffering face, heard the tone of her voice, submissive to fate and full of despair, there was a catch in his breath and a lump in his throat, and his eyes began to shine with tears.
> "My God! What have I done? Dolly! For God's sake! . . . Dolly, what can I say? . . . One thing: Forgive . . ." (*Anna Karenina*, Part 1, chap. 4)

Compare Levin's remorse when he sees the effect of the diary recounting his premarital debauchery on his betrothed, Kitty. He gives her the diary and then returns in the evening to see her:

> It was only when the same evening he came to their house before the theater, went into her room and saw her tear-stained, pitiful, sweet face,

miserable with suffering he had caused and nothing could undo, he felt the abyss that separated his shameful past from her dovelike purity, and was appalled at what he had done. . . .

"You can't forgive me," he whispered.

"Yes, I forgive you; but it's terrible!"

But his happiness was so immense that this confession did not shatter it, it only added another shade to it. She forgave him; but from that time more than ever he considered himself unworthy of her, morally bowed down lower than ever before her, and prized more highly than ever his undeserved happiness. (*Anna Karenina*, Part 4, chap. 16)

Should we count Oblonsky's emotion as a shallow instance of remorse, or as a relatively trivial analog of it? From what the novel gives us we cannot tell for sure, but the difference would be this. Remorse is a construal of oneself as having blameworthily violated some standard one is concerned to honor, and as being indebted for reparation for it. As the whole novel shows, Levin is deeply concerned for moral purity, and Kitty has become an embodiment of the standard of purity for him. He construes himself as indebted to her, by his blameworthy action, in a way that he can never pay, and this construal becomes dispositional. So, it is clear that his emotion is deep remorse. The question then is whether Oblonsky's "remorse" is shallow remorse or not remorse at all, but some trivial analog of it such as discomfort at the sight of intense and evident suffering and the construal of oneself as having (perhaps justifiably) caused it. Our reason for thinking that Oblonsky's emotion is not really remorse is that just a little bit later he justifies his behavior and blames Dolly: he is a sexually vital man and she has lost her good looks, and how vulgarly she shouted at him! And later in the morning, at a board meeting,

> "If they knew," he thought, bending his head with a significant air as he listened to the report, "what a guilty little boy their president was half an hour ago." And his eyes were laughing during the reading of the report. (*Anna Karenina*, Part 1, chap. 5)

It is possible that Oblonsky construed himself in terms that would qualify his emotion as remorse, but that this self-construal was extremely fleeting and based on an uncharacteristic and therefore shallow concern. This is possible because Oblonsky has access to concepts like blameworthiness, is rather intelligent, and is not unable to see things, at least momentarily, in ways that trade on his wife's point of view. However, I am inclined to think not in the present case. It seems more likely that he never felt remorse, that he did not even at the moment of his sobs appreciate the gravity of his delinquency, but responded instead in a more immediate and generic way to more outward features of the situation such as the look of misery on Dolly's face. But whichever diagnosis is more apt it is clear that Oblonsky's emotion is neither a painful indication of moral wellbeing nor a source of deep discomfort. Levin's remorse, by contrast, does express moral wellbeing and is a continuing source of discomfort with himself. But this source of his discomfort (his concern for purity) is also a source of gratifications in his wife and family that are not merely hedonic gratifications but also expressions of personal wellbeing of which Oblonsky is fundamentally incapable. It is for reasons like these that Tolstoy can present Levin as a flourishing man despite his frequent emotional pain, and Oblonsky as a pitiful specimen of humanity despite his irrepressible cheer.

Scope

We have seen that the *depth* and *import* of emotions, and not merely their pleasant or painful, satisfying or frustrating, character, affect their relevance to our happiness. Another relevant feature is *scope*. An emotion's scope is the breadth of its object in relation to one's life. Emotions take in more or less that is of import to one's life, and the more an emotion takes in, the more it affects one's happiness, for better or worse. A person's regret, for example, can take in a great deal or just a little bit. You might regret having bought a house in a certain neighborhood because the property values in that neighborhood dropped; or you might regret the career choice you made thirty years ago. You are regretting a larger piece of your life in the second case than in the first, and I am saying this difference makes the first regret less relevant to your happiness than the second. A person might regret his *whole* life, in which case it would count heavily towards his unhappiness. Or, again, a person might despair of getting an academic job, and this might be an important despair because getting an academic job is important to him. Yet such despair need not undermine his happiness. But were he to despair of himself (Kierkegaard 1983) – seeing no prospect of being the self he deeply wants to be – then he would be unhappy indeed.

The emotion that Wittgenstein expresses in instructing Mrs. Bevan, "Tell them I've had a wonderful life!" is an emotion of absolute scope – it is about Wittgenstein's life as a whole. Consequently, as a positive emotion, it weighs heavily against the many negative emotions that Malcolm says Wittgenstein experienced. But scope is just one factor in the relevance of an emotion to happiness, and can become of little importance if not combined with some of the others. A comment on these words of

Wittgenstein by J. N. Findlay would, if true, seem to undermine their status as evidence of Wittgenstein's wellbeing. Findlay says, "he died of cancer in 1951, saying that he had lived a wonderful life, which he certainly had, since, though he had never satisfied himself, he had aroused infinite admiration in many who were very intelligent indeed" (Findlay 1973: 175). (A thesis of Findlay's invidious essay is that Wittgenstein's influence was due less to the power of his philosophical ideas than to a powerful personal presence that struck awe into the hearts of those who met him.) Findlay seems to be saying that the satisfaction that Wittgenstein voices is the satisfaction of his vanity. This is not impossible. Wittgenstein himself testifies to his vanity, though he speaks of trying to quiet it (Wittgenstein 1953: x). But it seems unlikely that Wittgenstein would think that his life could be wonderful in virtue of his vanity's being satisfied, however richly. Of course, the rather trivial concern to be admired by highly intelligent people might be the concern on which his emotion is based, without his knowing it; people are often unaware of the basis of their emotions. But Wittgenstein was morally savvy about himself, and so seems unlikely to have been deceived or self-deceived here (see Monk 1990). These thoughts are speculative, but in any case my point is not biographical but philosophical. If an emotion is the satisfaction of vanity, it is too trivial to count towards happiness as wellbeing. Even absolute scope will not make it count.

Perhaps Wittgenstein's emotion was more like the one that Levin voices at the very end of *Anna Karenina*:

> This new feeling has not changed me, has not made me happy and enlightened all of a sudden, as I had dreamed, just like the feeling for my child. There was no surprise in this either. Faith – or not faith – I don't know what it is – but this feeling has come just as imperceptibly through suffering, and has taken firm root in my soul.
>
> I shall go on in the same way, losing my temper with Ivan the coachman, falling into angry discussions, expressing my opinions tactlessly; there will still be the same wall between the holy of holies of my soul and other people, even my wife; I shall still go on scolding her for my own terror, and being remorseful for it; I shall still be as unable to understand with my reason why I pray, and I shall still go on praying; but my life now, my whole life apart from anything that can happen to me, every minute of it is no more meaningless, as it was before, but it has the positive meaning of goodness, which I have the power to put into it. (*Anna Karenina*, Part 8, chap. 19)

The feeling that Levin calls "faith" (or "not faith") is a positive emotion of absolute scope. It seems to be based on the concern, characteristic (that is, deep) of Levin, for goodness that is at the same time sense-making of the activities and events of life. Though the terms of this construal are not the Christian doctrines concerning salvation, the construal seems to be analogous to the Christian sense of oneself as justified, in spite of one's own ongoing sin, by the transcendent power and goodness of Jesus Christ and the promise of resurrection in him.

Goodness

Let us turn to a specification of the import dimension. Evil emotions can be as important as good ones, and it is a thesis of classical moralities such as ancient Judaism, Christianity, Aristotelianism, and Stoicism that good emotions (both positive and negative) tend to promote, express, or constitute happiness, while evil ones (positive and negative) tend to promote, express, or constitute unhappiness. This claim is subject, in my view, to qualification by reference to the other happiness-relevant qualities (hedonic value, depth, and scope) that emotions can possess.

Consider Miss Havisham, a character in Charles Dickens's *Great Expectations*. Jilted on her wedding day, she stopped all the clocks in the house and caused the rooms to remain as nearly as possible as they were at that moment of crushing disappointment. She has not seen the sun since that day, and continues to wear her now yellowed wedding dress, entertaining such guests as she has in the presence of the rotting bridal cake amidst which the mice and spiders play. Her master passion is resentment against her lover and by extension against all men; she takes pleasure in her sad victimization as a mark of reproach against him and them. But the central delight of her life is her beautiful adopted daughter Estella, whom she has reared to be both seductive and cold, as her weapon for destroying young men's happiness.

Pip, the novel's main character, is Miss Havisham's main victim. As a child he is brought to the dismal house to play with Estella and fall in love with her, and thus to be made discontent with his destiny as an uneducated blacksmith and to have his heart broken. Miss Havisham delights in monitoring the progress of his ensnarement.

> Miss Havisham would often ask me in a whisper, or when we were alone, "Does she grow prettier and prettier, Pip?" And when I said yes (for indeed she did), Miss Havisham would seem to enjoy it greedily. Also, when we played at cards Miss Havisham would look on, with a miserly relish of Estella's moods, whatever they were. And sometimes, when her moods were so many and so contradictory of one another that I was puzzled what to say

or do, Miss Havisham would embrace her with lavish fondness, murmuring
something in her ear that sounded like "Break their hearts my pride and
hope, break their hearts and have no mercy!" (*Great Expectations*, chap. 12;
see also chaps. 8, 15, and 29)

Most will agree that Miss Havisham's delight is evil, and that its being evil
partly explains its role in her unhappiness. Its most straightforward connection to her unhappiness is her bitter remorse at the end of the novel for
the state of affairs that she had hoped for and delighted in, when the horror
of the evil she has done comes home to her, replacing the satisfactions of
her supposed revenge (chaps. 44–49).

Her remorse is triggered by Estella's announcement, in Pip's presence,
that she is going to throw herself away by marrying the arrogant and
loutish Bentley Drummle. Pip's response reminds Miss Havisham of her
own disappointed love, and she starts to feel compassion for Pip and
Estella.

> "What have I done! What have I done!" She wrung her hands, and crushed
> her white hair, and returned to this cry over and over again. "What have
> I done!"
>   I knew not how to answer, or how to comfort her. That she had done a
> grievous thing in taking an impressionable child to mould into the form
> that her wild resentment, spurned affection, and wounded pride, found
> vengeance in, I knew full well. But that, in shutting out the light of day, she
> had shut out infinitely more; that, in seclusion, she had secluded herself
> from a thousand natural and healing influences; that, her mind, brooding
> solitary, had grown diseased, as all minds do and must and will that reverse
> the appointed order of their Maker; I knew perfectly well. And could I look
> upon her without compassion, seeing her punishment in the ruin she was,
> in her profound unfitness for this earth on which she was placed, in the
> vanity of sorrow which had become a master mania, like the vanity of
> penitence, the vanity of remorse, the vanity of unworthiness, and other
> monstrous vanities that have been curses in this world?
>   "Until you spoke to her the other day, and until I saw in you a looking-
> glass that showed me what I once felt myself, I did not know what I had
> done. What have I done! What have I done!" And so again, twenty, fifty
> times over, What had she done! (*Great Expectations*, chap. 49)

Like Meursault, Miss Havisham is a "stranger" profoundly unfitted for this
earth where she is placed. She has committed a grievous wrong, but this act
and project are systematically connected to her twisted character and her
constructed daily environment and the patterns of behavior and social
interaction of her distorted life. Her project of using Estella to avenge
herself on men is sustained and given "sense" in the distorted perceptions

of her brooding seclusion. In a sort of maladjusted adjustment, these distortions enable her to take intense pleasure (a kind of pseudo-happiness) in what is bad – the exploitation of Estella to avenge herself on the innocent Pip. The human psyche and the world, in concert, provide healing influences, which, if used, can correct some of what is amiss in a life. The society of others, against which Miss Havisham shields herself, can be one such influence. Sorrow, penitence, remorse, a sense of unworthiness can also be healing influences, if rightly used to fit the person to herself and to the world in which she is placed. In Dickens's Christian outlook they are part of the appointed order of our Maker by which we are and / or can be adapted to our own nature and the nature of the world we inhabit.

Like Meursault, Miss Havisham has in her something "natural" that emerges emotionally at the end. In her the emotion is remorse, based on a concern to have done right by Estella and Pip, while in Meursault it is the agonies of facing death, based on his love of temporal existence. In both cases the concern is hidden or submerged earlier in the novel and, triggered by circumstances, becomes manifest in emotions towards the end. A difference is that Meursault's concern meets at the very end with its satisfaction, as his love of temporal life is adjusted to that life as it actually was – absurd, so that even the fact that it is ending is of "no importance." So, he can claim to be happy despite facing the end of everything that has had "meaning" to him. It now has meaning to him precisely as this utterly transient thing that has no other meaning than that: as "absurd." To construe the indifference of the universe as perfectly basic and OK is to construe such features of it as the guillotine that awaits him as "tender," and himself as happy. Like Levin's emotion at the end of *Anna Karenina*, this construal is of absolute scope. By contrast, Miss Havisham's new found concern to have done right by Estella and Pip is ultimately frustrated in the construal of herself as having done them irreparable and perhaps unforgivable harm, and she dies miserable in the vanity of remorse. This emotion too is of great, if not absolute, scope.

On my reading, Miss Havisham's unhappiness is not just a matter of her having intensely negative emotions at the end of her life – not even if they are of absolute scope. These elements are part of the picture, but I have been pressing the more classical notion that her unhappiness consists in her profound misattunement to her own nature and the nature of the world. On this account, people will *tend* to have intensely negative emotions if they are so misattuned; but in certain local environments, and subject to certain distortions of their own natures, they may have intensely pleasant emotions for a time, as Miss Havisham does. Also, persons who are rather well attuned to themselves and the universe, like Levin, may suffer great frustrations. The presence, in Levin's impinging world, of people like Vronsky, can make for some deep negative emotions; but the fact that the concerns on which these negative emotions are based express Levin's attunement to himself and the universe counts towards his happiness nevertheless. So, we have a good and classical reason for thinking that Miss Havisham is unhappy in the very midst of her malicious joys and hopes; indeed, *her* hope and joy are marks of her unhappiness.

We can imagine a Miss Havisham whose character or narrative was different from that of the novel. Imagine one whose concern for the wellbeing of others is even more submerged than Miss Havisham's – one who is unmoved by the scene that triggers her remorse. This would be a Miss Havisham who by virtue of her even greater misattunement to the universe and to herself was saved the pain of desperate remorse at the end. Or she might have been saved from this pain by simply dying in her vindictive joy. On the classical conception of happiness that I am promoting, these variations would not save Miss Havisham from unhappiness; they might even be thought to increase it.

Relativity to outlook

"There are so many conceptions of happiness," says Alexei Karenin in response to Oblonsky's suggestion that Karenin and Anna may as well divorce since they cannot make one another happy (*Anna Karenina*, Part 4, chap. 22). I have advocated and exploited a conception of happiness, found schematically in many moral, spiritual, and philosophical outlooks, according to which happiness is not just a preponderance of positive over negative affective tone (much less sensory pleasure), but a kind of double attunement, first to basic human nature and the nature of the universe, and secondly to the circumstances of one's life. This classical schema has room for considerable disagreement about what happiness is, since it allows for disagreement about human nature and the nature of the universe. I have perhaps made my reader uncomfortable by expounding the schema with examples that disagree with one another on substantive issues of what happiness is. Also, I have sometimes made normative judgments about characters' happiness or unhappiness that may have seemed arbitrary. In the present subsection I hope to assuage that discomfort somewhat by addressing head-on the relativity of concepts of happiness to concepts of human nature. I want to exploit some of the concepts developed earlier in this chapter, to compare the happinesses or unhappinesses in some of the literary examples I have been using, and note the disagreements of happiness-judgments that can be made about them. Then I want to explore the limits of this relativity.

Despite the fact that many readers of *The Stranger* (including me) are inclined to think that Meursault is a human wreck, on Camus's conception of the universe (or at least Meursault's), he is well attuned to it: his mother's death *is* of no importance, and he reacts to it with indifference; marriage *is* of little importance and he reacts to it with indifference; at the very end of the novel he is open to the "tender indifference of the world": whether he lives or dies *is* of no importance, and his death, being thus no disaster, strikes him as perfectly benign. Only at the beginning of chapter 5, where it first dawns on him that he is actually going to be executed, does he show something like the "normal" emotions. There he shows misattunement with such a nature and such a universe, in that he yearns for some hope of escape from the guillotine, and upon imagining himself as spectator (rather than object) of an execution, feels a "poisoned joy," and then, coming back to the reality of his situation, feels what seems to be terror.

Another way Meursault is unlike any character in Dickens or Tolstoy is that he comes very close to having none at all of what they would regard as distinctively human concerns. He is indifferent not only to mere social conformity, but also to his mother, to his girlfriend other than as sexually gratifying, to his work, and to his acquaintances (whom he accepts because they are there, but would not go out of his way for). He seems to have no sense of duty. Apart from his supposed passion for truth, Meursault is a paradigm case of a man without character (good *or* bad). It is this above all that makes him so "strange." His concerns all seem to be "animal" concerns: food, sexual contact with Marie, a dry towel in the washroom at work, relief from the blazing sunlight on the beach. When such desires are more or less satisfied, he is "happy." (In this he bears a distant resemblance to Oblonsky, except that Oblonsky has shallow analogues of moral emotions, and he also has an easily satisfied concern to please those around him.) This is a very different picture of happiness than that presented or presupposed by novelists like Tolstoy and Dickens.

On Dickens's conception of human nature and the universe, Miss Havisham is profoundly misattuned to both. Since human beings and the universe are made in the image of God, who is love, the way to be metaphysically attuned (to reflect "the appointed order of our Maker") is to love one's neighbor as oneself and respect the non-human aspects of the world or, failing that, to be penitent before a forgiving God and to hope for a better self and a better world to come. Thus Miss Havisham's malicious joy and hope in Pip's heartbreak is a great misattunement to herself and the universe, however well it may express attunement of that corrupt disposition to the local circumstances in which Estella is actually destroying Pip's happiness. The desperate remorse in which Miss Havisham dies expresses an attunement to herself and the universe, but is now a horrific misattunement to her local environment, in which the salient features are Estella's numbness to love and consequent self-destructive engagement to Drummle, and Pip's misery, all these being consequences of her own deliberate action. She has the healthy concern, but in a truthful construal of her situation it can only have the character of intense frustration. Dickens, disagreeing with Camus-Meursault, assumes that human beings need hope, and in particular a hope that transcends death. As Solomon puts it, God has "put eternity into man's mind" (Eccles. 3:11 *Revised Standard Version*). So, on Dickens's view of human nature and the universe, both Meursault and Miss Havisham are unhappy at the end, even though Meursault thinks he is happy. Meursault is unhappy because he is starkly out of attunement with his nature, while Miss Havisham is unhappy because her partial metaphysical attunement, towards the end of the novel, puts her out of attunement with her local circumstances, which she has so royally screwed up. On the other hand, on Camus–Meursault's view of human nature and the universe, Miss Havisham's unhappiness is *complete*; her emotional frustration at the end of the novel expresses a misattunement to herself and the indifferent universe she inhabits. It is not only painful, but also dysfunctional.

I have pointed out that, on the classical conception of happiness with which I think we still have some intuitive sympathy, judgments about people's happiness must be indexed to the judge's views of human nature and the universe, which may contrast starkly with the views of the person whose happiness is being judged. On this classical conception, Camus will judge Levin to be so thoroughly misguided as to have little in the way of real happiness; while Tolstoy will judge Meursault to be miserable in the highest degree – despite the protestations of both characters that their lives were good. By my choice of examples I may give the impression that people with divergent metaphysics typically judge (or should judge) one another to be very unhappy. But this field admits much scope for approximations. Differing conceptions of human nature and the universe may nevertheless overlap significantly, and no one, I suppose, more than approximates to attunement of either the metaphysical or the circumstantial variety.

Moral outlook apologetics

The concept of happiness in well-established reflective moral traditions is a kind of double attunement. And we have seen that the concept of the first kind of attunement varies with conceptions of human nature and the nature of the universe. I do not want to leave the reader with the impression that happiness is *simply* relative to world view, as though all world views were equally productive of happiness, if only they are properly assimilated. Rather, it seems that some world views are more adequate to human nature than others, and thus more productive of real happiness. It may be hard or even practically impossible to adjudicate to everyone's satisfaction between deeply thought-out moral traditions. But in principle such adjudication ought to be possible, and we can use a case of a pretty obviously weak philosophy of life, in comparison with one that has endured the test of great time, to illustrate how such an adjudication might go.

Alexei Vronsky, the man with whom Anna Karenina has her affair, is emotionally a good exemplar of his own philosophy of life, which is in part what has been called a morality of honor. His view is elitist and sexually liberated, hedonist and romantic. Tolstoy describes Vronsky's philosophy of life in a couple of passages whose tastiness is due in part to letting his scorn show through with uncharacteristic obviousness.

> In [Vronsky's] Petersburg world people were divided into two quite distinct classes. One – the lower class – commonplace, stupid, and, above all, ridiculous people, believed that a husband should live with one woman to whom he was married, that young girls should be virtuous, women chaste, and men virile, self-controlled, and strong; that children should be brought up to earn their bread and pay their debts, and other such nonsense. These were the old-fashioned, ridiculous people. But there was another class: the real people, the kind to which his set belonged, in which the important thing was to be elegant, handsome, broad-minded, daring, gay, and ready to surrender unblushingly to every passion and to laugh at everything else. (*Anna Karenina*, Part 1, chap. 34)

To construe this view on analogy with the classical views, of which Tolstoy's own is a variant, we would characterize it as holding that human nature is "realized" in the concern to be elegant, licentious, etc. That this sounds pretty silly is an indication that this view is not a well thought out moral outlook. The same thing is evidenced by the arbitrariness of the "principles" referred to in the next quotation, and by the fact that the outlook is best characterized in terms of behavioral rules rather than in a definite view of human nature and the universe.

Vronsky's life was particularly happy in that he had a code of principles, which defined with unfailing certitude what should and what should not be done. This code of principles covered only a very small circle of contingencies, but in return the principles were never obscure, and Vronsky, as he never went outside that circle, had never had a moment's hesitation about doing what he ought to do. This code categorically ordained that gambling debts must be paid, the tailor need not be; that one must not lie to a man but might to a woman; that one must never cheat anyone but one may a husband; that one must never pardon an insult but may insult others oneself, and so on. These principles might be irrational and not good, but they were absolute and in complying with them Vronsky felt at ease and could hold his head high. Only quite lately, in regard to his relations with Anna, Vronsky had begun to feel that his code did not quite meet all circumstances and that the future presented doubts and difficulties for which he could find no guiding thread. (*Anna Karenina*, Part 3, chap. 20)

The viability of Vronsky's outlook, and thus of his character as a basis for happiness, increasingly breaks down as the novel progresses. Anna nearly dies in giving birth to Vronsky's daughter and is briefly reconciled to her husband. Vronsky, in humiliation and despairing love for Anna, shoots himself but without completing a suicide. Anna and Vronsky both recover, realize they cannot be happy without each other's love, Vronsky resigns his military commission and Anna leaves her husband, and they flee to Europe with their daughter, where they live for their love, semi-isolated because of the irregularity of their social position.

Vronsky, meanwhile, notwithstanding the complete fulfillment of what he had so long desired, was not entirely happy. He soon began to feel that the realization of his desires brought him no more than a grain of sand out of the mountain of bliss he had expected. It showed him the eternal error men make in imagining that happiness consists in the realization of their desires. For a time after uniting his life with hers, and donning civilian clothes, he had experienced all the charm of freedom in general, of which he had known nothing before, and of freedom to love, and he was content, but not for long. Soon he felt a desire spring up in his heart for desires – *ennui*. Involuntarily he began to clutch at every fleeting caprice, mistaking it for a need and a purpose. Sixteen hours of the day must be filled somehow, living abroad as they were, in complete freedom, cut off from the round of social life that had absorbed so much time in Petersburg. As for any of the bachelor amusements he had enjoyed on previous travels abroad, he dared not even think of them: one attempt in that direction had produced such unexpected depression in Anna, quite out of proportion with the offence of a late supper with some acquaintances . . .

> As a hungry animal seizes upon everything it can get hold of in the hope
> that it may be food, so Vronsky quite unconsciously clutched first at
> politics, then at new books, then pictures. (*Anna Karenina*, Part 5, chap. 8)

But he errs in thinking it an "eternal error" to suppose that happiness
consists in the realization of one's desires. The crucial question is, which
desires? Vronsky's problem, someone might say, is that the desire from
whose fulfillment he proposes to make his happiness is not the right kind.
Compare someone else who thinks happiness may consist in getting what
you want. In an interview with Malcolm Muggeridge, Mother Teresa of
Calcutta speaks of the rigorous vows that young women take when they
commit themselves to her order, the Missionaries of Charity.

> Muggeridge: That is asking a lot, isn't it? You ask these girls to live like the
> poorest of the poor, to devote all their time and energy and life to
> the service of the poor.
>
> Mother Teresa: That is what they want to give. They want to give
> everything to God. They know very well that it's to Christ the hungry
> and Christ the naked and Christ the homeless that they are doing it. And
> this conviction and this love is what makes the giving a joy. That's why you
> see the Sisters are very happy. They are not forced to be happy; they are
> naturally happy because they feel that they have found what they have
> looked for. (Muggeridge 1986: 80)

The love of Christ in the person of the poor may not be as deliciously
exciting as the love of a sexually dazzling, culturally sophisticated woman;
but it is more sustainable over a lifetime because the object is intrinsically
more important. It is the kind of object that meets the deeper needs of the
human self. Thus we do not find Mother Teresa's spiritual daughters
becoming bored with their service, "clutching at every fleeting caprice,"
looking for ways to fill their days with excitement. These sisters' happiness
is not consequent on their having got what they *happened* to want, as
though the satisfaction of just *any* desire would be equally fulfilling. The
happiness of the sisters is confirmation of the Christian doctrine that human
beings are made for loving God above all things and their neighbors as
themselves, by a God who is love and who has ordered the creation to this
end. On the Christian view, this kind of sacrificial love is in the "design plan,"
we might say. So, it will not surprise a Christian (as it ought to surprise
Vronsky) if unusual happiness is to be found in a community in which God
is daily honored as the Lord of the universe and some of his needy creatures
are served in tenderness, mercy, and compassion. The Christian analysis of
Vronsky's failure to find happiness in the realization of his desires is that the

desires are misdirected, malformed; his passional formation fits neither his own nature nor the nature of the universe. It is as though, dazzled by Anna's loveliness, he makes her the object of a passion that is fittingly directed only to a very different kind of object. No wonder it's unsustainable.

Here one criterion for basic attunement is sustainable circumstantial attunement. We may think it evident that Vronsky's character is not well attuned to his nature and the nature of the universe, from the fact that acting on its characteristic motives and principles leads to dissatisfaction, *ennui*, and sorrow. And we may take it as evidence that Mother Teresa's younger associates' concerns express their true nature because, acting on them, they are conducted into a life full of joy and lacking in regrets, *ennui*, and disappointment. Such a comparison is very far from showing that the Christian conception of human nature and the nature of the universe is correct in its details (we have hardly gone into any detail at all). Many moral outlooks contrast with Vronsky's in similar ways, and our comparison does not adjudicate between those outlooks and Christianity. I have chosen a weak competitor so as to get as much agreement as I can that Christianity is a better basis for happiness; my point is that not all moral outlooks are equally good, and that the better ones are better in part because they are more realistic about human nature.

The case of Anna and Vronsky lends itself to one more point about the limits of this kind of argument, namely, that because which metaphysic "works" emotionally for an individual depends on circumstance and temperament and individual formation, such argument is always in principle open to the objection that the misattunement is due to these accidental factors. Maybe Anna's and Vronsky's bad circumstantial attunement is due not to non-negotiable features of human nature but to accidents of Russian culture in the late nineteenth century. Maybe a more liberal culture would make it possible for them to circulate freely in society. Or maybe their misery is an artifact of individual temperament. Maybe if Anna were less clingy and insecure in love, and thus less jealous, or if she were less maternal towards her son, and thus more willing to forsake him for Vronsky, or if Vronsky were more domestically inclined and thus less inclined to get bored when cooped up with Anna for long periods, she and Vronsky would be better attuned to their circumstances without a change in Vronsky's metaphysic of morals. The kind of argument I have just given can convince, but it will convince only those who adhere to certain in-principle contestable premises – for example, the premise that it is a good thing, based in non-negotiable features of human nature, for mothers to be committed to their sons and to demand fidelity in their partners. Vronsky's moral formation is fragile in the sense that it adjusts persons only to very special and rarely sustainable circumstances of privilege and wealth and is vulnerable to be undermined by probable circumstances such as pregnancies and jealousies and insecurities and prior commitments.

Circumstantial transcendence

The model of happiness offered in this chapter posits a double attunement – first to one's nature and that of the universe, and then, given that attunement, another attunement to one's circumstances. Both are subject to fortuity. The first attunement depends heavily on a moral upbringing that is far from available automatically with membership in the human race; it also depends somewhat on native individual temperament. So, even if the first kind of attunement requires choice, effort, and self-development from the individual, happiness is still deeply subject to what has been called "moral luck." The second attunement is usually fostered by the individual arranging her world, as far as she can, so that the particular situations of her life accommodate her concerns and thus evoke positive emotions. In this way the first attunement may help promote the second. Thus the virtue of industry is an adjustment to one's nature and the nature of the universe; and a large part of its purpose is to dispose its possessor to contribute to the formation of the situations of her life so that they satisfy some of her concerns. However, the situations of one's life cannot be perfectly controlled by one's own choices and efforts; ever so much practice of industry may be undone by a drought or a global financial crisis or intelligent miscalculation. And besides this, attunement to one's nature and that of the universe may actually dispose one to create situations that frustrate some of one's concerns, or to "demand" of situations features that the situations stubbornly refuse to have. For example, the virtue of justice, as a metaphysical attunement, may dispose one to contribute causally to situations that are disadvantageous or dangerous to oneself and one's family, or to wish passionately that situations were just that stubbornly resist being so.

Disharmonies between metaphysical attunement and circumstantial attunement may be explained in two ways. One way is the approach we took to Vronsky's moral outlook (though we admitted that it falls short of being a coherent metaphysical adjustment). A chief reason for dismissing it was that it so strongly tends to create situational maladjustment for its practitioners: it regularly sets them up for frustration. One might try to say

the same about Christianity, namely, that a thorough metaphysical attunement on the Christian prescription (such as one finds among the saints and
martyrs) would set one greatly and frequently at odds, emotionally, with
the situations of life in this world. Jesus says to his disciples, "Because you
do not belong to the world, but I have chosen you out of the world –
therefore the world hates you" (John 15:19 *New Revised Standard*). Such an
interpretation might seem borne out by the very fact of martyrdom and its
frequency in the history of the church among those who take their
Christianity seriously. Think of the woes of the apostle Paul (2 Cor.
11:23–29), Joan of Arc, and Dietrich Bonhoeffer, most of which could
have been avoided by their having a less strictly Christian character. Like
Vronsky's lifestyle, Christianity tends to get you in trouble, and the reason
that most "Christians" don't get into trouble is that they are not
thoroughly metaphysically attuned in the distinctively Christian way.

The other way of explaining the disharmony between metaphysical and
circumstantial attunement lays the blame not on the metaphysics, but on
the state of the world: the world is somehow "out of joint" with the true
metaphysics. Christians explain the discrepancy by saying that the world is
"fallen"; it is a spoiled creation. So, it is not to be expected that people who
are correctly adjusted metaphysically will feel comfortable with a life "in
the world." Whether or not it seems plausible that the entire world has
been spoiled, it is very clear that some parts of it (say, Vronsky's social
world) are more spoiled, by the standards of some metaphysics (say,
Tolstoy's), than other parts (say, the social world of the Russian peasants).
If Levin's emotional discomforts, when he circulates in Vronsky's social
world, constitute no objection to the viability of Levin's metaphysical
attunement, then the fact of the apostle Paul's persecutions, stemming
from his metaphysical attunement to Jesus Christ, need constitute no
objection to Christianity.

But the parallel between the apostle's circumstantial "misattunement"
and Vronsky's is incomplete in a way that is crucial for our discussion.
Vronsky's misattunement shows up in negative emotions of frustration,
ennui, anger, and depression, while the apostle, in the midst of his persecutions, is full of joy, gratitude, and hope. The apostle's "misattunement"
is not emotional, but merely external, and so is not relevant to the question
of happiness. Somehow, the apostle's metaphysical attunement begets an
emotional attunement to his situation despite the outward conflicts.

This leads us to observe a relation between metaphysical attunement
and circumstantial attunement that we have not yet commented on. In
some moralities the metaphysics quite directly supplies materials for a

construal of life-situations, so that for persons practiced in the outlook, metaphysical and circumstantial attunements coalesce. A Christian example is the apostle's recommendation that Christians give thanks in all circumstances (1 Thess. 5:18), and it is probably a clue to how he maintained his cheer in some very trying situations (2 Cor. 6:1–10). What Christians see with the eyes of gratitude are not just the local circumstances, which in themselves may not provide reasons for gratitude; they give thanks for or rejoice in their salvation in Christ or the providential care of God, which are not exactly local circumstances, but ones that transcend all local circumstances and are part of the Christian's metaphysic. But the local circumstances are seen, in various ways, in the light of the transcendent one. For example, after being flogged for their witness to Jesus in Jerusalem, some disciples "rejoiced that they were considered worthy to suffer dishonor for the sake of the name [of Jesus]" (Acts 5:41 *New Revised Standard*). Or the rejoicing might have in view the improvement in character that the suffering is likely to occasion (see Jas. 1:2, Rom. 5:3–5). Or circumstances of misfortune might simply be construed, in terms of the consideration of God's favor in Christ, as merely temporary and unworthy to be compared with the glory that God has in store (Rom. 8:18). In such everyday use, it is as though the Christian metaphysics comes to determine the character of ordinary local circumstances. And for a wide variety of circumstances *such* metaphysical attunement forestalls the kind of circumstantial misattunement that erodes the happiness of many.

A similar coalescence of metaphysic and local circumstances is found in Stoics. In the passage that I quoted from Marcus Aurelius near the end of Chapter 2, he claims that the universe is reasonable and therefore good. Every state of affairs that arises in it conforms to the highest rational standards and thus contributes to this goodness. Stoic metaphysical adjustment consists in one's own rationality tracking emotionally the rationality of the universe, so that one appreciates from the heart the value (to the universe) of such events in one's own life as contracting tuberculosis or getting maimed. The local circumstances are construed as instantiating the metaphysical "circumstance" that the whole is beautiful and good because of the character of its parts.

Emotions such as Stoic joy in the harmonious beauty of the universe or Christian gratitude for the privilege of suffering as one's Lord suffered are especially constitutive of happiness as conceived respectively in these traditions because and insofar as they exhibit those features that we discussed in earlier sections of this chapter. First, they are hedonically positive, and though I have argued that hedonic positiveness is a defeasible happiness-making property and is not sufficient by itself, still it is an important element in happiness. Second, it seems possible (if rare) for a person to experience these emotions in a shallow way, perhaps as a sort of dreaming Christian or Stoic, or an esthete who plays with these world views. If they are shallow, they will not contribute much to Stoic or Christian happiness. Third, they satisfy the import and goodness conditions, since these positive emotions are about the most important and best things, according to these world views. And, last, though they are about some very local circumstances (the fact of this little band of persons being flogged on a given day, or the fact of this individual having tuberculosis), they have great scope because of the metaphysical terms in which those local circumstances are construed.

Objective and subjective happiness

I realize that the concept of happiness on which the present chapter has traded is not the one that first comes to modern English speakers' minds. Prior to reflection on cases like that of our self-stimulator, we are likely to feel confident that *happiness* is a thoroughly subjective concept – that, as one social scientist who researches happiness says, "If you feel happy, you are happy – that's all we mean by the term" (Jonathan Freedman, quoted in Myers 1992: 27). And even if we are impressed by our hesitancy to say that the self-stimulator is a happy person, we may still be inclined to say he is happy "in one sense of the word." This I admit. But I have commended a more classical and biblical concept of happiness, one that is far richer and more interesting than our modern subjective concept. Now I want briefly to consider why we should hold onto this classical concept – that is, why we should not give in to the advice some people have given me to divide the concept into two and to say that happiness is just life-satisfaction, however achieved, and the emotional wellbeing that I have been calling metaphysical attunement is something else (perhaps eudaimonia).

Since I am not denying the existence or propriety of the concept of happiness as mere feeling good or life-satisfaction, the question is whether I may be permitted the richer, more classical concept *in addition*. I take it that the objection to the two-condition concept that I have proposed is not that it is incoherent, but that it is inconvenient (confusing). And that objection is not really about the concept, but about the word, "happiness." So, the objection is that employing the word "happiness" for this two-condition concept is confusing, because we are so used to using "happiness" for the mere life-satisfaction concept. But the question whether the inconvenience is great enough to warrant dropping the word depends on whether it is really important to hold the two conditions together in the way the classical concept does, and, if this is important, whether any other word than "happiness" better captures the two-condition concept. If it is important to be able to hold the two conditions together in one concept, and if no better word than "happiness" can be found for this concept, then perhaps we had just better live with the supposed inconvenience. After all, people get used to conceptual innovations all the time, as well as learning older concepts that have fallen out of currency. In fact, many readers of Aristotle and the Bible have adapted well to the translation of "eudaimonia" as "happiness" and "makarios" as "happy."

Is it important that we have a concept for which both metaphysical and circumstantial attunement are conditions? A kind of importance that it has for my project has to do with the concept of a human virtue. A virtue, classically conceived, is an engrained personal disposition which is at the same time an actualization of essential human potentialities given the environmental conditions under which human beings live, *and* promotes life-satisfaction – that of the possessor of the virtue and that of persons with whom the possessor lives. Thus this concept of a virtue refers implicitly to both of the conditions of the classical concept of happiness.

This argument may make the importance of the classical concept of happiness seem to depend on a special, and perhaps arcane, intellectual project (for discussion, see de Sousa 2011: chap. 5). I do not think the project is arcane. The basically classical concept of a virtue is as strong a contender today as ever it was, and an understanding of the virtues is fundamental to an articulate consciousness of our humanity. And such consciousness is the business of every well-developed person.

Furthermore, as I argued early in this chapter, I do not think that we modern English speakers are entirely bereft of the classical concept of happiness. The mere satisfaction concept dominates, but I do not think it is entirely strange to us to say that the self-stimulator is both perfectly subjectively satisfied with his life, and yet not a happy person. I have not denied that the classical concept of happiness is weak among us; but neither do I think it has been completely lost (see Annas 2011: chap. 8). We have other words that are ambiguous as between a subjective and an objective reference. For example, we can say, "The color of the car is very important *to her*, but it isn't very important."

That we are still sensitive to the objective concept is suggested by the fact that many serious and reflective people do not want to be satisfied with their life under just any conditions. For example, they would not want to be "happy" under conditions of religious illusion, even if it were seamless. One way to express this concern is to say that for them the ideal of happiness includes objective wellbeing.

Conclusion

In the effort to move ahead into some definite, if general, account of the nature of happiness, I have blurred over many questions about what is right and wrong about configurations of character and emotional responses and patterns of responses to the situations of life. An adequate account of the good human life can be given only in the context of a fairly detailed discussion of the affective dimensions of particular virtues such as justice, courage, self-control, humility, generosity, gratitude, forgivingness, sense of duty, and sense of humor. The final chapter of this book moves one step closer, prolegomenon-wise, to such a discussion.

9

Diversity and connection among the virtues

Introduction

Aristotle comments that

> people who talk in generalities, saying that virtue is a good condition of the
> soul, or correct action, or something of the sort, are deceiving themselves. It
> is far better to enumerate the virtues, as Gorgias does, than to define them
> in this general way. (Aristotle 1998 [*Politics* 1.13])

We see examples of such efforts at generality in some modern accounts of
virtue, such as Kant's "Virtue is the strength of a human being's maxim in
obeying his duty" and "Virtue is . . . the moral strength of a *human being's*
will in fulfilling his duty, a moral *constraint* through his own lawgiving
reason, insofar as this constitutes itself an authority *executing* the law"
(Kant 1996a: 524, 533 [*Doctrine of Virtue* IX, 6:394; XIII, 6:405]; italics
original), and Julia Driver's recent effort (2001: chap 4) at a consequentialist reduction. I noted in Chapter 5 that Aristotle's own gesture in generality, his doctrine of the mean, is equally unenlightening (though I think it's
less distorting than these modern efforts) and, fortunately, little more than
a cover for his Gorgian enumeration, or, even better, his conceptual
explorations of particular virtues.

I argued in Chapter 1 that, rather than use the concept of a virtue to
contrive a new way of grounding ethical concepts in the hierarchical
manner of modern ethical theories, a virtue-oriented approach to ethics
should play to its strength by focusing on particular virtues and analyzing
them deeply enough to make the analysis yield insights that can contribute
to our wisdom. No such analysis of a particular virtue has appeared in this
book. Even the current chapter, which focuses on virtues, remains at too
abstract an altitude to have much potential, in itself, to express or induce
wisdom. We must reserve that task for another work. This final chapter is
part of the "prolegomena" to such work.

In earlier chapters I attempt to identify various roles that emotions play in aspects of the moral life – in moral knowledge, in our actions, our relationships, and our happiness or misery – and the current chapter continues that endeavor. Here I try to clarify some ways that emotions and emotion dispositions enter into the structure and expression of virtues. A correlated aim of this chapter, which broadens it beyond the focus on emotions, is to reinforce the anti-theoretical drift of Chapter 1 by stressing the structural diversity of the virtues. I think that efforts to give very general accounts of the nature of virtues can actually undermine our understanding of them; at a minimum such accounts tend to work against the richly detailed understanding of the moral life that a wisdom-seeking virtue-oriented study of ethics can yield. In this final chapter, I aim to do two things. I'll discuss, first, a variety of ways the virtues differ from one another; and, second, a variety of ways they depend on each other, thus producing something at least remotely like a "unity of the virtues."

These two aims belong together. One of the worthy motives of the modern theoretical impulse was to achieve something like completeness or adequacy of description of the moral life. To understand the moral life – and this is surely the chief legitimate aim of moral philosophy – is to grasp its various parts not only in depth of detail and difference, but also in connection with one another. Wisdom is a kind of understanding, and understanding is by nature (more or less) synoptic. The trouble with theories like those of Kant or Driver is that they achieve synopsis rather by reduction than by connection. Thus for Kant all virtue is a version of the sense of duty, and for Driver any disposition that dependably produces good consequences is a virtue. In their very different ways, each of these reductions distorts the concept of virtue and so renders the discussion of it less able to induce wisdom. For a discussion of virtues that is not reductive, see Swanton 2003.

I'll identify five ways that virtues differ from one another, without claiming that these are the only ones. I will discuss situational differences, differences in the way emotions figure in them, differences in psychological structure, differences in the way the concept of the virtue or some concept very close to it figures in characteristic deliberations, and differences due to peculiarities of moral tradition.

Kinds of differences among virtues

Situational differences

Try to imagine a person with one and only one virtue. She has exemplary justice, say, but completely lacks courage, kindness, humility, gratitude, and forgivingness. Or she is perfectly courageous, but has no justice or sense of duty or generosity. If we can conceive of such a person at all, we must admit that she is dysfunctional – not well adapted to live a human life. We may even doubt whether a person *can* have justice or courage without having any other virtues. And the same doubt arises for each of the virtues. This is not at all to deny that a single virtue may be a special or salient mark of a virtuous individual – as, say, forgivingness is of the mature Nelson Mandela, or compassion of Mother Teresa of Calcutta – or that a person might be courageous or industrious or humble without being very compassionate.

Why does it strain credulity to imagine a person with only one virtue? I propose that each of the virtues adapts us for some particular kind of situation that arises with some frequency in any normal human life. The person who had only justice or only courage would, thus, be well adapted to only one or some of the generic kinds of situations of a human life, and left unfitted for the several remaining ones. Virtues incline and enable us to respond in various ways to situations – perceiving, feeling, judging, deliberating, acting – and the different virtues adapt us for these functions in relation to different kinds of situations. Because virtues incline and enable us to function in a variety of ways, and not only to act or behave well, I will use the more general word "function" when talking about what the virtue inclines and enables us to do.

What counts as a situation here? I propose that a situation is a configuration of factors that is relevant to our perceiving, judging, deliberating, or acting. An example would be the one I used in Chapter 6 of the parent whose young child is walking on a wall too close to the edge. Here the situation includes (1) that the adult is the parent of the child; (2) that the child is out of immediate reach of the parent; (3) that the wall is high enough to make a fall from it nasty; (4) that the child is treading close to the edge of the wall. The parent responds to this situation with fear for the child, and this emotion exemplifies a virtue that we might call *parental solicitude* – a disposition to look out for the wellbeing of one's children. The situation of danger to one's child is one for which the virtue of parental solicitude adapts a person to function well. A situation need not have the kind of physical and sensory immediacy of the one just described. You can be in the situation of being now indebted to a great teacher when you were in high school years ago, or the situation of having a sick friend who is physically absent from you, or the situation of having money in the bank that you can conceivably do without while being committed to a cause that needs the money badly, or in the situation of being married to a certain man. For purposes of thinking about the virtues, situational elements can include mental events and states such as appetites, desires, and emotions, because some virtues are designed to enable us to handle or respond properly to such events and states. Let me now give a quick rundown of the situation types in which some typical virtues fit us to function properly.

Compassion adapts or fits a person to function well where another is suffering: to notice the suffering, to feel compassion, to judge well concerning how to help, and to act helpfully. This remark alerts us to an aspect of the import of "adapts" or "fits." This notion of adaptation is eudaimonistic rather than Darwinian. Fitness here is not the ability to survive and reproduce, but the ability and inclination to go on in the manner of an excellent human specimen. Thus it is an ethical fitness, and so is relative to an ethical notion of functioning well. Compassion is a way of living well even when it costs dearly in terms of Darwinian fitness or pleasure or bodily and mental health. (Of course, if one's health deteriorates too much as a result of one's compassion, one can be disabled for compassion.) Adaptation of persons to situations in this sense is not only to the direct or immediate benefit of the adapted person, but also to the benefit of others with whom he or she has to do. The help that compassion motivates is directly to the benefit of the sufferer, and indirectly to the benefit of the compassionate person himself. It benefits him in that, if for no other reason, it makes him a better specimen of humanity.

Justice – the disposition to judge and feel and act justly adapts us to situations in which goods are to be distributed, rewards and punishments meted out, or payment made or received (trade). Again, when we say that justice adapts us to such situations, we are assuming that adaptation encompasses benefiting one's community as well as oneself, as we are assuming for most, if not all, of the virtues that follow. *Forgivingness* adapts us to situations in which some moral offense has been perpetrated against us or persons very closely associated with us, by someone with whom we need to interact benignly or with whom (or with whose memory) we will live better if we do.

Courage adapts us to act effectively in situations of threat and situations in which we have fear that would, without the virtuous functioning, make us less able to act appropriately. Other virtues that belong to the class that I call "virtues of will power" are *patience, perseverance, longsuffering,* and *self-control.* The first three of these adapt us to situations that require extended time, either in waiting (patience) or in accomplishing something (perseverance), or simply in enduring (longsuffering). Self-control adapts us to a variety of situations that tend to evoke untoward emotions like anger and impatience, and appetites like those for food, drink, and sex. Self-control is the model for at least an aspect of courage, patience, and perseverance, because the situations to which these adapt us are ones that evoke emotions and urges that are, at least in context, untoward. If we take *temperance* to have reference only to bodily appetites, as Aristotle does, then it adapts us to situations in which objects of such appetites are presented to us. They may be presented in imagination; and here the imagination is subject to the virtue, so that what is apprehended as being presented depends to this extent on the state of our character.

Not all *sense of humor* is a virtue. Some is even vicious. But when it is a virtue, the sense of humor adapts the agent rightly to see situations that present some incongruity that is of (usually negative) moral interest, yet without being tragic. *Generosity* adapts a person to situations in which he or she is in a position to give, as a gift, something of his own that will be of use, pleasure, or other benefit to another; while *gratitude* adapts one to situations in which one receives such a gift from another.

A *sense of duty* adapts an agent to situations in which he lacks the intrinsic motivation to perform actions that some of the other virtues (justice, generosity, and compassion, for example) would provide intrinsic motivation for. The sense of duty, like the virtues of will power, illustrates that the "situation" to which a virtue can adapt us is sometimes internal to the agent, or at any rate has an internal dimension. The difference is that the sense of duty makes up for a missing or weak attraction to the good, whereas the virtues of will power mostly manage existing but untoward attractions (e.g., lust) and repulsions (e.g., fear). *Humility* enables the agent to function well in situations that invite responses characteristic of vanity, arrogance, snobbery, conceit, and the like.

Practical wisdom adapts a person to situations that require deliberation or moral perception from the agent – that is, to all the other situation types. This remark alerts us to the fact that the kinds of situations are not only disparate, but differentially distributed. Some of them occur every day in a normal human life, while others occur more rarely. Other virtues adapt us to "situations" that are constant states of our universe. If Christians are right about the nature of God, then what we call *faith* is a virtue that adapts us to the "situation" of God's existence, his having a certain nature and performing and having performed certain actions. If Christian doctrine is true, then not to have faith is to be maladapted to the universe in a very fundamental way.

This remark alerts us to the fact that a scene from life may exemplify situations of more than one type. For example, a situation can be such as to call for faith, courage, justice, and generosity – because, in addition to the relevant constant state of the universe, it contains a threat that might deter right action, it calls for a distribution of goods or allotment of reward or punishment, and such distribution can be effected by the agent's giving a "gift," something good that he does not owe to the recipient. (That the recipient is owed the good does not imply that any particular agent owes him the good.)

The traits by which we become able and disposed to respond appropriately to this array of situation types (and, no doubt, others) are virtues because these situations are typical and generic for human beings, in virtually any human community, and the particular patterns of response associated with each trait are thought to be appropriate or excellent, given what human beings are. Such situation types are foci of the virtues because they afford opportunities for excellent human functioning as well as improper functioning. To be a good human being is to be ready for such situations. However, as the above reference to faith suggests, some of the situation types are controversial, being challengeable on the basis of one or another possible metaphysical view.

The strand of personality psychology called "situationism" (see Doris 2002, Alfano 2013; for evaluation, see Adams 2006, Russell 2009, and Snow 2009) holds that character-traits (including, perhaps especially, virtues) are greatly overrated as determinants of behavior, and that we should look first to situational factors rather than to character traits as explaining human behavior. A variety of empirical studies and historical cases seem to show a woeful degree of behavioral inconsistency among people to whom common sense attributes traits. These results lead some situationists to call into question the existence of such traits and the internal coherence of personality. According to Doris, classical virtue theorists like Aristotle held that virtues are robust and global traits. A trait is "robust," according to situationists, if it strongly predicts behavior of a type to which the trait disposes an individual (say, compassionate actions to a compassionate person, just actions to a person with a virtue of justice, etc.), where "strongly" entails that the person will exhibit such behavior across a rather wide variety of trait-proper situations. And personality satisfies "globalist" requirements if it is made up of a non-conflicting set of robust traits. Situationists also appear to assume, contrary to Plato and Aristotle, and most of the classical tradition, that ethicists who focus on the virtues are committed to the view that robust and globalist virtues are very widespread in the human population. Situationism of the Doris variety is the view that, while there may be some modest traits, they are not robust; situational variables other than the kinds I have identified are much more important in the explanation of behavior than traits. And it holds that what traits people do have do not amount to a coherent set. Such situationists emphasize observable behavior to the neglect, one may think, of subjects' internal processes of motivation, understanding, and evaluation of situations (Snow 2009); and perhaps they also oversimplify the variety of traits that go to make up the moral personality and the subtle situational interactions among the traits. They also perhaps underestimate the usefulness of the concept of *akrasia* in explaining inconsistent behavior without giving up on the idea of traits. (For further discussion, see Roberts 2007.) Let me illustrate some of the subtle interaction of such factors by looking at chapter 16 of Alan Paton's (2003) *Cry, the Beloved Country*.

Steven Kumalo is a good man, but not perfect. He is a conscientious pastor in the Anglican Church, but the narrator tells us that he was once sorely tempted to commit adultery with one of his parishioners. He is generally humble, but has occasional moments of vain self-display. He is gentle and truthful, but in one episode he lies to his brother out of a motive of revenge. He is compassionate, but is capable of moments of cruelty, followed by repentance and shame. These descriptions suggest that Kumalo's virtues fall short of being "robust." In chapter 16 he goes to visit the girl who is pregnant by his son Absolom, who has strayed from the strait ways of his village and his family under the influence of Johannesburg, and now has murdered a white man. Steven's mission is one of justice and benevolence in the midst of his personal distress: he wants to offer the wayward girl adoption, as the mother of his grandchild, into the family where she can live well and her child can be reared properly. He realizes that his son may well be condemned to death, leaving the child fatherless and the girl to stray into more irregular liaisons and a further disastrous life, all of which is likely to be disastrous for his grandchild. So, he goes to offer her marriage to his son and a permanent home in his village.

The situation in which Kumalo is acting is unique in his life. Of course, it resembles situations he has dealt with before, but it is extraordinary for its degree of impact on his personal interests and in its special details. Indeed, the whole experience of Johannesburg is very foreign to his habits of action, judgment, and feeling. He is outside his element, so his virtues are under situational strain. After telling the girl the shocking news of her "husband's" action and imprisonment, he asks whether she wants to marry Absolom. She is confused and does not know how to answer, but becomes enthusiastic when she realizes that Kumalo is offering to provide a home for her. He warns her that the place he is proposing is liable to be boring compared with Johannesburg, and asks about her family background. Her parents quarreled and her father finally left in disgust about his wife's drinking; because the girl "could not understand" the man who replaced her father, she left home. To live alone? No, to live with her first "husband." How many have there been? Three. And what happened to the first two? They were "caught."

– And now the third is caught also.

He stood up, and a wish to hurt her came into him. Although he knew it was not seemly, he yielded to it, and he said to her, yes, your third is caught also, but now it is for murder. Have you had a murderer before?

He took a step toward her, and she shrank away on the box, crying, no, no. And he, fearing that those outside might overhear, spoke more quietly to her and told her not to be afraid, and took a step backwards. But no sooner had she recovered than he wished to hurt her again. And he said to her, will you now take a fourth husband? And desperately she said, No, no, I want no husband any more.

And a wild thought came to Kumalo in his wild and cruel mood.

– Not even, he asked, if I desired you?

– You, she said, and shrank from him again.

– Yes, I, he said.

She looked round and about her, as one that was trapped. No, no, she said, it would not be right.

– Was it right before?

– No, it was not right.

– Then would you be willing?

She laughed nervously, and looked about her, and picked strips of wood from the box. But she felt his eyes upon her, and she said in a low voice, I could be willing.

He sat down and covered his face with his hands; and she, seeing him, fell to sobbing, a creature shamed and tormented. And he, seeing her, and the frailty of her thin body, was ashamed also, but for his cruelty, not for her compliance.

He went over to her and said, how old are you, my child?

– I do not know, she sobbed, but I think I am sixteen.

And the deep pity welled up in him, and he put his hand on her head. And whether it was the priestly touch, or whether the deep pity flowed into the fingers and the palm, or whether it was some other reason – but the sobbing was quietened, and he could feel the head quiet under his hand. And he lifted her hands with his other, and felt the scars of her meaningless duties about this forlorn house.

– I am sorry, he said. I am ashamed that I asked you such a question.

– I did not know what to say, she said.

– I knew that you would not know. That is why I am ashamed. Tell me, do you truly wish to marry my son? (Alan Paton, *Cry, the Beloved Country*, pp. 103–04)

The episode recounted in this excerpt is an "outlier" for Steven, an unfamiliar and stressful situation in which to exhibit his moral traits. And we see "inconsistency" in his behavior. At one moment he is cruel and imperious, and almost immediately he turns compassionate and contrite. If we looked only at his behavior, and did not have the cognitive-motivational account that is supplied by the novel's narrative context, we might find him puzzling and think that in fact no traits lie in the background. But if we read the story with even minimal sensitivity, we have no trouble understanding the behavior in terms of Kumalo's virtues and the gaps in his virtues. And the way we do so is to track his behavior as a set of responses to the changing situation as he experiences it emotionally. This is not to say that he himself would anticipate his responses to this situation; he not only does not know exactly what situation he is getting into, like most of us he has an imperfect understanding of his dispositional liabilities. He surprises and disappoints himself. Were he to find himself in a relevantly similar situation in the future, he might display less akrasia; but then again, he might not.

He wouldn't be in the situation at all were it not for his justice towards the girl and her child, as supported by his benevolence. He is on a mission of mercy and justice, and one that, because of the pain and uncertainty he can anticipate, requires courage. And the anger he displays towards the girl, which makes him want to hurt her, is a morally admirable distress at the sordidness of her history and his son's part in it. This virtuous concern, therefore, is a causal factor in the background of his cruelty. His anger is, of course, not a perfectly wise emotion, given that she is a mere child, caught in a web of degradation and injustice for which she is not personally responsible. As the situation develops – her response to his desperate lecherous proposal and his shamed response to her shame and distress – he sees this clearly and his anger is replaced with compassion and a return to his original mission of kindness and justice. We can well imagine a less virtuous, more narcissistic man turning back to the justice project without the intervening repentance, or without, at any rate, the expression of penitence that contributes to her response of trust.

An episode like this may seem to bespeak a dominance of situational determinants over trait determinants of behavior. It does bespeak a man who in the everyday context of his village life, where the situations he encounters are more uniform and he is better habituated to them, would display much more consistent behavior. But because of the novel's partially internal look at the mind of the character, it can show how, even in the extreme situations of Kumalo's life crisis, situation and traits work together to explain behavior.

Differences in the ways emotions figure in the virtues

This book follows in the long tradition of Plato and Aristotle, the Stoics, Thomas Aquinas, Adam Smith, David Hume, and Søren Kierkegaard, of giving major importance, in the contemplation of virtues, to the idea of an emotion (passion, sentiment). Thus I have devoted the whole of a previous volume to the nature of the emotions, and most of the present one to considering the various ways they can have broadly moral properties. A volume that is to follow this one will contemplate in much greater detail and intensity a variety of major virtues, with a primary focus on emotions' involvement in them. Let me now give a quick accounting of the various ways emotions can figure in the virtues.

Justice is a concern for justice as an attribute of situations, human relationships, institutions, and persons (I call this "objective justice" to distinguish it from the virtue). As such a concern, the virtue is a disposition to the whole range of emotions that can be based on the concern – joy, hope, gratitude, anger, indignation, guilt, sorrow, admiration, emulation, etc. – depending on the situational vicissitudes of the thing whose attribute of objective justice or injustice is in question. Thus when an injustice is corrected, the just person will be glad, and maybe grateful to those who had a hand in the correction, and may admire somebody whose virtue was particularly in evidence in bringing about the correction.

Compassion the virtue is a disposition to feel compassion the emotion and to act on it. Thus it appears that the virtue gets its name from the emotion. But the emotion appears to be based on a concern for the wellbeing of members of whatever group of persons or other beings the virtue inclines one to feel compassion for. This concern is called benevolence. So, compassion is really a kind of benevolence. Or is it *simply* benevolence? Compassion, as benevolence, would then have the same structure as justice, and be a disposition to a whole range of emotions, not just the one emotion (type) of compassion. Out of concern for the sufferer's wellbeing, the compassionate person may feel disappointed if the sufferer refuses ready help, or regretful that circumstances prevented his relief from suffering, or joyful at seeing his suffering relieved by others. And if suffering were not even in the picture, the compassionate person might take pleasure in contemplating somebody's health and happiness. But it seems odd, in that case, for us to attribute the virtue of compassion, rather than just to say that the person is kind or benevolent. After all, compassion fits its possessor for situations in which there is suffering. I'll return to this question at the end of this section.

Forgivingness is a disposition to give up or not feel anger towards persons who deserve one's anger, and to do so in one or more of a particular range of *ways* of giving up or not feeling it. These ways distinguish forgivingness from other strategies of anger-management or extirpation, such as condoning the wrong, satisfying the anger, and Stoic strategies. The primary emotion involved in forgiveness is anger (some say resentment, which is a species of anger); but the motivation for forgiveness, when it's an action, may be benevolence or similar concerns (also, it may be a sense of duty). This virtue, then, involves emotion quite differently from justice and compassion.

Humility is a disposition *not* to have the emotions characteristic of vanity, arrogance, conceit, egotism, hyper-autonomy, grandiosity, pretentiousness, snobbishness, impertinence (presumption), haughtiness, self-righteousness, domination, selfish ambition, and self-complacency (see Roberts and Wood 2007). Each of these vices involves a concern-laden self-understanding that generates a variety of emotions that will be more absent in the humble person than in the unhumble, and ideally absent altogether. Unlike courage and other self-control virtues, humility paradigmatically does not involve any active mastery of emotion; it is instead a disposition not to feel or otherwise have the kinds of emotion in question. But not just any absence of the interests and thought patterns characteristic of these vices is humility; just as forgivingness involves a *way* that anger is put away or fails to arise, humility presupposes *some* rather intense concern or "ruling passion" (in the most virtuous case some other virtue like justice or compassion or love of truth) that overrules the concerns of vicious pride. It is thus indirectly or incidentally a disposition to a range of emotions in something like the way justice is. Thus the humble person is emotionally "blind" to aspects of situations that will be quite obvious and perceptible to the vain or dominating person.

Courage is paradigmatically a disposition to manage one's fear in the interest of some end, though the "management" may be so habitual as to be inexplicit; courage may also, in some cases, be fearlessness (but it can't be a generalized fearlessness), and a thrilling at threats may be an ingredient in it. Patience is a disposition to manage the emotion of impatience, though here too the management may not be explicit; patience is sometimes attributable in the absence of a disposition to impatience. Perseverance is a disposition to manage emotions that result from delays, setbacks, extensions, and sheer duration of projects and / or to be little subject to such emotions; some of the emotions in question are disappoint-ment, frustration, boredom, and despair. More positively, perseverance can be associated with hopefulness. Self-control, as its name may suggest, is more purely a self-management virtue than the others, and has more general application to untoward emotions (anger, joy, fear, despair, com-passion – any emotion that can be inappropriate in a circumstance yet insistent enough to require management) as well as appetites and desires: thus appetites for sex, food, and drink; the kinds of appetites characteristic of addictions; anger and envy, among the emotions; and urges to buy things and dominate conversations, among the desires.

A sense of humor is a disposition to be amused by what is comical; thus amusement is the (non-standard) "emotion" to which this virtue is a disposition. But in conformity with Aristotle's idea that virtue consists in the disposition to feel emotions that are "right" in various ways, a virtuous sense of humor is not just a strong disposition to be amused, but a disposition to be amused *properly* – or better, *excellently*, and that is to say, to perceive *significant* incongruities for what they are. Such amuse-ment expresses the virtue; but it does not express it in the way that compassion expresses compassion or anger at injustices can express justice, because it bears a different relationship with concerns (amusement, as an emotion-like state, is not a concern-based construal). Relatedly, neither amusement nor the sense of humor motivates action characteristic of the virtue in the way that the other emotions motivate actions characteristic of the virtues they express.

Generosity has a balanced double concern structure: first, a concern for the wellbeing of persons other than oneself, and second, a concern for the goods that can be given to those persons (both *as* goods-that-can-be-given and as goods-for-oneself). As concerns in this balanced structure, generos-ity is a disposition to a variety of emotions. Gratitude is a disposition to feel the emotion of gratitude upon receiving gifts. It has an analogous double-concern structure (for the giver and for the gift received) that co-ordinates in the virtuous personality with that of generosity, so that generosity is a "criterion" for gratitude and gratitude a "criterion" for generosity. A gratitude that is not generous in attributing good motives to the benefactor falls short of the best gratitude, and a generosity that refuses to acknowledge its indebtedness to the grace of others or of others to its own grace falls short of the best generosity.

The sense of duty is a concern to do one's duty, which is an indirect concern to do the actions characteristic of virtues such as compassion, justice, generosity, truthfulness, and other "passional" virtues (that is, virtues that are concerns or based in concerns). As a concern to do one's duty, the sense of duty is a disposition to such emotions as joyful relief (when one finds that one has done one's duty, especially in a difficult situation), and guilt or shame (when one fails conspicuously to do one's duty), and anxiety (when one both wants to do one's duty and strongly wants not to do that thing that happens to be one's duty). Emotions associated with the sense of duty are reflexive: joy or pride that I did my duty, anxiety that I may not do my duty, sadness, shame, regret or guilt that I failed to do my duty. The sense of duty can also be a concern to feel certain emotions, for example, the concern to feel the Christian emotion of *agape* for one's neighbor or for God.

Practical wisdom is the disposition to proper judgment and perception that is entailed by the other virtues, both individually and in conjunction. As we saw in Chapter 3, these moral epistemic powers depend on emotions. Thus any and all the emotions expressive of the virtues will be characteristic of practical wisdom, and they will be one of the important sources of its deliberations and judgments. Full-blown practical wisdom requires a wide range of emotional sensitivities, in a modulated (flexibly adjustable) balance.

The previous section gave a quick run-down of the situation types for which various virtues fit their possessors. The reader will remember that my account of emotions makes their "objects" normally not things, but situations. Emotions are concern-based *construals*: perceptual *constructions* of *com*plex situations in various ways, out of the elements that the situations are taken to involve. This is a major connection, then, between these two kinds of differences – the virtues differ according to the kind of human situation for which they fit their possessor, and the emotions grasp the evaluative significance of the situations they are about. Compassion is a particularly clear example of this intersection: the virtue of compassion fits the subject to address situations that contain sufferers, and the emotion of compassion is the construal of the situation in terms of a sufferer in need of succor. Here we have the answer to the question I raised above: given that compassion as a virtue is really a disposition to a *range* of diverse types of emotion, why does the virtue take its name from compassion in particular among these emotions? The answer is that the kind of situation the virtue especially applies to is exactly the kind that this particular emotion lights up and motivates the subject to assuage.

Let me add a general remark about the relation between emotions and virtues, one that is implicit in the above rundown. I just referred to emotions that are "expressive of the virtues." Emotions connect to virtues in two broad ways. Some emotions *express* the virtues, while others are *managed, dispelled* or *missed out* by the virtues. Thus anger at injustices may express the virtue of justice, regret can express generosity, and, of course, gratitude expresses gratitude and compassion compassion. In contrast, while anger is related to self-control, it would be wildly wrong to say that anger expresses self-control. Fear is the emotion that courage most characteristically has to do with, and impatience is the emotion that patience most has to do with, but fear does not express courage, nor does impatience express patience (much less does vain self-exultation express humility). In these last cases, the virtue is, in one way or another (and there are several possibilities here), opposed to the emotion; but in the former cases it is harmonious with it. That emotions figure in the virtues in these two broad kinds of ways corresponds to the fact that emotions can be either good or bad morally, either intrinsically or pragmatically (see Chapter 2).

Structural differences

Virtues also differ from one another in salient psychological and conceptual structures that are related to their situation-specificity and their emotional differences. The schema that I will offer here, like any other general schema for virtues, is an invention consequent on observation. It is not the only possible, perhaps not even the best, way of dividing up the territory. I will note three pairs of "opposite" properties according to which virtues can be categorized. My aim is not to make a hard and fast categorization, for, as we will see, virtues can fall in more than one of the offered categories, because they can have or lack more than one of the properties defining the class. Also the "same" property can vary a little from case to case. Still, I think the categorization will be instructive, as it involves identifying properties of virtues.

Long ago, I distinguished *passional virtues* from *virtues of will power* (Roberts 1984). The idea is that some virtues are based on an essential "passion" – that is, a concern for a definite type of thing. For example, justice as a personal virtue is based on a concern for just states of affairs, actions, institutions, people, and so forth; compassion is based on a concern for the wellbeing of people (and of whatever other kind of beings the virtue is a disposition to feel compassion for); the generous person is concerned for the wellbeing and pleasure of others; the sense of duty is the concern to conform to the dictates of duty; and so forth. People who lack the concerns requisite for these virtues cannot have the virtues in question. The virtues of will power, by contrast, are not based on any particular type of concern or passion, though actions exemplifying them require some motivation or other. For example, a self-controlled person has to have *some* motivation for exercising self-control, but the virtue itself does not involve any particular kind of motivation. A person may control his emotions or appetites out of a sense of justice or compassion, or he may control them out of a desire for reputation or monetary gain or pleasure or self-preservation. I argue that the same is true of such virtues as courage and perseverance. Earlier I argued that the special mark of the virtues of will power is that they are self-management skills. The self-controlled person exemplifies this virtue by practicing a skill of managing his anger, lust, envy, appetite for food, or whatever.

We can also distinguish *detachment virtues* from *virtues of immediacy*. The detachment virtues are personal excellences that involve, in some salient way, an ability to "stand back" or "detach" or "divide" oneself from some feature of oneself. The way the detachment works varies quite a bit among the virtues in this class. Practical wisdom, for example, involves the ability to assess one's own immediate perceptions, emotions, and judgment-impulses from a point of view differing from those immediacies. This is not the only way that practical wisdom makes judgments, however, because there is much in the judgment of practical wisdom that is immediate: the person of practical wisdom has the power to perceive and judge, relatively unre-flectively, the truth about practical situations. Practical wisdom's power of detachment works through reflection and deliberation. A sense of humor presupposes a power of detachment, as does a sense of duty, though these differ from one another in how they accomplish the detachment. It is not hard to see that the virtues of will power, to the extent that they are self-management skills, depend on powers of detachment and therefore on some of these other virtues.

The virtues of immediacy, by contrast, are characterized by an "attached" response-disposition. As a passion for justice, the virtue of justice is not a power of detachment (it is precisely an attachment to, or love of, justice), though justice could not operate in an individual who had no practical wisdom, and a sense of humor and a sense of duty are also a big help. Other virtues of attachment are compassion and generosity, though generosity also involves detachment from whatever one gives away.

Self-control of appetites is a detachment virtue and thus bears a very different relation to appetites than does temperance of appetites; temperance involves neither self-transcendence nor active control since proper appetite is characteristic of it. It seems that there should be emotional analogs of temperance, that is, virtues that consist in a disposition to well-tempered emotions – emotions that quite spontaneously take the right object for the right reason in the right degree of intensity and duration, etc. Aristotle's virtues of mildness (*praotês*) and courage (*andreia*) are virtues of "temperate emotion" on this model. I see no reason why we shouldn't talk analogously of temperate hope, temperate regret, temperate embarrassment, temperate admiration, and so forth, since in all such cases it is possible for the emotion to get its object "right" in the various requisite ways, and some people conceivably develop a smooth and deep disposition to have such emotion. In regard to their psychological structure, all such virtues would stand in contrast with their self-control analogs.

A third important contrast is that between the *virtues of requirement* and the *virtues of grace*. The sense of duty is perhaps the paradigm virtue of requirement, given that it is a disposition to do what is required, *as required*. To act from a sense of duty is to act on the consideration that the action is required. Other virtues of requirement are justice and truthfulness. Actions most characteristic of these virtues are done not from a sense of duty, but from a concern for justice and truth; yet justice and truth are kinds of things that are required, and the just person understands that they are. Payment of a strict debt (a debt of justice), for example, is not optional, not a matter of choice as a gift is, but is required. Yet one can perform it gladly, and thus in a sense not *as* required; one heartily *wants* justice to be done, so that no thought to the effect that *this is something I MUST do* enters in. Truth is similarly required in situations fitting that virtue (this is not to say that the truthful person is always required to tell the truth). If justice, truthfulness, and the sense of duty are dominated by the concept of *requirement*, the virtues of generosity, gratitude, forgivingness, and compassion are dominated by the concept of a *free gift*. Gifts are not required, nor are thanks in response to them; or, rather, when the generous person is acting most characteristically of generosity, she does not give her gift as required, but as "free" from requirement, either as requiring that she give what she gives, or as requiring acknowledgment or a return from the gift's recipient. If the grateful person treats his responsive "return" for a gift as strictly required, then his attitude is not most characteristic of gratitude. Something similar can be said of forgivingness and compassion.

Differences in how reasons figure in deliberation and emotion

Some virtues supply reasons for acting and feeling. For example, the just person, being concerned that justice be done, acts for the sake of justice when he acts justly. He acts to bring about or preserve justice in the situations and institutions of his world, and is glad to see injustices rectified and sorry to see them prevail. If asked, why did you do that? he'll say things like, "It would have been unfair to do otherwise" or "I promised to do so" or "He was owed an explanation" or "It was only fair that the family should know the state of the evidence against him." The same family of motivation explanations will be relevant in case the just person is asked why he feels as he does about an action or event or institution that exemplifies justice or injustice: "You simply don't make an accusation like that and then refuse to back it up" or "They had a right to equal pay!" or "Because Sue treated Melody so unfairly."

Compassion, truthfulness, and generosity are other virtues that supply reasons for action and emotion because their very structure involves caring about some kind of thing: about the relief of suffering, about the truth, or about the wellbeing of others. Why did the compassionate person volunteer for Hospice? – to ease the suffering of the dying and their caretakers. (Contrast: to keep himself from being bored in retirement.) Why did the truthful scientist announce the failure of his long-held and hard-won hypothesis about the causation of the tides? Because he cared more about truth than about the comforts of intellectual success. (Contrast: because he was going to be found out by his colleagues anyway, and wanted to avoid embarrassment.) Why did the generous person give such a large proportion of her wealth to charities? Because she believed in the good the charities were doing. (Contrast: to get her name on published donor lists.)

So, some virtues carry their characteristic reasons within them, so to speak. It is plausible to think that for such virtues the reasons characteristic of them are a major constitutive or individuating factor. Justice differs from generosity and compassion and truthfulness by way of its distinctive reasons; and so on for each of the virtues of this kind. We might even say that such virtues are defined by their characteristic reasons.

Other virtues are individuated not by characteristic reasons, but by the kinds of circumstances that call for them (taking "circumstances" in a broad sense that includes "internal" or psychological factors). Some virtues belonging to this class are perseverance, patience, courage, and self-control. Daniel Russell (2009: chap. 6) apparently thinks that virtues across the board are individuated by their characteristic reasons. Let's test this idea by considering courage. If I am right, courage will not be individuated by characteristic reasons, because it doesn't have characteristic reasons. When a person acts courageously, he certainly acts for a reason, but the reason will not be characteristic of courage.

Russell cites reasons for courage offered by Rosalind Hursthouse: "[1] 'I could probably save him if I climbed up there,' [2] 'Someone had to volunteer,' [3] 'One can't give in to tyrants,' [4] 'They'll suffer if I don't get to them'" (Russell 2009: 183–84). These are indeed plausible responses to the question, "Why did you act as you did?" where the action was courageous. But I think these reasons derive from virtues other than courage, for example, from compassion [1, 4], generosity [2], and justice [3]. We would need a little more context to determine more precisely what the motive was in each of the cases. As courageous, all of these actions have something in common, but it isn't the motive. It is instead that the situations that give rise to these reasons characteristic of compassion, generosity, and justice are *also threatening*, so that courage is needed to perform them. So, they are situations that call for two different virtues: compassion and courage, generosity and courage, or justice and courage.

In response to this suggestion, Russell might say that in these situations the reason deriving from the other virtue provides also reason not to let oneself be deterred by fear (or by the threat). That seems true, but it would also be an admission that the fundamental reason derives not from courage but from one of the motivational virtues. For example, the reason one faces the threat in [1] is a compassion-style reason. But it seems to me that courageous actions need not be motivated virtuously at all. Another "reason for courage" might be, "If I don't, my $10,000 guitar will burn up" or "If I don't, we'll never pull off this robbery." So, perhaps non-virtuous and even vicious reasons can also be reasons for courageous action. My thesis is not that courageous actions don't have reasons, but that the reasons for courageous actions are not distinctive of the virtue of courage. They do not individuate it. They do have something in common, though: they are all reasons not to be deterred by threatening circumstances. But that is *all* they have in common: the fact that they are strong enough to precipitate action despite threats. What individuates courage is not any particular kind of motive, but the kind of circumstance in which it fits an agent to act. And what makes courage a virtue is not that it aims at some good end, but that it broadens the fitness of an agent to act (for whatever end). Analogous accounts will individuate perseverance, patience, and self-control.

Differences in degrees of maturity

Although we must endorse a distinction between virtues and mere simulacra, I will argue that the distinction is not precise. If something of a continuum separates these extremes, some traits that occupy positions towards the virtue end will be virtues, albeit imperfect ones, and some that occupy positions towards the simulacrum end will be simulacra, but no definite rule will mark the transition from the one area to the other.

Mark Alfano (2013) discusses a study by Richard Miller, Philip Brickman, and Diana Bolen (1975) that compares the effectiveness of exhortation with that of virtue labeling in fostering tidy behavior in fifth graders. One group were asked repeatedly to keep their classroom tidy; the other were falsely complimented repeatedly and in various ways for being unusually tidy. "After a brief increase in tidiness, the exhortation group settled back into its old routine, but the labeling group exhibited higher levels of tidiness over an extended period" (178). Alfano mentions other studies that confirm the greater effectiveness of virtue labeling as compared with exhortation in bringing about reliable behavior characteristic of virtue, and says that the favored explanation of the effect is by way of self-concept. On this explanation, the fifth graders behaved tidily because they came to think of themselves as tidy. It would be wrong, according to Alfano, to attribute the *virtue* of tidiness to them, since thinking oneself tidy is not a reason characteristic of the virtue of tidiness. The truly tidy person is one who appreciates the value of tidiness. Thus he or she acts for reasons such as *a tidy room is more pleasant* or *a tidy room allows for more efficient work*. But on the self-concept explanation of the virtue labeling effect, the fifth graders' reason for their tidying actions was something like *I am tidy* or *the teacher says I'm tidy*, and these are not reasons characteristic of the virtue. Alfano concludes that since the labeling effect is virtue-like, but not properly virtue, we may call it "factitious virtue," that is, virtue that is both artificial (got up) and not the real thing.

However, it seems to me that, granting that virtue labeling works by way of self-concept (which is plausible), we still need reasons to explain the subjects' actions. On Alfano's explanation of the results, if the experimenters had gone on to ask the subjects *why* they were tidying up, they would have said "I'm tidy" or "The teacher says we're tidy." But if the subjects did give such an odd response, the obvious next question would be, "Yes, but how does your being tidy supply a reason for tidying up?" One kind of answer would be that the students like the approval they get for being tidy and want more of it, or that they are afraid of losing the teacher's approval if they don't deliver on the attribution. Students who acted only on this kind of reason would clearly not be exhibiting the virtue, no matter how consistent their tidying behavior, and I don't think we would be inclined to attribute even factitious virtue to them. They would be people of whom Aristotle says that they do virtuous deeds, but not as the virtuous person would do them (*Nicomachean Ethics* 2.4).

Here is another possibility. People pick up pretty early in life what Wittgenstein might call the deep grammar of virtue-concepts. An important part of understanding a virtue-concept is a grasp of the reasons a person must be sensitive to if he possesses the virtue in question. (As per the previous section, this will hold for only some virtues.) I would not be surprised to find out that fifth graders know that the virtue-specific reason for tidy action is an appreciation of tidy rooms for their appeal and utility. If so, then a fifth grader who construes herself as tidy will construe herself also as appreciating tidy rooms for their appeal and utility. So, if the experimenter asks her why she's been so tidy lately, she might say, "Tidy rooms are more pleasant and better places to work." Alfano has pointed out to me that such a self-attribution of a reason for acting, consequent on a self-construal as a tidy person, might be a confabulation. Maybe the truth is that self-construal as tidy directly caused the subject to emit tidy behavior, and she makes up something in response to the request for a motive. Or maybe she really wanted the teacher's approval, and made up the virtue-specific reason either to cover up her real reason or without knowing what her real reason was.

Yes, confabulation is a distinct possibility. But it's not the only one. Another, which may or may not rule out confabulation in any particular case, is what we might call Stanislavskian role-playing (see Stanislavski 1936). On this scenario, the agent, upon having the virtue attributed to him and knowing the motivational grammar of the virtue-concept, takes on the role of the tidy person, not exactly as his own but by way of "putting it on" in the manner of a Stanislavskian method actor. But in taking on the role he also takes on the emotions and other motives characteristic of the role that he's playing. He actually feels the emotions and desires of the person he's portraying. When in the role, he has a heartfelt appreciation of tidy rooms. In one way, these emotions and desires are not his; they belong to the role he's playing. But, in another way, they are his: this person differs starkly from someone who is simply confabulating. Of course, he might be confabulating and, unbeknownst to himself, playing a role à la Stanislavski. Now it seems to me that if the agent is feeling the reason in this way, then he is accessing a sensitivity that is *actually in himself*, even though he's currently getting it up by playing the role. The virtue attribution has triggered the role-playing, which is "natural" to him in the sense that he can get into the role in virtue of sensitivities that exist (perhaps dormantly) in him. Here, it seems to me, we have adequate reason for talking about factitious virtue. The agent is not virtuous – after all, his behavior and feelings are the product of role-playing – but there is something virtuous about him, that would not have manifested itself without the artifice of the virtue-attribution. And his actions qualify as virtuous both by what they effect (a tidy room) and by the character of their motivation (the appreciation of a tidy room).

The difference between such virtue as I have just described and real, mature virtue will be the depth of the ingress of the concern and understanding characteristic of the virtue. The maturely tidy person will not be playing a role when he behaves tidily; he will be "playing himself" (more or less). He will not need to "put on" tidiness because *he* will be tidy. I wouldn't be surprised to find out that most people's virtue – to the extent they have it – is mostly factitious. It is a relatively fragile product of the expectations of one's circle accepted in the form of implicit self-attribution, plus a knowledge of the grammar of the virtues involved, and an ability to play the roles "with feeling."

Differences due to peculiarities of moral tradition

Another kind of diversity among the virtues belongs to the fact that they come in contestable and diverse metaphysical and narrative settings. Virtues are connected, in their logic, with what those who exemplify them believe about human nature and the world we live in. Often this kind of background will profoundly differentiate virtues that go by the same name. For example, the kind of compassion that Aristotle, following the Greek tragedians, describes in *Rhetoric* 2.8 requires that the agent construe the sufferer as not to blame for his suffering (see Nussbaum 2001: 304–27). This condition on compassion is contradicted by the Christian tradition (see Luke 15:11–32). This is just one of several respects in which Christian compassion differs in its logical structure from "tragic" compassion. These differences can be plausibly traced to differences in ethics and metaphysics between traditions. I suspect that the difference I have mentioned is made by the centrality of the idea of forgiveness in the Christian tradition, as compared with the tradition that Aristotle represents.

Thus in one sense I do not think there is such a thing as *the* virtue of compassion; rather, there are *versions of compassion*. This may sound reminiscent of moral relativism or a kind of anti-realism in ethics, but I do not intend it this way. For example, it seems to me that believing that Christian compassion is real compassion (because it gets the world right) is perfectly compatible with admitting that other versions of compassion are out there, and are adhered to by intelligent, thoughtful people. I discussed realism with respect to the emotions in Chapters 4 and 5. Most writers about the virtues write in the "modern" style, supposing that tradition should be irrelevant to the structure of the virtues.

The very lists of the virtues differ strikingly from tradition to tradition. Aristotle's list differs radically (with just a bit of overlap) from that of the New Testament. In light of Aristotle's picture of the great-souled man (*Nicomachean Ethics* 4.3), it is hard to imagine that humility, which is so important on the Christian list, would appear on his list of the virtues. The Stoics' list differs from Nietzsche's, which is a modernization of an ancient heroic list. Another example of a virtue that appears to appear on both the Christian and Aristotelian lists is generosity / liberality. But a closer look at these virtues will reveal, I think, that the one virtue has a rather different motivational structure from the other. Actually, we have here two virtues, whose difference can be explained by reference to other aspects of the different outlooks to which they belong.

Kinds of interdependencies among virtues

Virtues not only differ from one another in a variety of ways; they also lock into each other, thus forming a kind of web of character traits such that a weakening in one virtue can cause sagging or underperformance in another. Such interdependency seems to be due to the fact that the situations of life often make more than one kind of demand on virtue. For example, justice depends on courage because many of the situations that call for just action also contain threats to the person who would act justly. Courage enables the doing of justice in situations where, without courage, fear would impede action. In this way courage allows also the development of the virtue, by enabling actions that contribute to habituation in justice. But the dependency is in the other direction as well. I have said that courage and other virtues of "will power" or self-control are indifferent with respect to motivation. Thus if actions characteristic of these virtues are themselves to be substantively virtuous, they need "imported" or "borrowed" motivation to make them fully virtuous, and this must come from substantive virtues like justice and compassion.

Substantive virtues also depend on one another. Compassion and generosity and forgivingness temper and humanize justice, which otherwise might be mechanical or cold. And in doing this they do not just mitigate justice (though that is a sometime danger that practical wisdom can hope to minimize), but they actually make justice more just by minimizing the anger of the person whose injustice is being corrected. These "gift" virtues can have this effect even if the only expression of them is attitudinal, the outward practical decision being one of simple justice. I think, too, that the very existence of these softer virtues depends on justice. If generosity is a disposition to give to another what one does not owe him, it is clearly conceptually dependent on the concept of what is owed, thus on the concept of justice. Similarly, forgiveness is appropriate only where there has been some transgression, that is, some injustice. Merely not holding an offender accountable for his injustice against oneself is not forgiveness but condonation; so the virtue of forgivingness is possible only to someone who has a strong enough sense of justice that he can refrain from insisting on full justice without condoning the offender's wrong.

Conclusion

This chapter has been only the barest sketch of the virtues. It does not exemplify the kind of contemplation of virtues that I think can contribute materially to the wisdom of those who think it through. Thus it does not fulfill the promise of Chapter 1. For that, it has been far too sketchy, abstract, and under-illustrated. But I hope that, in conjunction with the chapters about the epistemic, the practical, the relational, and the eudaimonic ethical functions of human emotions, it can serve to suggest their centrality to the constitution and functioning of the virtues. All of the other functions combine in the proper emotional functioning that is so largely constitutive of the virtues, allowing us to speak of a fifth function, namely, the aretaic function of emotions.

I hope in the not too distant future to publish a volume that will fulfill the promise of Chapter 1. The volume I envision will treat a number of main virtues both individually and organically, going into sufficient depth to map the deep structure of virtues in the various kinds of diversity outlined in the present chapter, but at the same time to show their structural relations within the moral personality.

References

Adams, Robert M. (1999). *Finite and Infinite Goods*. Oxford University Press.
(2006). *A Theory of Virtue*. Oxford University Press.
Alfano, Mark (2013). *Character as Moral Fiction*. Cambridge University Press.
Alston, William P. (1991). *Perceiving God*. Ithaca, NY: Cornell University Press.
Annas, Julia (2011). *Intelligent Virtue*. Oxford University Press.
Anscombe, Elizabeth (1958). "Modern Moral Philosophy," *Philosophy* 33: 1–19.
Aquinas, Thomas (2003). *On Evil*. Translated by Brian Davies and Richard Regan. New York: Oxford University Press.
Aristotle (1980). *Nicomachean Ethics*. Translated and edited by W. D. Ross, revised by J. L. Ackrill and J. O. Urmson. Oxford University Press.
(1934). *Nicomachean Ethics*. Translated by H. Rackham. Cambridge, Mass.: Harvard University Press.
(1998). *Politics*. Translated by C. D. C. Reeve. Indianapolis, Ind.: Hackett.
Austin, Michael, and Doug Geivett (2012). *Being Good: Christian Virtues for Everyday Life*. Grand Rapids, Mich.: William B. Eerdmans.
Bagnoli, Carla (ed.) (2011). *Morality and the Emotions*. Oxford University Press.
Bechara, Antoine, Hannah Damasio, Daniel Tranel, and Antonio Damasio (1997). "Deciding Advantageously Before Knowing the Advantageous Strategy," *Science* 275: 1293–95.
Becker, Gary (1978). *The Economic Approach to Human Behavior*. University of Chicago Press.
Blackburn, Simon (1985). "Errors and the Phenomenology of Value," in Ted Honderich (ed.), *Morality and Objectivity*. London: Routledge and Kegan Paul, pp. 1–22.
Blum, Lawrence (2011). "Empathy and Empirical Psychology: A Critique of Shaun Nichols's Neo-Sentimentalism," in Carla Bagnoli (ed.), *Morality and the Emotions*. Oxford University Press, pp. 70–193.
Brady, Michael (2011). "Emotions, Perceptions, and Reasons," in Carla Bagnoli (ed.), *Morality and the Emotions*. Oxford University Press, pp. 135–49.
Callahan, Sidney (1988). "The Role of Emotion in Ethical Decision-Making," *Hastings Center Report* 18: 9–14.
Camus, Albert (1955). *L'Étranger*. Edited by Germaine Brée and Carlos Lynes. New York: Appleton-Century-Crofts.
(1988). *The Stranger*. Translated by Matthew Ward. New York: Alfred A. Knopf.

Conrad, Joseph (1960). *The Secret Sharer* and *The Heart of Darkness*. New York: New American Library.

D'Arms, J., and D. Jacobson (1994). "Expressivism, Morality, and the Emotions," *Ethics* 104: 739–63.

(2000). "The Moralistic Fallacy: On the 'Appropriateness' of Emotions," *Philosophy and Phenomenological Research* 61: 65–90.

(2003). "The Significance of Recalcitrant Emotions," in Anthony Hatzimoysis (ed.), *Philosophy and the Emotions*. Cambridge University Press. 127–45.

Damasio, Antonio (1994). *Descartes' Error: Emotion, Reason, and the Human Brain*. New York: Avon Books.

Dancy, Jonathan (2004). *Ethics Without Principles*. Oxford: Clarendon Press.

de Sousa, Ronald (2011). *Emotional Truth*. Oxford University Press.

Deigh, John (1994). "Cognitivism in the Theory of Emotions," *Ethics* 104: 824–54.

(2004). "Primitive Emotions," in Robert C. Solomon (ed.), *Thinking About Feeling*. Oxford University Press.

(2011). "Reactive Attitudes Revisited," in Carla Bagnoli (ed.), *Morality and the Emotions*. Oxford University Press, pp. 197–216.

Dickens, Charles (1999). *Great Expectations*. Edited by Edgar Rosenburg. New York: W. W. Norton.

Döring, Sabine (2003). "Explaining Action by Emotion," *Philosophical Quarterly* 53: 214–30.

Doris, John (2002). *Lack of Character: Personality and Moral Behavior*. Cambridge University Press.

Dostoevsky, Feodor (2008). *Notes from Underground* and *The Gambler*. New York: Oxford University Press.

Driver, Julia (2001). *Uneasy Virtue*. Cambridge University Press.

Epictetus. *Enchiridion*. http://classics.mit.edu/Epictetus/epicench.html.

Evans, C. Stephen (2004). *Kierkegaard's Ethic of Love*. Oxford University Press.

Findlay, J. N. (1973). "My Encounters with Wittgenstein," *Philosophical Forum* 5: 167–85.

Gibbard, Alan (1990). *Wise Choices, Apt Feelings*. Cambridge, Mass.: Harvard University Press.

Gladwell, Malcolm (2005). *Blink: The Power of Thinking Without Thinking*. New York: Little, Brown, and Company.

Goldie, Peter (2000). *The Emotions: A Philosophical Exploration*. New York: Oxford University Press.

(2010). *The Oxford Handbook of Philosophy of Emotion*. Oxford University Press.

Greenspan, Patricia (1988). *Emotions and Reasons: An Inquiry into Emotional Justification*. New York: Routledge.

(1995). *Practical Guilt: Moral Dilemmas, Emotions, and Social Norms*. New York: Oxford University Press.

Hare, John (2005). Review of Linda Zagzebski's *Divine Motivation Theory*. Notre Dame Philosophical Reviews. http://ndpr.nd.edu/news/24314-divine-motivation-theory.

Helm, Bennett (2001). *Emotional Reason: Deliberation, Motivation, and the Nature of Value*. Cambridge University Press.

(2010). "Emotions and Motivation in Neo-Jamesian Accounts," in P. Goldie (ed.), *The Oxford Handbook of Philosophy of Emotion*. Oxford University Press, pp. 303–23.

Hume, David (1896). *A Treatise of Human Nature*, ed. L. A. Selby-Bigge. Oxford University Press.

(1983). *An Enquiry Concerning the Principles of Morals*, ed. J. B. Schneewind. Indianapolis, Ind.: Hackett.

(1985). *Essays Moral Political and Literary*. Edited by Eugene F. Miller. Indianapolis, Ind.: Liberty Classics.

Hursthouse, Rosalind (1991). "Arational Actions," *Journal of Philosophy* 88: 57–68.

(1999). *On Virtue Ethics*. Oxford University Press.

Jacobson, Daniel (2005). "Seeing by Feeling: Virtues, Skills, and Moral Perception," *Ethical Theory and Moral Practice* 8: 387–409.

James, William (1884). "What Is an Emotion?" *Mind* 9: 188–205.

Joyce, Richard (2009). Review of *The Emotional Construction of Morals*. *Mind* 118: 508–18.

Kant, Immanuel (1996a). *Practical Philosophy*. Translated and edited by Mary J. Gregor. Cambridge University Press.

(1996b). *Religion and Rational Theology*. Translated and edited by Allen W. Wood and George di Giovanni. Cambridge University Press.

Kawall, Jason (2009). "In Defense of the Primacy of the Virtues," *Journal of Ethics and Social Philosophy* 3: 1–21.

Kierkegaard, Søren (1983). *The Sickness Unto Death*. Translated and edited by Howard V. Hong and Edna H. Hong. Princeton, NJ: Princeton University Press.

(1998). *Works of Love*. Translated and edited by Howard V. Hong and Edna H. Hong. Princeton, NJ: Princeton University Press.

Louden, Robert (1992). *Morality and Moral Theory: A Reappraisal and Reaffirmation*. New York: Oxford University Press.

(1997). "On Some Vices of Virtue Ethics," in Roger Crisp and Michael Slote (eds.), *Virtue Ethics*. Oxford University Press, pp. 201–16.

MacIntyre, Alasdair (1981). *After Virtue*. Notre Dame, Ind.: University of Notre Dame Press.

(1988). *Whose Justice? Which Rationality?* Notre Dame, Ind.: University of Notre Dame Press.

(1990). *Three Rival Versions of Moral Inquiry*. Notre Dame, Ind.: University of Notre Dame Press.

(1999). *Dependent Rational Animals*. Chicago, Ill.: Open Court.

Mackie, John (1977). *Ethics: Inventing Right and Wrong*. Harmondsworth: Penguin Books.

Malcolm, Norman (1958). *Ludwig Wittgenstein: A Memoir*. London: Oxford University Press.

Marcus Aurelius (1997). *Meditations*. Translated by George Long and edited by William Kaufman. Mineola, NY: Dover.

Matthews, Gareth (1980). "Ritual and the Religious Feelings," in Amélie Rorty (ed.), *Explaining Emotions*. Berkeley: University of California Press, pp. 339–53.

Miller, R., P. Brickman, and D. Bolen (1975). "Attribution Versus Persuasion as a Means for Modifying Behavior," *Journal of Personality and Social Psychology* 31: 430–41.

Monk, Ray (1990). *Wittgenstein: The Duty of Genius*. New York: Viking.

Muggeridge, Malcolm (1986). *Something Beautiful for God*. San Francisco, Calif.: HarperSanFrancisco.

Murphy, Mark (2002). *An Essay on Divine Authority*. Ithaca, NY: Cornell University Press.

Myers, David (1992). *The Pursuit of Happiness: Who is Happy and Why*. New York: William Morrow and Company.

Noë, Alva (2000). "Experience and Experiment in Art," *Journal of Consciousness Studies* 7: 123–36.

Nussbaum, Martha (1990). *Love's Knowledge*. Cambridge University Press.

  (2001). *Upheavals of Thought: The Intelligence of Emotions*. Cambridge University Press.

Paton, Alan (2003 [1948]). *Cry, the Beloved Country*. New York: Scribner.

Pelser, Adam (2010). "Belief in Reid's Theory of Perception," *History of Philosophy Quarterly* 27: 359–78.

Plantinga, Alvin (2011). *Where the Conflict Really Lies: Science, Religion, and Naturalism*. New York: Oxford University Press.

Prinz, Jesse (2004). *Gut Reactions*. Oxford University Press.

  (2006). "The Emotional Basis of Moral Judgments," *Philosophical Explorations* 9: 29–43.

  (2007). *The Emotional Construction of Morals*. Oxford University Press.

Rawls, John (1971). *A Theory of Justice*. Oxford University Press.

Reid, Thomas (1997). *An Inquiry into the Human Mind on the Principles of Common Sense*. Edited by Derek R. Brookes. University Park: The Pennsylvania State University Press.

Roberts, Robert (1984). "Will Power and the Virtues," *Philosophical Review* 93: 227–47.

  (1988). "What an Emotion Is: A Sketch," *Philosophical Review* 97: 183–209.

  (1994). "The Philosopher as Sage," *Journal of Religious Ethics* 22: 409–31.

  (2003). *Emotions: An Essay in Aid of Moral Psychology*. Cambridge University Press.

  (2007). "Situationism and the New Testament Psychology of the Heart," in David Lyle Jeffrey (ed.), *The Bible and the Academy*. Grand Rapids, Mich.: Zondervan Publishing Company.

  (2009a). "Justice as an Emotion Disposition," *Emotion Review* 1: 36–43.

  (2009b). "The Sophistication of Non-Human Emotions," in Robert W. Lurz (ed.), *Philosophy of Animal Minds*. Cambridge University Press, pp. 218–36.

(2010). "Emotions and the Canons of Evaluation," in P. Goldie (ed.), *The Oxford Handbook of Philosophy of Emotion*. Oxford University Press, pp. 561–83.

(2013). "Temperance," in Kevin Timpe and Craig Boyd (eds.), *Virtues and Their Vices*. Oxford University Press.

(unpublished). "Generosity and Gratitude in *Bleak House*."

Roberts, Robert, and W. Jay Wood (2007). *Intellectual Virtues: An Essay in Regulative Epistemology*. Oxford: Clarendon Press.

Robinson, Jenefer (2005). *Deeper than Reason*. Oxford University Press.

Russell, Daniel (2009). *Practical Intelligence and the Virtues*. New York: Oxford University Press.

Sacks, Oliver (1970). *The Man Who Mistook His Wife for a Hat*. New York: HarperCollins.

Salmela, Mikko (2011). "Can Emotion be Modeled on Perception?" *Dialectica* 65: 1–29.

Searle, John (1983). *Intentionality*. Cambridge University Press.

Seneca (1995). *Moral and Political Essays*. Edited by John M. Cooper and J. F. Procopé. Cambridge University Press.

Sherman, Nancy (1997). *Making a Necessity of Virtue: Aristotle and Kant on Virtue*. Cambridge University Press.

(2010). *The Untold War*. New York: W. W. Norton.

Slote, Michael (2001). *Morals from Motives*. New York: Oxford University Press.

Smith, Michael (1998). "The Possibility of Philosophy of Action," in J. Bransen (ed.), *Human Action, Deliberation and Causation*. Dordrecht: Kluwer Academic Publishers, pp. 17–41.

Snow, Nancy (2009). *Virtue as Social Intelligence: An Empirically Grounded Theory*. London: Routledge.

Sommers, Christina Hoff (1993). *Vice and Virtue in Everyday Life*. 3rd edn. Fort Worth: Harcourt Brace Jovanovich.

Sorabji, Richard (2000). *Emotions and Peace of Mind*. Oxford University Press.

Stanislavski, Constantin (1936). *An Actor Prepares*. New York: Routledge.

Stocker, Michael (1976). "The Schizophrenia of Modern Ethical Theories," *Journal of Philosophy* 73: 453–66 (widely anthologized).

Swanton, Christine (2003). *Virtue Ethics: A Pluralistic View*. Oxford University Press.

Tappolet, Christine (2002). "Long-term Emotions and Emotional Experiences in the Explanation of Actions," *European Review of Philosophy* 5: 151–61.

(2010). "Emotion, Motivation, and Action: The Case of Fear," in P. Goldie (ed.), *The Oxford Handbook of Philosophy of Emotion*. Oxford University Press, pp. 325–45.

Timpe, Kevin and Craig Boyd (eds.) (2013). *Virtues and Their Vices*. Oxford University Press.

Tolstoy, Leo (1996). *A Confession*. Translated by David Patterson. New York: W. W. Norton.

(1998). *Anna Karenina*. Translated by Louise and Aylmer Maude, with introduction and notes by W. Gareth Jones. Oxford University Press.

Tversky, Amos, and Daniel Kahneman (1986). "Rational Choice and the Framing of Decisions," in R. M. Hogarth and M. W. Reder (eds.), *Rational Choice: The Contrast Between Economics and Psychology*. University of Chicago Press, pp. 67–94.

Watson, Gary (1990). "On the Primacy of Character," in Owen Flanagan and Amélie Rorty (eds.), *Identity, Character, and Morality*. Cambridge, Mass.: MIT Press, pp. 449–69.

Wiggins, David (1987). "Truth, Invention, and the Meaning of Life," *Needs, Values, Truth*. Oxford University Press, pp. 87–137.

Williams, Bernard (1985). *Ethics and the Limits of Philosophy*. Cambridge University Press.

Wittgenstein, Ludwig (1953). *Philosophical Investigations*. Translated by Elizabeth Anscombe. New York: Macmillan.

Zagzebski, Linda (1996). *Virtues of the Mind: An Inquiry into the Nature of Virtue and the Ethical Foundations of Knowledge*. Cambridge University Press.

(2003). "Emotion and Moral Judgment," *Philosophy and Phenomenological Research* 66: 104–24.

(2004). *Divine Motivation Theory*. Cambridge University Press.

Zajonc, Robert (1980). "Feeling and Thinking: Preferences Need No Inferences," *American Psychologist* 35: 151–75.

(1984). "On the Primacy of Affect," *American Psychologist* 39: 117–29.

Index

218